Sharing Lives

Sharing Lives explores the most important human relationships which last for the longest period of our lives: those between adult children and their parents. Offering a new reference point for studies on the sociology of family, the book focuses on the reasons and results of lifelong intergenerational solidarity by looking at individuals, families and societies. This monograph combines theoretical reasoning with empirical research, based on the Survey of Health, Ageing and Retirement in Europe (SHARE). The book focuses on the following areas:

- adult family generations, from young adulthood to the end of life, and beyond;
- contact, conflict, coresidence, money, time, inheritance;
- consequences of lifelong solidarity;
- family generations and the relationship of family and the welfare state;
- connections between family cohesion and social inequality.

Sharing Lives offers reliable findings on the basis of state-of-the-art methods and the best available data, and presents these findings in an accessible manner. This book will appeal to researchers, policymakers and graduate students in the areas of sociology, political science, psychology and economics.

Marc Szydlik is Professor of Sociology at the University of Zurich. He previously worked at the German Institute for Economic Research, the Max Planck Institute for Human Development, the Free University of Berlin and the University of Erfurt. He was a visiting scholar at Harvard, Columbia, Oxford, Stanford and Cambridge Universities, and has published widely in the field of generations.

T0413951

Routledge Advances in Sociology

Sharing Lives
Adult Children and Parents

Marc Szydlik

Routledge
Taylor & Francis Group

LONDON AND NEW YORK

First published 2016
by Routledge
2 Park Square, Milton Park, Abingdon, Oxon OX14 4RN

and by Routledge
711 Third Avenue, New York, NY 10017

First issued in paperback 2018

Routledge is an imprint of the Taylor & Francis Group, an informa business

British Library Cataloguing-in-Publication Data
A catalogue record for this book is available from the British Library

Library of Congress Cataloging in Publication Data
Names: Szydlik, Marc, author.
Title: Sharing lives: adult children and parents / by Marc Szydlik.
Description: Abingdon, Oxon; New York, NY: Routledge, 2016.
Identifiers: LCCN 2015035958 | ISBN 9781138125711 (hardback) |
    ISBN 9781315647319 (ebook)
Subjects: LCSH: Parent and adult child.
Classification: LCC HQ755.86.S99 2016 | DDC 306.874–dc23
LC record available at http://lccn.loc.gov/2015035958

ISBN 13: 978-1-138-59624-5 (pbk)
ISBN 13: 978-1-138-12571-1 (hbk)

Typeset in Times New Roman
by Swales & Willis Ltd, Exeter, Devon, UK

Cover painting: *Family portrait of father, mother, son and daughter*, by Marie Brøgger.

Contents

Figures and tables

Figures

Tables

Preface

This book has come a long way. Over twenty years ago, at the Free University of Berlin, I began studying generations. More than ten years ago, I started working at the University of Zurich, expanding my previous research on selected aspects of intergenerational relations to a much broader perspective as well as to international comparisons. This book brings together these various strands of research.

The aim is to capture the relationships of adult children and parents – comprehensively and in depth. The book's concern is with family generations per se, but also with the relationship of family and state, of private and public intergenerational solidarity. It addresses consequences of lifelong solidarity, including connections between family cohesion and social inequality. What are the reasons for and results of lifelong intergenerational solidarity – for individuals, families and societies?

Above all, the questions pursued are about sharing lives. In what way are adult daughters and sons connected with their mothers and fathers, and vice versa? Do we still find strong, perpetual bonds across separate households, or are the generations rather preoccupied with their own lives with no relevant attachment? How frequent are conflicts? Are quarrels and fights a typical reality of adult family generations? In regard to support, do daughters and sons care for their elderly parents, and do adult children benefit from lifelong financial transfers from their parents, all the way to notable inheritances?

This book could not have been written without the most valuable help of many people. Since it goes back a long way, I am still much obliged to Martin Kohli, Karl Ulrich Mayer, Jürgen Schupp and my former colleagues Harald Künemund and Andreas Motel-Klingebiel.

Gratitude is owed to all – previous and current – members of the Research Group AGES (LAbour, Generation, Stratification) at the University of Zurich: Ariane Bertogg, Martina Brandt, Christian Deindl, Corinne Igel, Bettina Isengard, Ronny König, Corinne Krohn, Franz Neuberger, Klaus Preisner and Tina Schmid. I am especially grateful to Ronny König for his invaluable work and great patience with the figures and tables. Many thanks also go to Stephan Elkins at SocioTrans for correcting my English as well as to Gerhard Boomgarden and Alyson Claffey at Routledge for their great support.

x *Preface*

Sincere thanks belong to those who have been conducting the SHARE survey on which this study is based: to the researchers and administrative staff of the survey, and of course, to the tens of thousands of survey respondents.

The many helpful discussions with colleagues at scientific conferences, the audiences of public lectures, journalists and students in research seminars are greatly acknowledged.

I am indebted to the Swiss National Science Foundation for contributing funding to the generation project, and to the University of Zurich for providing very supportive working conditions.

Finally, my deepest thanks go to my family and friends.

August 2015   Marc Szydlik

1   Introduction

Mother, father, daughter, son. Those who make up our family generations are some of the most important people in our lives. For many, they are even the most important ones. Acquaintances live their own lives, neighbours move away or are left behind, colleagues change from job to job, friends may come and go, even partners can drift away – but family generations have the potential for lifelong solidarity. For many, no relationship lasts longer than the connection between parents and children.

Today, this is truer than ever before. Longer lives dramatically increase the time generations may spend together. When parents live as long as eighty or ninety years, relations with children may last five, six or even seven decades. Nowadays, we are able to accompany our closest relatives for the longest time ever in human history. This applies particularly to the shared lives of family generations in adulthood.

Increased longevity is one crucial part of demographic change. Lower fertility is another. Fewer children of the previous generation mean fewer siblings and cousins of the next generation, which again enhances the significance of parent-child relationships. Both demographic factors, longer lives and lower fertility lead to the same result: we have fewer family members of the same generation, and more of a different one. Intergenerational relations have become more and more important (Lauterbach 1995, Nave-Herz 1998, Bertram 2000, Bengtson 2001, Noack and Buhl 2004, Saraceno 2008, Swartz 2009).

This is one way to approach the bonds between adult children and parents. An alternative, very different reading insinuates crisis, conflict and alienation. According to that, families are in crisis, and their members are either in permanent conflict with or in total isolation from one another. In times of individualisation, flexibilisation and globalisation, close family members are thought to play an increasingly less important role in our lives. Fewer marriages, more divorces, more singles, fewer children, smaller households, increased geographical mobility: all these developments are seen as indicators of a 'crisis of the family'.

This 'crisis' can be represented by two scenarios. One scenario is conflict. Here, family members struggle to find common ground, internal and external pressure leads to permanent quarrels and fights, understanding and respect is non-existent, and a solution is not in sight. The second scenario is autonomy, which can also be described in terms of alienation, isolation or individualisation. This scenario applies most notably to adult generations. 'Out of sight, out of mind' is the adage that seems most apt. In this perspective, rapid cultural, economic and technological change alienates parents and their adult children, who live separate lives, and whose interaction may be limited to no more than sending an occasional, brief electronic message from wherever they happen to be. This scenario also fits a presumption by Talcott Parsons (1942) claiming that married and employed adult children no longer have a continuous attachment to their parents.

How can one decide between the above scenarios? Does solidarity, conflict or autonomy reflect reality more accurately? In fact, longer lives and fewer children are no proof of actual lifelong intergenerational solidarity. These developments only represent a *potential* for real connections between (adult) children and parents. The fact of having more joint lifetime offers the opportunity to spend this time together, but does not mean that people actually do so. Having fewer siblings and cousins may potentially lead to family generations turning to one another. In order to find out whether adult children and parents do indeed share their lives – and do not just live in parallel yet separate worlds – we need thorough empirical investigations.

Questions

The following are the general questions in this book:

- Do family generations share their lives? Are we more likely to find proof of solidarity, conflict or autonomy?
- How strong is the connection between adult children and parents exactly? To what extent do they care for one another, including giving and receiving time or money, and how often are they in conflict?
- Who maintains stronger intergenerational relationships: the lower or higher educational classes, the rich or the poor, women or men, natives or migrants? Are there relevant differences between countries?
- Which factors are responsible for greater or lesser intergenerational cohesion? What is the role of opportunities and needs, and how important are family structures and cultural contexts?
- What is the connection between the welfare state and intergenerational relations? Does the welfare state reduce or strengthen family solidarity?
- What is the relation between family solidarity and social stratification? Does intergenerational cohesion affect social inequality?

In answering these questions, a number of comparisons will be drawn. In order to learn more about a specific situation, it is necessary to compare it with other circumstances. This applies to comparisons of individuals, generations (e.g., parents with children), families, population groups (e.g., in regard to education, income, gender and migration) and whole societies, including different extents of welfare state support and social inequality. In this perspective, international comparisons allow the identification of best-practice examples that can serve as models for current and future policy considerations. Furthermore, this book compares all-important features of intergenerational relations, including obligations, contact, conflict, space, money, help, care and inheritance.

Theoretical reasoning and empirical evidence

The ideal of scientific research is to connect theoretical reasoning with empirical research. By this, theoretical ideas are put against reality, and empirical results are placed within a theoretical framework. When it comes to explaining inter-generational relations, there is not an abundance of theoretical frameworks to turn to (Nauck and Steinbach 2010: 1061). In the following chapters, this book draws on a theoretical model that has been developed explicitly for the study of family generations (although it can be applied to other interpersonal connections as well). The aim is to employ a theoretical framework to describe and explain intergenerational relations. On this basis, empirically testable hypotheses can be developed to link theory and empirical evidence.

The model, which will be described in greater detail later on, identifies four groups of factors that are thought to be responsible for more or less intense relations between (adult) children and parents: opportunity, need, family and cultural-contextual structures. Thereby three levels of analysis are distinguished, namely individuals, families and societies. This general theoretical model is applicable to all aspects of intergenerational relations, and will therefore be employed in all analyses throughout this book.

The empirical investigations are based on the Survey of Health, Ageing and Retirement in Europe (SHARE). This huge representative survey offers the best available information on adult family generations, including such information for a whole range of European countries, from north to south and west to east. In fact, intergenerational relations are a core theme of this survey. Among other things, SHARE offers comprehensive information on the existence of family generations, the geographical distance between them, obligations towards children and the elderly, intergenerational contact, conflict, coresidence, current monetary transfers, help, care and inheritance. This allows the investigation of generations in great detail and breadth. The survey makes it possible to look into a whole range of highly relevant aspects of intergenerational relations and gain a comprehensive picture thereof.

A particular advantage is that the survey asked all respondents in all countries about all these individual aspects in exactly the same manner. This guards against the problem of incomparability, which studies based on diverse surveys and questionnaires typically face. For example, when asking about giving help to another person, 'help' needs to be defined in the exact same way. This is precisely what the Survey of Health, Ageing and Retirement in Europe does, thus providing a solid foundation for comparing individuals and families across societies.

The respondents are at least 50 years of age. The survey gathers extensive information not only on the interviewees themselves but also on their parents and children. The analyses include over 39,000 respondents with 12,500 child-parent and over 82,000 parent-child relationships.

No fewer than fourteen countries are compared in this book, namely: Sweden, Denmark, Ireland, the Netherlands, Belgium, France, Germany, Poland, Czech Republic, Austria, Switzerland, Italy, Spain and Greece. Additionally, separate results are documented for West and East Germany.

All numbers presented in the figures refer to the first segment of the corresponding bar. Multivariate analyses are documented in the Appendix. In the chapters, coefficients are 'transformed' into pluses and minuses according to the magnitude of the effect.

Outline of the book

Chapter 2 introduces the theoretical framework for the following analyses. Before addressing family generations in more detail, we need to know more about generations in general. Thus, the chapter starts with an overview of labels and concepts of generations, distinguishing between generations in family and society. Furthermore, it is necessary to discuss the term 'intergenerational solidarity' and hereby identify a number of solidarities. Also, the relation between solidarity and conflict will be discussed. Ambivalence is another term that has been used in research on intergenerational relations, and this chapter shows that neither solidarity and conflict, nor solidarity, conflict and ambivalence need to be opposites. In fact, they can be reconciled with one another. The chapter goes on to provide an outline of the theoretical model, which already leads to a number of hypotheses for the empirical analyses. Finally, connections between family and society will be addressed. When conducting international comparisons, it is necessary to define the theoretical framework applied. Here, welfare states play a major role. Moreover, the scope is expanded to include connections between private intergenerational solidarity and social inequality by employing a life course perspective.

After having set the theoretical framework, *Chapter 3* provides the first general empirical information. The aim here is not yet to present detailed analyses, but to give a first overview of potentials and types of contemporary intergenerational relations, drawing on the notion of the so-called 'crisis of the family'. Before addressing intergenerational cohesion, the chapter explores how many people actually have living family generations with which they could possibly interact. How common are multigenerational families, and how many respondents have living parents and children? A second immensely important prerequisite of direct interaction is geographical distance. This distance may range anywhere from generations living within the same four walls all the way to family members living very far apart. Thirdly, obligations may play a relevant role, too. The extent to which population groups perceive a sense of obligation towards the previous and next generations will be determined. After discussing the potential for intergenerational family relationships, a general typology will be introduced, identifying eight different types within four categories, based on summarised forms of intergenerational solidarity and conflict.

Chapter 4 starts the more detailed and thorough analyses by analysing contact. All the empirical chapters are structured in the same way: following a brief outline of the corresponding form of intergenerational cohesion, previous research is documented and hypotheses are developed on the basis of the general theoretical model. The empirical section begins with the wording of the chapter's topic in the questionnaire and proceeds with the presentation and discussion of the empirical results, offering a summary at the end. Chapter 4 investigates the most general form of intergenerational cohesion. How often, if at all, do adult children and parents stay in touch, even if they no longer live in the same household? Is there empirical truth in the notion of individualised family members, or do we rather find strong connections? And if so, are there differences between parents and children, higher and lower social classes, women and men, migrants and natives? When explaining different extents of intergenerational contact, the empirical investigations draw on relevant micro, meso and macro factors.

Conflict is the topic of *Chapter 5*. The aim is to explore whether notions such as 'battle' or even 'war of generations' actually reflect general reality. Although there are all kinds of intergenerational relations, the first question here concerns general patterns. Do generations mainly quarrel and fight? Or are these relations of a more or less harmonious nature? The second question refers to population groups: where do we find more conflict? The third question deals with conflict factors: Can individual opportunities and needs, on the one hand, and family and societal structures, on the other, be made responsible for intergenerational controversy? For example, this chapter will investigate whether the 'strain hypothesis' offers a suitable approach for analysing conflict. Do family members with little financial means and greater health problems report disputes with parents and adult children more frequently? Furthermore, connections between family conflict and the welfare state will be investigated. Do more social benefits come with fewer disputes amongst parents and children, and are there connections between family conflict and social stratification?

The following chapters investigate functional solidarity across the life course: space, money, time and inheritance. They follow the main transfer routes. Space, money and inheritance are mainly provided by parents to children, whereas time transfers tend to go in the opposite direction. *Chapter 6* starts with space. Living together – or not – may have valuable advantages. At the least, doing so saves money since one common household is less expensive than several. However, adult generations sharing the same space, to some degree, goes against the norm of and wish for autonomy, and comes with compromises in daily life. Thus, it is of particular interest to find out how many parents and adult children live together, and which generations do so. Does it really make sense to conclude the existence of a 'crisis of the family' from the fact that coresidence is less common among contemporary families than it has been in the past? The argument would be less convincing if adult family generations living together were to do so out of necessity. In this perspective, it will also be crucial to compare individuals, families and especially countries. Are there influences of public expenditure on families' living arrangements, and what impact do wealth and poverty have?

Chapter 7 addresses money. Financial transfers tend to run down the family line, supporting the so-called 'cascade model'. This being the case, the chapter concentrates on monetary transfers from parents to adult children. The focus is on current transfers; more precisely, financial assistance or gifts given during the last twelve months. Who gives money, and who receives it? Of particular interest are the resources of parents and the needs of children. How important is the financial situation of the transfer giver? Does every daughter and every son receive something, or are need structures the main trigger of such transfers? In this respect, it will be important to consider the employment situation of the adult child. Moreover, are siblings competitors when it comes to receiving (larger) sums of money from their parents? Is there reciprocity of money and time? Another crucial theme is the connection between private transfers and social inequality. Since it is one of the main topics of this book to investigate the consequences of intergenerational family solidarity for social stratification, this question needs to be given particular attention when researching intergenerational flows of money.

Who helps, who cares? This is the subject of *Chapter 8*, which deals with time. At the centre of attention are two forms of support that adult children may provide to their parents: (a) help with household chores and paperwork and (b) personal care. One especially important task is the empirical examination of the so-called 'crowding-out' and 'crowding-in' hypotheses. The question is whether the welfare state is more likely to encourage the retreat of relatives when it comes to taking care of parents in need, or whether family support is actually enhanced, since public services take over especially strenuous tasks, thus opening up opportunities for family members to provide other forms of support. In the former, a strong welfare state would 'crowd out' family solidarity; in the latter, there would be 'crowding-in'. However, this is not the only issue addressed in this chapter. First of all, the chapter investigates how many adult children support their (elderly) parents in general, and addresses the question of reciprocity. Is there some kind of exchange of time (from adult children) and money (from parents)? Such an empirical result would imply that family members are more likely to support one another if they receive something in return.

The last empirical *Chapter 9* investigates inheritance. First of all, it answers the question whether these mortis causa transfers are a topic for a book on intergenerational family relations. In other words, do inheritances really stem primarily from parents, or do other bequeathers also play a significant role? Additional questions that are addressed refer to the time and extent of the inheritance, and the chapter examines whether there are population groups that have higher or lower chances of receiving a bequest. As in the previous empirical chapters, relevant factors affecting intergenerational transfers will be determined. Again, individual opportunities and needs as well as family and cultural-contextual structures will provide the framework for the empirical investigations. Are there connections between welfare state expenditure and the assets that are bequeathed? As in the case of current transfers, a particular focus is the connections between family relations and social inequality. What are the consequences of intergenerational solidarity for social stratification? Do most inheritances favour those who are in greater need, or is wealth that is handed down the family line more likely to benefit population groups that are already in a considerably better economic situation?

Finally, the book closes with a general summary of the most important results and draws a number of conclusions, especially with regard to the connections among intergenerational cohesion, welfare state regulations and social stratification.

2   Concepts and contexts

Generations

Labelling

What are 'generations'? According to suggestions by scholars, writers and journalists, there are a great number of different generations. For example, there has been talk of pre-war, war, post-war, founding, rebuilding, economic miracle, baby boomer, turnaround, reform, Gulf War and Intifada generations, of Adenauer, Brandt, Kohl, Schröder, Merkel, Berlusconi, Blair, Obama, Putin, Sarkozy, Thatcher, Benedict and Francis generations, as well as of global, grey, heir, hippie, internship, jobless, maybe, me, no-future, power, problem, project, protest, silver, single, stress, welfare, white-collar, wimp, youth and yuppie 'generations'.

Furthermore, we read about abandoned, abused, affluent, alternative, authentic, bankrupt, betrayed, casual, chosen, conformist, consumerist, demanding, digital, emotional, enquiring, fatherless, forgotten, greedy, helpless, heroic, heterogeneous, hybrid, indifferent, later-born, liberated, lost, love, materialistic, misled, moralistic, narcissistic, open-minded, optimistic, post-alternative, post-materialistic, pragmatic, pseudo-political, pubertal, rebellious, sceptical, security-oriented, seeking, self-centred, selfish, shocked, silent, spoiled, stolen, superfluous, transcendental, unsure and wild 'generations'.

The list does not end there. Other labels refer to numbers, places, objects, activities, music genres and brands, such as: '68, '78, '89, '90, '97, '99, millennial, G4, 13th, 50-plus, 60-plus, 70-plus, €700; Berlin, east, Europe, Fulda, PISA, Prague, Tenerife and Weimar; cell phone, chips, chocolate, clutter, gel, grill, iron, jeans, laptop, sandwich, smartphone, tape deck, TV and vodka; action, care, click, coffee shop, cuddle, cyber, doer, fun, helper, Internet, model, online, party, playback, spectator, thrill, upload and user; beat, disco, hip hop, jazz, pop, raver, rock and techno; Facebook, Gameboy, Golf, Google, MTV, Nintendo, Siemens, Tamagochi and YouTube.

Even single letters are sufficient as labels for a new 'generation', as evidenced by generations A, B, C, D, e, J, P, Q, V, X, XXL, XTC, Y, Z and @. At any rate, journalists, writers and scholars seem to have become obsessed with generational labelling. Many of those who have coined a new generational label would probably agree to applying only one specific term to a certain group of people, just as long as it is their own term.

In view of this 'generation labelling mania', it seems appropriate to consider various concepts of 'generation'. In the following, generations in the narrow sense are discussed, before adding a few further usages of the term (see Szydlik 2000: 19ff.).

Generations in family and society

'Generation' is a multifaceted concept. To clear a path through the jungle of generational terminology, we can generally identify generations in family and society. Furthermore, it is helpful to distinguish between generations, cohorts and age groups.

Family generations refer to the micro level and describe family lineage: grandparents, parents, children, grandchildren etc. They represent generations in the original sense of the word 'generate' (to bring into being). Accordingly, Vern Bengtson suggests applying the term mainly when referring to generations in this sense: 'And we should use the term generation primarily to reflect ranked-descent ordering of individuals within families' (Bengtson 1993: 10f.). In the same vein, Tamara Hareven argues: 'A generation designates a kin relationship (e.g., parents and children or grandparents and grandchildren); it encompasses an age span often as wide as 30 years or more' (Hareven 1995: 16). Empirically, intergenerational family relationships are frequently described as dyads, which represent relations between two individuals. The relationship between daughter and mother constitutes a dyad, and the relationship of the same daughter to her father another dyad.

Generation concepts come up against difficulties and disagreement when the aim is to describe *social generations*. In this case, what is meant by 'generation' is often only vaguely defined. This also holds true for the majority of the generational labels listed above. Even among generation researchers there is no agreement as to the criteria to be applied in identifying specific social generations. We encounter a number of fundamental problems:

- Many of the suggested generational labels refer to individuals who hardly have any key experiences or clearly defined sociocultural attributes in common.
- These individuals do not appear as a collective actor in the public arena, nor can we speak of any common awareness or shared sense of representing a specific generation.
- Many generational labels merely take up short-term trends and fashions. This contributes to the impression of 'generation' being an arbitrary concept.
- A generational label is especially questionable when more or less vague cultural attributes are assumed for a group of people who do not share any particular political or economic conditions.
- Oftentimes, the creators of generational labels project subjective perceptions of individual characteristics, or the characteristics of small groups, onto entire populations.

- It is often unclear where precisely the line is drawn between those who just barely still belong and who no longer belong to the proposed 'generation'.
- The concept of generation is frequently greatly overextended. It is much more useful to distinguish between 'generation', 'cohort' and 'age group'.

In principle, 'social generation' is a concept that refers to the meso or macro level. It comprises individuals who were born within a period of a few years and who share everlasting significant commonalities. Thus, a social generation is, by definition, also a birth cohort. The members of a cohort belong to the same group of people throughout their entire lives.

This concept is in stark contrast to that of age groups: as people get older, their age group changes. Members of a young age group, over time, enter a middle-aged age group until they belong to an old age group. Thus, the term 'young generation' would be a contradiction in terms if it were to imply age groups. However, it would be much more appropriate when referring to stable traits of a specific birth cohort or even to a family generation. In any case, for the sake of clarity, it is helpful to exercise some caution in using the concept of generations in connection with 'age groups'.

Equating the concept of cohort with social generation would neglect important aspects as well. 'Generation' means more than 'cohort' does. Cohorts are more or less random aggregations of people born within a few years. The concept of cohort therefore involves a greater degree of arbitrariness. Social generations, on the other hand, have additional characteristics in common beyond the period of birth alone. This adds another substantial dimension to the concept of cohort (e.g., common experiences).

People who are merely born in the same time period (i.e., members of a random cohort) thus do not form a social generation per se. Only with regard to some cohorts are we justified in speaking of a 'generation'. A generation comprises a certain cohort, but a specific cohort does not constitute a generation. This is already emphasised in Karl Mannheim's seminal work:

> [W]e pointed out that mere co-existence in time did not even suffice to bring about community of generation location (. . .). In order to share the same generation location, i.e. in order to be able passively to undergo or actively to use the handicaps and privileges inherent in a generation location, one must be born within the same historical and cultural region. Generation as an actuality, however, involves even more than mere co-presence in such a historical and social region. A further concrete nexus is needed to constitute generation as an actuality. This additional nexus may be described as *participation in the common destiny* of this historical and social unit.
>
> (Mannheim 1952: 303; 1928: 309)

Family and social generations are generations in the literary and strict sense. Besides using the term 'generation' for age groups or cohorts, there are additional concepts that are sometimes more, sometimes less related to the concepts of family or social generations:

Demographic generations are based on the average difference between the year of birth of parents and children.

Entry generations refer to the time of entry into an institution such as the labour market, a firm or an association.

Immigrant generations are mostly defined in terms of their native country: the 'first generation' was born in the country of origin, whereas the term 'second generation' mostly refers to their children, who were born in the host country.

Pedagogical generations refer to the relation of teachers and pupils.

'*Present generation*' puts currently living persons into one category, whereas the term '*future generation*' may refer to people who have yet to be born or are still quite young. Sometimes there is talk of 'future generation*s*', which indicates a number of subsequent generations without really explaining them.

Technology generations are based on cohorts who grew up with the emergence of some new technology, for instance, computers (Sackmann and Weymann 1995; Korupp and Szydlik 2005; Sackmann and Winkler 2013).

Political, cultural and economic generations

Social generations can be distinguished further in political, cultural and economic generations. When Mannheim speaks of generations in his influential work, published in 1928, he is referring to *political generations*. By this, he distinguishes three relevant aspects, which are: 'generation location *(Generationslagerung)*', 'generation as an actuality *(Generationszusammenhang)*' and 'generation unit *(Generationseinheit)*'. *Generation location* refers to individuals who are born into the same historical and social community. This group of people does not yet constitute a generation. Generation location, however, bears the potential for a generation as an actuality, i.e., a generation location can crystallise into a generation. *Generation as an actuality* comprises individuals who were not only born at the same time into the same historical and social community, but who also share the common 'destiny' of this historical and social unit. In particular, major societal events are constitutive of generations (e.g., wars, major social upheaval etc.). Finally, *generation units* are based on 'formative and interpretive principles [which] form a link between spatially separated individuals'. These units are 'characterized by [. . .] an identity of responses, a certain affinity in the way in which all move with and are formed by their common experiences' (Mannheim 1952: 306; 1928: 313). That is to say, generations as an actuality can comprise generation units that are in conflict with one another in terms of their opinions, goals and behaviours.

Mannheim's approach remains very useful today to identify political generations or to distinguish between political generations and mere cohorts. For instance, if we apply his terminology to the West-German '68 generation, we can hold that the West Germans born in the 1940s share a common generation location, whereas those who were, to some degree, active at the time (mostly university students) make up the core of the respective generation as an actuality. Generation units were the extra-parliamentary opposition movement of the West German political left, on the one hand, but also conservative student associations, on the other (Kohli and Szydlik 2000).

Cultural generations comprise cohorts that are characterised by specific shared (life) experiences, attitudes and styles. Mannheim's terminology can be applied in this context as well. At first glance, the majority of the generational labels listed above seem to fall into the category of cultural generations. Scepticism is nevertheless in order here. It is questionable whether one should actually speak of a 'generation' when referring to (parts of) age groups or cohorts without any shared generational consciousness, let alone any presence as a collective actor. Another objection is that many of the labels listed above merely refer to short-lived features; one is even tempted to speak of fashions. By contrast, social generations are marked by cohorts sharing specific commonalities that clearly distinguish them from previous and subsequent cohorts, while the defining characteristics they have in common are not short-lived but leave an imprint on these cohorts over their entire lifetime.

In fact, most of the said labels are highly problematic. One may be tempted to attract attention by introducing a new terminology, and to highlight certain aspects related to small groups that are then projected onto whole cohorts. Certain attitudes and behaviours encountered in certain small groups may even be observed to a lesser or greater degree among other members of the same cohort. Nevertheless, according to Mannheim, much more is required if we want to speak of a 'generation' (as an actuality).

Again, we can take the '68 generation as an example of a cultural generation. At the centre of attention in this context is less its involvement in extra-parliamentary political opposition than its ultimate success in advancing a more liberal way of life; and in this respect, this generation is not only different from preceding but also from succeeding cohorts. Especially as a cultural generation, the '68 generation was quite successful. At the same time, this example testifies to the fact that in cases where using the term 'generation' is justified, political and cultural generations are often linked.

Economic generations are formed less by way of political or sociocultural commonalities, but instead, are cohorts whose members share specific economic opportunities or risks. Specific structural conditions – for example, via the labour market, economy or state – affect the life chances of the members of an economic generation. These conditions may be created by the respective generation itself or may be the product of external causes. For instance, the time of labour market entry can be an important determinant of career pathways. Depending on the business cycle, the existence of excess labour supply or a labour shortage, as well as the specific economic situation, a cohort may encounter specific opportunities or risks. Members of large cohorts may be subject to greater competition for education and employment opportunities compared to members of small cohorts. At the same time, the type of commodity production and the dominance of the primary, secondary or tertiary sector at the time of labour market entry may lead to substantial inequality between cohorts (Easterlin 1980).

In general usage, the term 'generation' is frequently referred to in the context of welfare state redistribution. In order to identify underlying ideas and motives, it again makes sense to differentiate between generations, cohorts and age groups.

This also applies to debates on the so-called 'intergenerational contract' in welfare state contributions and benefits. Many of these discussions are difficult simply because it is not clear who precisely the debate is about: is it about age groups, cohorts or indeed generations? What criteria are applied in classifying a group of people as being advantaged or disadvantaged? Where precisely do we draw the line as to who belongs to this group of people, and who does not (e.g., which cohorts specifically)?

Clarifying the underlying concept is also important in the debate on 'intergenerational justice' with regard to the welfare state. In this context, conflicts over the distribution of welfare benefits and burdens are sometimes even referred to by the (ineffable) expression 'a war of generations'. First and foremost, the 'intergenerational contract' refers to age groups rather than to cohorts or even generations: to avoid poverty in old age, the economically active population supports pensioners and thus becomes entitled to receiving support in old age as well. However, when the terms 'age group' and 'cohort' are used interchangeably, this results in a conflict of objectives between two kinds of justice: justice between age groups versus justice between cohorts. Should priority be given to offsetting inequalities between current contributors and pensioners, or is the main objective to reduce discrepancies in cases where public redistribution affects birth cohorts to different degrees over their entire lifetime? Answering these questions may also reveal more or less hidden controversies, for instance, when members of better-off groups in particular are interested in retreating from what they perceive to be 'unjust' public intergenerational redistribution. Some policy proposals that suggest *less* inequality between cohorts would thus lead to *more* inequality between age groups and social classes instead. Some discussions about *inter*generational justice tend to neglect or even disguise the much more relevant *intra*generational discrepancies between those who are economically better and worse off (see Kohli 2005).

In any case, it would be difficult to consider current contributors and pensioners as economic generations in the light of the generation concept presented above. First of all, today's contributors will be tomorrow's pensioners, just as today's pensioners were once contributors themselves. Therefore, we do not find an affiliation with a certain generation over an entire lifetime. Moreover, neither contributors nor pensioners constitute a group composed of members within a narrow birth range. Referring to 16–60 year olds as a 'generation' would contradict the concepts referred to above, just as reference to 60–100 year olds would. We may be able to speak of generations when welfare state arrangements benefit or disadvantage certain cohorts significantly and permanently (welfare state 'winners' or 'losers'; Thomson 1989; Leisering 2000). This may be the case, for instance, when higher social security contributions are accompanied by lower pensions in old age. Nevertheless, it is not such an easy task to clearly identify specific 'welfare generations' (May 2013).

Breaking down social generations into political, cultural and economic generations does not intend to imply that they are not at all connected. Economic generations can be political and cultural generations at the same time. In fact, one might argue that a social generation emerges especially when a specific cohort distinguishes itself economically as well as politically and culturally from previous and subsequent cohorts. The '68 generation is a case in point when arguing that the political involvement of many members of this generation was not least rooted in a sense of economic security. In fact, the emergence of political and cultural generations can be based upon a specific economic situation. For example, a cohort's collective economic situation may lead to the pursuit of more conservative or more progressive ideas and goals.

All in all, identifying social generations involves major challenges, especially when considering Mannheim's seminal work. Three simple conditions cast doubt on the applicability of most of the labels mentioned above: first, a generation encompasses a birth cohort; second, the members of this cohort share relevant (political, cultural or economic) experiences and characteristics; and third, these characteristics are lifelong and, ideally, separate a specific generation from the previous and following cohorts.

These identification problems, which are typical of social generations, do not exist when referring to family generations. In the following and throughout this book, the term 'generation' is used in the literal sense, namely in regard to parents and children.

Solidarity and conflict

What is 'intergenerational solidarity'? First of all, usage of the term depends on the concept of generation applied (see above). For example, the term is used when referring to the public 'intergenerational contract', i.e., the young and middle-aged working population supports elderly pensioners. When it comes to family generations, the basic source is the concept of solidarity suggested by Vern Bengtson and colleagues. This very influential and widely used concept is defined in general terms: 'For the sake of clarity, we employ 'solidarity' (. . .) as a meta-construct subsuming characteristics of intergenerational bonds in families' (Roberts et al. 1991: 12). Six dimensions are proposed in more detail: affectual, associational, consensual, functional, normative and structural solidarity (e.g., Bengtson and Roberts 1991; Lawton et al. 1994).

Conceptualising intergenerational family solidarity across various dimensions has the benefit of taking into account its multifaceted nature. However, instead of employing this division into six dimensions, here the emphasis is placed on drawing a clear distinction between the potential for solidarity and actual solidarity. This applies especially to structural, normative and consensual solidarity. In this perspective, intergenerational solidarity can be described adequately in terms of affectual, associational and functional solidarity (see Szydlik 2000: 34ff.).

Bengtson and Roberts define '*structural solidarity*' as an '[o]pportunity structure for intergenerational relationships reflected in number, type, and geographic proximity of family member' (1991: 857). It therefore refers to the opportunity or the potential for intergenerational solidarity. The mere existence of (many) family members such as parents and adult children does not necessarily mean that they are (closely) connected with one another. In fact, they may have no relationship at all. A similar thing applies to geographical distance. Apart from coresidence as a form of functional solidarity (see below), residential proximity between non-coresident generations can rather be seen as a crucial prerequisite for intergenerational solidarity.

'*Normative solidarity*' is defined as '[s]trength of commitment to performance of familial roles and to meeting familial obligations' (Bengtson and Roberts 1991: 857), and describes the degree to which individuals feel obliged to practise solidarity. To what extent are family members convinced that they ought to support one another? So-called 'normative solidarity' is not necessarily focused on relationships with individual parents and children, but revolves around attitudes towards the family in general (see Silverstein et al. 1994: 252). It also represents a general principle that does not necessarily have to accord with actual action (Lawton et al. 1994: 35). Again, this involves 'only' a potential for solidarity but not intergenerational solidarity as such.

'*Consensual solidarity*' describes commonalities between individuals in terms of values, attitudes and beliefs. To what extent do family members agree in political, economic and cultural matters? Do they share the same opinions on political parties, unions or churches? Do they subscribe to the same values and lifestyles, or do they display major differences in this respect? Although assessing 'consensual solidarity' involves comparing the views of certain family members, the opinions themselves do not necessarily refer to any specific relative of another generation. There may be consensus on a certain issue, but no more than that. Such a consensus may foster intergenerational family solidarity but does not necessarily have to do so.

Intergenerational family solidarity refers to bonds and interactions between family members of different generations. In this sense, it is interindividual, personal and dyadic in principle. It comprises a wide range of facets, which can be classified into three dimensions: the affectual, associational and functional dimensions of solidarity. Although these dimensions can be linked to one another, this does not necessarily have to be the case. Whether and to what degree they actually overlap is ultimately an empirical matter. The associational and functional dimensions refer to the element of action involved in solidarity, whereas the affectual dimension points to the existence of emotional bonds.

Thus, it is suggested that, in principle, there are three dimensions of intergenerational family solidarity:

- *Affectual solidarity*: sense of affiliation and common bond between people (emotional closeness, affection, sense of community)
- *Associational solidarity*: shared activities and interaction (frequency and kind of contact)
- *Functional solidarity*: the giving and taking of money, time and space (monetary transfers, assistance in the form of time and coresidence).

Affectual solidarity describes emotional bonds and affection. A measure for such bonds is the emotional closeness of the relationship between family generations such as adult children and parents (e.g., Szydlik 1995, 1996, 2000, 2008a; Bertogg and Szydlik 2016). Affectual solidarity refers to the subjective sense of a common bond and a feeling of togetherness between individuals, hence, this also implies that the other is significant to one's own life.

Associational solidarity pertains to shared activities and interaction. It refers to the question of whether individuals are involved with one another in the first place and, if so, how frequently they are in contact. Different kinds of contact are subsumed by the dimension of associational solidarity, for instance, meeting in person, talking on the phone, writing, spending a holiday together or providing personal help and care.

Functional solidarity is another dimension of family solidarity related to action. It comprises three 'currencies' of intergenerational transfers, namely the giving and taking of money, time and space (see Soldo and Hill 1993). Thus, functional solidarity can be divided into three subdimensions: monetary transfers, assistance in the form of time and coresidence. *Monetary transfers* include voluntary or involuntary financial assistance, which may occur once or repeatedly, on a regular or irregular basis. They also refer to gifts of money and things, loans and bequests. *Assistance in the form of time* involves a wide range of services. It includes, for instance, helping in the household, in the garden, doing repair work, running errands, providing care, looking after grandchildren and offering advice, consolation and encouragement. *Coresidence,* that is, sharing the same household, can go hand in hand with financial support, but also with giving and saving time. A person who pays no or only modest rent saves money, and so do those who share a household with others compared to a single-person household. This applies in a similar manner to saving time with regard to chores, such as cleaning, home maintenance and doing the laundry. Thus, we can argue that coresidence is not quite on a par with the other two modes of transfer but is subordinate to the giving and taking of money and time. Moreover, this underscores that the three basic 'currencies' cannot always be neatly separated. Time can be 'translated' into financial transfers in cases where outside help would have to be engaged instead. Conversely, financial transfers can serve to pay for help and care services.

Solidarity and conflict

What is the relationship between solidarity and conflict? One way of thinking about this is to treat them as opposites. From this perspective, a relationship between people is marked either by solidarity or conflict, and furthermore, is rated as either 'good' or 'bad'. However, this perspective is not applied here. On the contrary, it is argued that solidarity must not be mistaken for harmony. Accordingly, the opposite of solidarity is not conflict. Relationships based on solidarity are not necessarily characterised by an absence of discord. Also, more solidarity is not inevitably 'better' per se (see Bengtson et al. 2002: 571). Here are just a few examples of affectual, associational and functional solidarity:

- The relationship between adult children and their parents can be *too* close if either the parents cling to their adult children, or adult children have such close emotional ties to their parents that they are unable to move toward independence.
- Frequent contact may be seen as a helpful means to avoid loneliness and promote family integration. However, not all contact is perfectly voluntary and without friction.
- From a superficial perspective, we might be inclined to view intergenerational transfers as a generally 'positive' aspect of intergenerational solidarity. After all, family members often support one another in cases of financial difficulties. Such transfers, however, may also represent dependence, come with implicit or explicit demands and may put a strain on both transfer givers and receivers (Chapters 5 and 7). Also, adult children caring permanently for elderly parents might not be in the interest of either the children or their parents (Chapter 8).

Accordingly, all conflict is not necessarily and always 'bad'. Obviously, there are intense, destructive fights. However, to some extent, open disagreement and debate between family members can also provide an opportunity for negotiating opposing opinions and wishes (see Stierlin 1974: 180f.). Respectful discussions permit the parties involved to explain their different views, which can contribute to improving mutual understanding and further developing the relationship (Chapter 5). One can even treat such conflict as an element in human bonding. A person who engages in respectful debates with another person may be showing his or her interest and the wish to maintain that relationship. A person who no longer has anything to say to the other, who has broken off the relationship, is no longer inclined to argue with that other person either.

If we agree that solidarity and conflict are not opposites per se, it follows that intergenerational relations are not necessarily marked by either cohesion or dispute. In fact, both forms of interpersonal behaviour can occur in the same relationship, even at the same time, and sometimes they presuppose one another. Conflict can be a reaction to solidarity, for instance, in times of monetary transfers to adult children or personal care for frail elderly parents. Help and care can place an excessive burden on families and thus lead to quarrels. Conversely, as mentioned above, sharing and respecting different views can enhance cohesion. However, bitter controversies may also lead to diminished contact or even termination of the relationship. We should be cautious about painting a picture of intergenerational conflict that is too pessimistic or too optimistic. The impact of controversy on a relationship depends not least on its frequency and intensity. For example, previous analyses indicate that noteworthy conflict between family generations is quite rare, but if it does occur, it may lead to avoiding the other person (Szydlik 2008a).

Figure 2.1 depicts the possible connections between interpersonal solidarity and conflict. It positions human relations in a space defined by four poles: symbiosis, autonomy, harmony and hostility. These extremes are connected by a solidarity

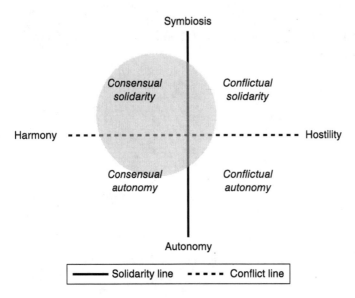

Figure 2.1 Solidarity and conflict

line and a conflict line, respectively. Their positioning in the figure implies that conflict does not preclude support, and a close relationship between generations may be accompanied by disputes as well. The solidarity line connects 'total symbiosis' and 'absolute autonomy'; the conflict line ranges from 'complete harmony' to 'outright hostility'. Total symbiosis and absolute autonomy represent two ends of an imagined continuum along which the specific intergenerational relationships can be positioned closer to one end or the other. The same applies to the continuum between complete harmony and outright hostility.

Of course, the four poles represent extremes that are rarely found in reality. Nevertheless, in order to identify the spectrum, it makes sense to have a brief look at these extremes. *Total symbiosis* implies an absolute connectedness between family generations. There is no room for a person's own individual perspective; the only possible unit is 'we'. In this case, adult children and their parents live together, the children never manage to separate from their parents, and the generations spend all available time together; if one person is in need, the other helps without hesitation and limitation. On the other side of the continuum, *absolute autonomy* means the complete absence of any bond, which at the same time involves total independence of the family generations. There is no contact at all, no postcard, no mail, no emotion and even no thinking of the other person. *Complete harmony* would imply that there is no discussion whatsoever: all parties are always in concord over every aspect, even minor ones; everyone agrees on every single word that the other person says, and there exists a perfect consonance of opinions in all matters, ranging from politics to lifestyle and small everyday decisions. The other side of the continuum marks *outright hostility*. Here, we have permanent unresolvable conflict.

Every single word is disputed, loud discussions are endless, and since we are imagining an extreme pole, all-out conflict may also involve strong emotional and physical abuse, as well as the involvement of the police, lawyers and the courts.

Since total symbiosis, absolute autonomy, complete harmony and outright hostility are extraordinary exceptions, the great majority of the relations can be expected to be located somewhere between these four poles. In order to fill this theoretical model with empirical results, the grey area gives a preview of the following analyses. Of course, the figure offers only a very general view of adult family generations, neglecting differences between forms of solidarity and degrees of variation in child-parent and parent-child relationships.

- Most parents and adult children find themselves within the category of *consensual solidarity* (tight and close; see Table 3.1). These relations are marked by profound solidarity and weak conflict. All in all, parents and adult children rarely report noteworthy controversies. If disputes occur, they do not tend to be excessive. The generations show strong bonds, help each other when in need and are in frequent contact.
- *Conflictual solidarity* (strained and entangled) means that family generations are very close to one another, which becomes apparent by frequent contact, and at the same time, we observe considerable conflict. Some of these controversies may go back to difficult situations of need, which are at least partly met by intergenerational support. All in all, this category represents the second smallest group.
- Relations with frequent conflict and low solidarity can be labelled as *conflictual autonomy* (obligatory and divided). On the one hand, there are considerable controversies; on the other, contact is less frequent. In this case, the generations are possibly in the process of more or less permanent separation (Szydlik 2008a: 107f.). The empirical results indicate that these relations form the smallest group of all.
- Last but not least, *consensual autonomy* (customary and separate) defines a situation in which the generations do not quarrel with one another (anymore) and there is also not much contact. In some cases, the relationship has ceased to exist, be it after a long struggle, be it in terms of the adage, 'Out of sight, out of mind'. This is the second largest group, but still much smaller than consensual solidarity (see Figure 3.5).

Theoretical model

The following theoretical model provides the basis for explaining intergenerational relations. The aim is to understand which family generations lead which relationships – and why. Why do some adult children and parents show more cohesion than others? The ONFC model (based on opportunity, need, family and cultural-contextual structures) links the descriptive solidarity-conflict model with corresponding explanations. It offers a general conceptual framework for more detailed theoretical reasoning as a basis for empirical analyses. Throughout this book, the model is applied to all empirical multivariate analyses, including contact, conflict, space, money, time and inheritance. In doing so, the model connects theoretical assumptions with empirical investigations.

Originally, the model was developed to explain emotional closeness between parents and adult children (Szydlik 1995). In the meantime, it has found widespread use for addressing a host of intergenerational issues, such as the provision of living space, help and care as well as financial transfers between generations (e.g., Szydlik 2000, 2004, 2008a; Brandt et al. 2009; Leopold and Schneider 2010; Steinbach and Kopp 2010; Deindl 2011; Isengard and Szydlik 2012).

The three circles at the centre of Figure 2.2 symbolise the three solidarity dimensions addressed in the previous chapter, namely affectual (emotional closeness), associational (contact) and functional solidarity (giving and taking of money, time and space).

Which factors influence intergenerational relations? The diverse determinants can be classified into four groups, namely opportunity, need, family and cultural-contextual structures. In so doing, three levels of analysis are distinguished: individual, family and society. Intergenerational relations are generally dyadic, which means that essentially two people are involved (e.g., adult child and parent), each with specific opportunities and needs. This relationship is embedded in a family and, beyond that, in a societal context. Among the groups of factors are influences and dependencies (represented by arrows).

The general model provides a tool for developing appropriate hypotheses as a basis for empirical research. Therefore, a variable may be attributed to opportunities in one case, whereas the same variable may represent a hypothesis referring to need structures when explaining another aspect of intergenerational relations. Since one and the same variable may be involved in various hypotheses, the ONFC model 'forces' the researcher to decide what the main hypotheses are. Of course, this decision has to be reviewed in the light of the corresponding empirical results.

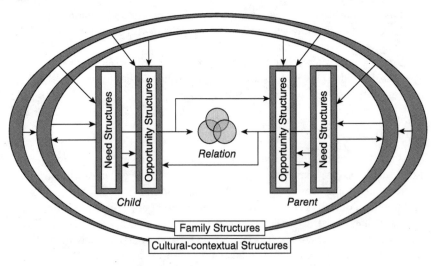

Figure 2.2 Theoretical model (ONFC)

In the following, the four groups of factors as well as the applicability of the model will be illustrated by briefly naming a number of relevant hypotheses for the empirical analyses of this book. Those (and further) hypotheses will be illustrated in more detail in the corresponding chapters.

Opportunity structures

Opportunity structures reflect opportunities or resources. They enable, promote, hinder or prevent social interaction. To interrelate with someone typically requires suitable conditions and means. Opportunities describe favourable circumstances for social interaction and comprise all kinds of available resources (see Foa and Foa 1980; Foa et al. 1993), such as skills and abilities, knowledge and information, money, goods, time, health, power, status and social ties.

Frequent personal *contact* amongst adult generations can be expected to depend on living in close proximity. It is much easier to meet somebody on a regular basis when people live in the same neighbourhood. Good health is another prerequisite that facilitates the ability to meet. Moreover, financial resources, including a prospective bequest, might foster intergenerational contact.

Since *conflict* is likely to emerge especially under stressful conditions, financial resources may increase concord. Additionally, conflict between people requires contact, so that a high frequency of contact provides potential opportunities for more quarrelling. However, conflict may also lead to less intergenerational cohesion.

With regard to *space*, a likely prerequisite for adult children and parents coresiding is the availability of living space. A sufficient number of rooms offers the opportunity to share the same four walls. At the same time, educational and financial resources may provide the means for greater independence and thus for separate residences of adult family generations.

Financial resources are also likely to play an important role in the giving of *money*. Supporting relatives in the form of monetary transfers depends on having sufficient means at one's disposal, via household income or savings. Furthermore, one cannot preclude that frequent contact offers more opportunities to give and receive.

Closer geographic proximity is likely to enable adult children to give *time* in the form of personal help or care to a parent. The health of potential helpers and carers may be a crucial resource, too, since people in poor health are less able to help others. Conversely, if the parents possess financial resources, this may lead to better chances of being helped or cared for by an adult child.

Research has shown that *inheritances* mostly stem from parents. Adult children are therefore more likely to have received a previous inheritance if their parents have already passed away. Conversely, adult children have a greater chance of expecting a future bequest if their parents are still alive.

Need structures

Need structures indicate the needs for social interaction. They also include desires, goals, interests, motives, wants and wishes of individuals, for themselves or for significant others. In fact, a whole range of needs can be listed (e.g., Maslow 1943, 1954; Max-Neef et al. 1991; Kenrick et al. 2010). In the context of intergenerational relations, needs, for example, can be of a financial nature (i.e., during education, unemployment or due to insufficient financial savings in old age), they can stem from health problems (be it a short-term or long-term illness or even one requiring lifelong help or care), there can be a need for information and advice, or there can be emotional needs (i.e., for appreciation, belonging, consolation, understanding, self-determination). Moreover, parents may want the best for their children and wish to support them throughout their whole lives and even thereafter (see Table 2.1), and adult children may feel the need to spend time with their elderly parents. The underlying premise is that human behaviour is not least guided by needs and wants (including the implicit wish to comply with norms), the fulfilment of which depends on opportunities that are influenced by immediate and general contexts. Human relations are embedded in meso and macro structures, which enable, hinder or mediate individual behaviour.

From this perspective, opportunities and needs may be intertwined (represented by arrows in Figure 2.2). The needs of one person may correspond with the opportunities of the same or another person, and they may match or contradict the needs of another. For example, a child's need for monetary support may be met by parental resources, or the care needs of a frail parent may contradict an adult child's wish for self-determination. In any case, the fulfilment of one person's needs may depend not only on that person's own opportunities but also on the resources and needs of the other person, as well as on the conditions, norms, regulations, traditions etc. of family and society. Furthermore, although intergenerational relations can play a part in addressing and fulfilling individual needs, there is also a need for independence from symbiotic relationships, persistent demands, continuous control and strict regulation.

Financial needs may motivate generations to stay in *contact*, and monetary transfers, including presents, may nurture the bonds between adult children and parents. It is an empirical question whether older people's greater need for attention and support leads to more intergenerational contact. The same is true for the consequences of poor health.

Strenuous situations can lead to *conflict*. This can apply to situations of financial need, for instance, when one generation transfers money to the other. Health problems may also evoke conflict, especially when relatives need intense help or even care. In contrast, one might hypothesise that age decreases the desire to engage in controversies with the next generation.

Parents providing *space* is much more probable when adult children are comparatively young. This is a time when they may still need to live with their parents, owing to a lack of sufficient financial resources of their own. Adult children in education are also more likely to coreside with their parents, in contrast to children in gainful employment.

Naturally, adult children who are still in education are much more in need of *money*. In general, it is younger adult children in particular who need financial support from their parents. A similar situation applies to the unemployed.

Furthermore, the needs of elderly parents for help and care may lead to reciprocity in terms of monetary 'rewards'.

Elderly parents in poor health are in special need of considerable *time* transfers by their adult children, be it due to a short-term or long-term illness, or even a condition requiring intense care. Conversely, one could argue that adult children with greater financial needs are more likely to help or care for their parents.

Poor people are in much greater need of an *inheritance* than wealthy ones. The analyses will show whether respondents with no property are actually more likely to receive a bequest. At the same time, helping and caring for elderly parents in need may increase the chances of receiving a 'gratification' in the form of a future inheritance.

Family structures

The relation between parent and child is embedded in family structures. They include, for example, family size and composition, earlier family events as well as family roles and norms. Factors of this kind are number of children, marital status, gender combination of the dyad (daughter-mother, daughter-father etc.) and socialisation, even going back to early childhood. For instance, growing up with divorced parents may have lifelong consequences for the intergenerational solidarity of adult children with both parents.

We can assume that mothers and daughters have the most frequent intergenerational *contact*, especially compared to fathers and sons. We can also expect relatively few contacts in relationships with divorced fathers. Additionally, having more children may lead to somewhat fewer meetings and conversations with each adult child.

Since women in particular are deemed responsible for assuming help and care tasks for their elderly parents, it is quite likely that daughters, in contrast to sons, have more *conflict* with their parents. The existence of grandchildren may reduce controversies between parent and an adult child, owing to the middle generation's 'gatekeeper' position.

It can be expected that adult children without a partner are much more likely to still share living *space* with their parents. Married children can be assumed to be more likely to have left their parents' home. This also applies to adult children who are parents themselves. Overall, it is adult sons who are more likely to still live with a parent.

Family structures may also play a role when it comes to giving *money*. Since resources are generally limited, it is likely that in larger families there will be fewer transfers per person. In other words, the more children, the less money for each adult child. Correspondingly, the existence of grandchildren may reduce the direct transfers to adult children as well.

The obvious hypothesis is that daughters much more often than sons spend *time* helping and caring for their parents. However, when parents (still) have a partner, help and care from adult children should be less probable. Having siblings and children of one's own may also reduce the time spent in supporting one's parents.

A similar situation applies to *inheritance*. The number of siblings, and hence the number of competitors for an inheritance, may play an important role when it comes to receiving wealth from parents. This may also be the case with regard to (grand) children if they emerge as additional 'competitors' for the bequests from parents.

Cultural-contextual structures

Cultural-contextual structures represent societal conditions in which intergenerational relations develop. These include social, political, economic and cultural conditions as well as rules and norms of institutions and groups. Cultural-contextual as well as family structures represent factors in their own right. However, they can be interrelated (family norms can be generalised and societal regulations may 'translate' into family features), and they may also have strong influences on individual opportunities and needs (indicated by arrows in Figure 2.2). The term 'culture' is used in a broad sense, including characteristics of migrants as well as institutions and structures at societal level, such as welfare state regulations and social stratification.

Regarding intergenerational *contact*, one can develop contradicting hypotheses on the basis of welfare state regulations: higher social and family expenditure might 'crowd out' family cohesion or, on the contrary, lead to closer intergenerational contact as a result of easing the burden of intense care tasks. Deciding this controversy requires empirical analyses.

Generating clear hypotheses is a much easier task in the case of family *conflict*: it can be argued that a strong welfare state leads to considerably less difficult situations for family members due to public support in the form of money or services. Correspondingly, greater poverty in a society might also be associated with more intergenerational controversies.

Assuming that adult children and parents, at least at some point, would prefer to live in their own *space*, more public financial support, such as social benefits and family allowances, should decrease intergenerational coresidence amongst adults. Conversely, greater poverty may lead to more family generations living within the same four walls.

A stronger welfare state that relieves families of financial burdens and thus leaves resources for the private transfer of *money* might lead to more intergenerational transfers. This may also apply to countries with more wealth per capita, whereas poverty may lead family generations to spend less money on others.

The extent of social and family expenditure may also play a role in the kind and extent of *time* transfers that adult children provide to their (elderly) parents. A stronger welfare state is likely to unburden adult children of intense care tasks. The question is whether this will lead to more frequent but less burdensome help.

Wealthy countries most probably offer better chances of bequeathing substantial sums from one generation to the next. By contrast, poverty is likely to be associated with lower chances of receiving an *inheritance* – both in the past and future. Furthermore, we can expect considerably fewer bequests for migrants compared to the native population.

Solidarity, conflict and ambivalence

As elaborated above, the ONFC model is a helpful theoretical tool for empirically investigating both solidarity and conflict. The model can be used to study all forms of intergenerational cohesion, including affectual, associational and functional solidarity as well as various forms and extents of controversies. But what about another term that has been used in the realm of generation research, namely 'ambivalence' (e.g., Lüscher and Pillemer 1998; Connidis and McMullin 2002a, b; Connidis 2015. For a critical review see, for example, Bengtson et al. 2002; Hogerbrugge and Komter 2012)? Since a few – partly different, partly intertwined – 'ambivalences' have been suggested, we first need to outline what is actually meant by the term.

Much research has addressed 'psychological ambivalence', suggesting mixed, contradictory or conflicting feelings of individuals, and implying both 'negative' and 'positive' emotions at the same time (e.g., Pillemer et al. 2007: 775; 2012: 1106). Mixed emotions may occur, for example, when individuals feel both affection and aversion toward another person. From this perspective, 'ambivalence has a relatively long history in psychiatry, psychoanalysis, psychotherapy, and psychology' (Connidis and McMullin 2002b: 599; Lüscher 2002). Thus, besides identifying cases experiencing mixed and contradictory emotions, research has tried to identify the impact of ambivalences on individual well-being, including depression, neuroticism and psychological distress (e.g., Lowenstein 2007; Fingerman et al. 2008; Kiecolt et al. 2011).

'Sociological ambivalence' refers to contradictory norms (Lüscher and Pillemer 1998: 415, based on Merton and Barber 1963 and Coser 1966). Those normative contradictions may then give rise to ambivalences at the individual level. Examples are 'conflict between norms regarding solidarity with children and expectations that adult children should become independent' (Pillemer et al. 2007: 776). Connidis and McMullin treat 'ambivalence as structurally created contradictions that are experienced by individuals in their interaction with others' (2002a: 559). This perspective sheds light on contradictions in social structure and thus in social roles. For example, having frail elderly parents can lead to severe ambivalence due to conflicting job demands and family obligations. Moreover, not caring for grandchildren may result in more 'structured ambivalence' – defined as 'the contradiction between behaviour and cultural norms' – when living in a country where grandchild care is highly obligatory (Neuberger and Haberkern 2014: 171). From this perspective, one might debate whether ambivalences 'designate contradictions in relationships between parents and adult offspring that cannot be reconciled' (Lüscher and Pillemer 1998: 416) or whether 'social actors regularly attempt to reconcile ambivalence or risk living in a constant state of inaction' (Connidis and McMullin 2002a: 563).

Further forms of ambivalence have been suggested as well, for example, with regard to incongruent forms of solidarity, including relationships that are emotionally close but involve only infrequent contact (Silverstein and Bengtson 1997: 433; Bengtson et al. 2002: 571). The concurrent appearance of solidarity and conflict has also been perceived as ambivalent (Steinbach 2008: 120; Ferring et al. 2009: 256ff.; Kiecolt et al. 2011: 373; Lendon et al. 2014). Furthermore, '[a]mbivalence may also be viewed as a collective ambivalence of mixed feelings across multiple children – positive with some children but less positive with others' (Ward et al. 2009: 162).

Of course, empirical studies of ambivalence depend crucially on its definition and measurement. Although there have been approaches to operationalise 'ambivalence', no agreement on these issues has been reached. For example, should a survey ask people directly about mixed feelings, or should it employ a more indirect approach, or are both strategies in fact equally suitable (e.g., Kiecolt et al. 2011; Suitor et al. 2011; Lendon et al. 2014)?

The ambivalence hypothesis underlines that intergenerational relationships involve contradictions, paradoxes and dilemmas, such as between closeness and distance, dependence and autonomy, obligation and self-interest, harmony and conflict, or loyalty and opposition. Solidarity can be the result of coming to terms productively with ambivalence. The ability to acknowledge and deal with those contradictions can be seen as an important prerequisite for long-lasting cohesion. Previous notions along the lines of 'intimacy at a distance' (Rosenmayr and Köckeis 1961, 1963) or 'inner closeness through outer distance' (Tartler 1961) point in the same direction.

Solidarity and ambivalence neither compete with one another (e.g., Bengtson et al. 2002: 573; Giarrusso et al. 2005), nor is the concept of solidarity impaired by these contradictions and dilemmas. Depending on its definition, ambivalence can be integrated into the solidarity-conflict model. If the concurrent existence of solidarity and conflict is the issue, the area of 'conflictual solidarity' in Figure 2.1 could be labelled as 'ambivalence'. If the focus is on 'psychological ambivalence', mixed feelings might be addressed within a broad conception of affectual solidarity. However, it is quite difficult to subsume 'sociological ambivalence' into a pure solidarity-conflict model (see Curran 2002; Connidis and McMullin 2002b). The main reason is that this model rather reflects a description of human bonding, whereas explanations of such bonding get the short end of the stick. Thus, there is a need for a more thorough model that addresses the complex conditions of interpersonal relations, including individual, familial and societal factors. In empirical terms, the solidarity-conflict model rather reflects dependent variables (which may be interlinked), whereas the ONFC model (Figure 2.2) provides a broader perspective in order to achieve a thorough picture of solidarity and conflict.

In fact, the ONFC model can be used to identify a number of possible ambivalences. This applies to both contradictions *within* and *between* the four groups of factors (Szydlik 2000: 52f.). *Opportunity structures* include dilemmas between closeness and distance. It is not possible to live in the same home with one's parents and far away from them at the same time. The same applies to time: either a person spends actual time with a specific family member or the person does not. Contradictions apply especially to *need structures*: (adult) children and parents may want to be connected with one another, which may contradict the often simultaneous wish for autonomy. Needing time or money is often set against the desire for independence. The needs of one generation may contradict the needs of another. *Family structures* may involve ambivalence, too, for example, when caring for grandchildren as a form of intergenerational solidarity comes with interference in parenting. Furthermore, members of the middle generation in a 'sandwich' situation may experience mixed feelings as a result of concurrent obligations towards frail parents and dependent children. *Cultural-contextual structures* not least indicate differing norms: on the one hand, adult children are supposed to be independent and thus 'cut the cord' from their parents; on the other hand, general norms demand maintaining contact and exercising intergenerational solidarity. Another dilemma goes back to discrepancies between work and family, when job demands for geographical flexibility stand against obligations to care for (frail) parents.

Opportunity structures may contradict the other three groups of factors, for instance, when financial or time resources are set against one's wishes and needs or when a lack of resources forbids helping other family members. *Needs* for individual autonomy or solidarity may contrast conditions at the family or societal level. How should individuals react when family and society demand that they sacrifice their own needs in order to care for relatives? *Family structures* may contradict individual opportunities and needs as well as societal settings and demands. It may be helpful for families at large when specific family members take on tasks of intergenerational solidarity. However, this must not necessarily also be in the interest of the individual support provider. Furthermore, family-specific norms may not be in accordance with general norms. Last but not least, *cultural-contextual structures* may result in more or less ambivalence for individuals and families. For example, living in a strong welfare state with considerable public services and relatively few normative obligations requiring adult children to care for the elderly, may lead to less mixed feelings about having professionals care for one's parents.

Generation and state

Worlds of welfare

Is there a way to organise countries into a specific order based on their welfare systems, or must we assume that every single country features its own unique arrangements that do not correspond to any general pattern of any kind? These alternative perspectives are discussed in the following, leading to a 'third way' of theoretical reasoning and empirical investigation.

Three basic welfare regimes may serve as a starting point, namely the social-democratic, liberal and conservative model (Esping-Andersen 1990). However, it has been argued that the conservative model actually consists of two types, which has led to distinguishing a fourth model: the familistic regime (e.g., Leibfried 1992;

Lessenich 1994; Ferrera 1996, 1998). Additionally, these four models only refer to Western welfare states and neglect post-socialist countries. Furthermore, some countries cannot easily be assigned to one of the general welfare regimes, leading to the notion of 'mixed forms', or 'special cases'. In fact, theoretical 'ideal types' are rarely found in reality, which leads to the need to exercise some degree of discretion in assigning countries to the various types. For Europe, one can suggest the following general models:

1   *Social-democratic*: Compared to the other types, the social-democratic regime represents the strongest welfare state. It tends to focus on equality and offers comparatively generous social benefits to the whole population. The Scandinavian countries are prominent examples of this type of welfare regime. It is therefore especially fortunate that Sweden and Denmark are included in the Survey of Health, Ageing and Retirement in Europe, and thus in this book. The smallest of the 'three worlds' was developed by social democracy, in particular, promoting 'an equality of the highest standards, not an equality of minimal needs as was pursued elsewhere' (Esping-Andersen 1990: 27). The social-democratic welfare state seeks to compensate the effects of market forces; it aims to reduce social inequality and provide a high degree of social protection. Naturally, a strong welfare state is associated with high costs. Accordingly, the acceptance of high taxes is crucial. High employment also reduces unemployment costs and increases revenue from income tax and social security contributions. The high level of social service provision makes it easier for individuals – and especially for family caretakers – to combine family and work. In contrast to the other proposed welfare regimes, the social-democratic model is less contested with regard to its theoretical suitability for welfare state research. This also applies to the general assignment of the Northern European states to this type of welfare regime.

2   *Liberal*: At the opposite end of the market-state continuum, we find quite weak, even residual welfare states. In these market-oriented political economies, the welfare state only steps in when individuals prove to be in substantial need of social benefits. To the extent that benefits are provided at all, they are means-tested and quite modest. 'Benefits cater mainly to a clientele of low-income, usually working- class, state dependents. (. . .) The archetypical examples of this model are the United States, Canada and Australia' (Esping-Andersen 1990: 26f.). Less clearly attributable European examples are Great Britain (which unfortunately does not take part in SHARE), and to some extent, Ireland (which is included). Later on, Esping-Andersen responded to criticism that Great Britain is one of the countries that might be difficult to assign to one of the three regimes: 'Britain is mainly a problem because the typology does not take into account mutation. (. . .) Britain appears increasingly liberal. Britain is an example of regime-shifting or, perhaps, of stalled "social democratization"' (1999: 87). Ireland does not seem to fit the liberal model perfectly either, since this country is assigned to the group with medium labour market regulation, along with Japan, the Netherlands,

Finland, Norway and Sweden (1999: 85). In the liberal welfare regime, considerably lower social benefits come with lower general costs, and therefore lower taxes as well. Moreover, the state generally supports private insurance for social protection.

3 *Conservative*: Whereas social-democratic and liberal regimes focus more on individuals, the following two models move the family to the centre of attention. With regard to the strength of the welfare state, the conservative regime can be placed in between the social-democratic and liberal types. Conservative welfare states are not as comprehensive as the social-democratic ones, yet they are not as weak as liberal regimes either. A main feature is status protection. In contrast to the social-democratic type, the conservative welfare state is less inclined to compensate the effects of market forces, and is thus less geared toward achieving more equality in society. Social benefits tend rather to be a reflection of previous contributions to the public social security system, which means that inequality tends to be preserved. In contrast to the liberal type, the conservative welfare state does provide considerable social expenditure. However, in doing so, the model supports traditional family patterns, not least based on influences from the church. '[T]he state will only interfere when the family's capacity to service its members is exhausted. (. . .) In the conservative tradition, of course, women are discouraged from working; in the liberal ideal, concerns of gender matter less than the sanctity of the market' (Esping-Andersen 1990: 27f.). Three prominent country examples of conservative welfare regimes are included in the empirical studies in this book, namely Germany, Austria and France.

4 *Familistic*: Initially, 'familistic' states were subsumed under the conservative type. However, a distinct familistic regime was suggested later on to account for the situation in Southern European countries, including Italy, Spain and Greece (Leibfried 1992; Lessenich 1994; Ferrera 1996; Bonoli 1997; Trifiletti 1999; Flaquer 2000). Within the triangle of market, state and family as the main providers of social security, these countries are closer to the family angle. Responsibility for social security is assigned primarily to the family. A weak and even residual welfare state goes hand in hand with strong norms regarding family solidarity, and it is women especially who are made responsible for these tasks. In fact, when assessing welfare regimes, it makes sense to consider their effects on gender inequality (e.g., Sainsbury 1994; Haberkern et al. 2015). Nevertheless, there are also arguments suggesting that the Mediterranean countries can still be assigned to the conservative regime. For example, Castles concludes that 'the countries of Southern Europe must be seen as quite typical members of the Conservative family of nations, which happen to spend less than others in the grouping only because they are poor and have relatively youthful populations' (1995: 311). However, in his influential paper, Reher (1998: 203) distinguishes between 'strong and weak family systems', whereas the former applies to the 'Mediterranean region' and the latter to the 'center and north of Europe' (for recent developments, see Marí-Klose and Moreno-Fuentes 2013).

5   *Post-socialist*: Do the transitory Eastern European, post-'socialist/communist' countries form a welfare regime of their own? Various authors come to different conclusions. Bahle (2008: 104ff.), for example, offers 'alternative hypothetical scenarios'. Zukowski (2009: 28f., see also Cerami 2006) proposes that 'the new member states from Central and Eastern Europe form a unique welfare model.' Rys (2001: 180) argues that '[s]ome common trends are noted in healthcare but this does not seem to add up to a special model.' Ferge (2008: 158) concludes that 'welfare culture does not seem to be very different in the east and west of Europe.' King and Szelényi (2005) distinguish three general varieties of post-communism ('capitalism from without, above and below'). Kollmorgen (2009: 84) discusses three post-socialists welfare regimes on the basis of Esping-Andersen's model. Fenger (2007: 27) finds that 'the post-communist welfare states cannot be reduced to any of Esping-Andersen's or any other well-known types of welfare states.' In any case, one should not neglect the 'socialist' past when it comes to investigating contemporary families. This applies particularly to adult intergenerational relations, which are rooted in (previous) societal contexts during childhood, youth and early adulthood. SHARE offers information on Poland and the Czech Republic. Furthermore, long-term influences of the situation in the former German Democratic Republic will be investigated via separate analyses for East Germany.

6   *Special cases*: Some countries are particularly difficult to assign to a 'family of nations'. A good example is Switzerland, which is sometimes assigned to the liberal model, sometimes to the conservative regime, sometimes even associated with familistic countries and sometimes described as a 'mixed', 'hybrid' or 'special' case (e.g., Esping-Andersen 1990, 1999; Bonoli 1997; Ferrera 1998; Obinger 1998; Armingeon 2001; Wicki 2001; Arts and Gelissen 2002; Imhof 2006). In some ways, the Swiss insurance schemes tend to resemble the conservative model; in others, liberal ideas prevail. Health insurance is obligatory, but there is competition amongst insurance companies. The pension system consists of three pillars: public, occupational and private. '[M]ost scholars agree to qualify Switzerland as a mixed conservative-liberal welfare state (. . .) – possibly with a predominance of continental characteristics' (Oesch 2008: 537). An argument can also be made that a once rudimentary Swiss welfare state has developed over time into a state with more comprehensive social benefits (e.g., Nollert 2007). The 'special case' interpretation with regard to Switzerland is underscored by the Swiss federal system, which involves a variety of welfare designs within the same country (e.g., Armingeon et al. 2004; Obinger et al. 2005). Another example of a special case is the Netherlands. Even Esping-Andersen states: '[T]he Netherlands remains a Janus-headed welfare regime, combining both social democratic and conservative attributes' (1999: 88).

It needs to be pointed out that the previous classification of welfare regimes is definitely not the only one. Various typologies have been offered that assign welfare states to a larger or smaller number of 'families of nations', depending on what is identified as the main underlying principle(s) of differentiation. For example, Esping-Andersen's original model has been criticised for its negligence of gender aspects (e.g., Lewis 1992; O'Connor 1993; Orloff 1993; Anttonen and Sipilä 1996) as well as for discrepancies between the 'pure' theoretical models and empirical reality. For an overview of a number of welfare state typologies (which quite often resemble the one suggested by Esping-Andersen) as well as various classifications of countries, see Arts and Gelissen 2002 and Bambra 2007.

It is also noteworthy that there are a number of explanations for different political economies, focusing on, amongst other things, historical and cultural backgrounds, educational systems, labour market structures, family allowances, social protection and social stratification. Unsurprisingly, these various aspects are linked to a whole range of consequences for individuals and families over the whole life course, including success in education and vocation, career mobility, income inequality, fertility, housing, family stability, compatibility of family and work, and retirement (e.g., Mayer 2001, 2004; Szydlik 2002).

There are even classifications with a particular focus on families. For example, Todd (1983, 1990: 29ff.) speaks of four historical family forms in Europe: *'famille nucléaire absolue, famille nucléaire égalitaire, famille souche, famille communautaire'* [absolute nuclear family, egalitarian nuclear family, stem family, communitarian family]. Lewis (1992) suggests a 'male-breadwinner family model'. Leitner (2003) identifies varieties of familialism by differentiating between 'explicit, optional, implicit and de-familialism'. Saraceno and Keck (2010: 675) propose a 'three-fold conceptualisation of familialism by default, supported familialism and de-familialisation'.

In any case, one needs to ask to what extent there is any regime typology at all that can serve as the basis for identifying international differences in intergenerational relations.

Worlds or states?

Should we refer to 'worlds of welfare', or is it more appropriate to focus on states when investigating intergenerational relations? To answer this question, we need to consider a number of issues:

- Regime typologies are often 'ideal types' that reflect theory rather than reality. They refer to theoretically distinct concepts that are supported by reality to a greater or lesser extent. Quite often, these theoretical ideal types are based on a single core country, which is surrounded by a few peripheral countries that are more or less similar to the core country.
- The assignment of a country to a specific regime depends strongly on the selected criteria. One could, for example, concentrate on (a combination of) care, culture, economy, education, employment, family, gender, history, norms, pensions, policy, religion, rights, social stratification or/and welfare designs.

- Regime types offer somewhat debatable coherence. Within these 'worlds', we may find huge discrepancies. One indication supporting this observation is that the former conservative type was later divided into two 'worlds', leading to the identification of the aforementioned distinct familistic model. There are also considerable differences between countries that are supposed to belong to the same regime.
- Countries with 'mixed backgrounds', as well as those that are located on the periphery of regime types, are quite likely to fall between typologies. Some countries are even described as 'special cases'. These countries stand outside the proposed typology to varying degrees, which means they cannot be ascribed to a specific type at all, or they form types of their own, consisting of a single, specific country.
- How can pronounced historical discrepancies between parts of the same country be taken into consideration? Germany, in particular, comes to mind here. It will still take a long time until all the effects of the different conditions in the 'former' Federal Republic of Germany and the German Democratic Republic have disappeared.
- The risk of lumping together countries into single 'worlds' can also be assessed by considering differences within countries that did not formerly belong to distinct political and economic regimes. In some cases, profound regional differentiation can be observed, not least owing to divergent economic conditions and developments.
- Countries change. For example, the Eastern European post-'socialist' states have been in fundamental transition, which makes it no easy task to decide whether they form a unique welfare regime or whether these countries are taking different paths, which may or may not lead to one of the previously proposed welfare types.

Suggesting 'worlds of welfare' offers great advantages, but we also need to avoid the pitfalls. Drawing on theoretical and empirical research on 'families of nations' provides helpful prerequisites for investigating intergenerational relations. Instead of number crunching without theory, we are offered relevant ideas and findings on international similarities and differences. Instead of a far too detailed preoccupation with all kinds of historical, economical, political, cultural etc. peculiarities of fourteen individual countries, we are now able to conduct international generation research with reference to general welfare models, thus taking a middle course between drowning in too much detail on the one hand, and neglecting important international differences on the other.

Nevertheless, although providing a helpful background, these general 'worlds' represent rather rough outlines of welfare states. The closer one looks, the more relevant details emerge, and the less convincing some of the general models appear. Of course, they represent theoretical 'ideal' types. In reality, however, when investigating countries, we find mixtures of theoretically pure forms of political economies that are, to a greater or lesser extent, close to the theoretical 'idealisations'. Therefore, when addressing intergenerational solidarity, it makes sense to conduct thorough empirical analyses of countries instead of prematurely grouping a number of states into an ideal-type 'regime' and, in doing so, running the risk of neglecting crucial differences. At the very least, one needs to conduct empirical analyses of countries before conclusively identifying the same pattern for a number of states.

In the following, the fourteen countries under consideration will not be lumped together into three, four or five groups per se. Instead, all countries – and additionally two parts of one country in the case of East and West Germany – will be subjected to empirical investigation.

Family in context

Identifying differences between the countries is a crucial first step. One would like to know whether intergenerational relations depend largely on the country where the adult children and parents live. The second step involves introducing other relevant factors into the empirical analyses. Different intergenerational relations in different countries might simply be the product of different population characteristics. In statistical terms, we therefore need to control for those characteristics.

There is also a third step. It is important to find country similarities and disparities while controlling for relevant characteristics of individuals and families. It seems natural to interpret these results on the basis of theoretical reasoning. For example, if we find more intergenerational care in Italy than in Sweden, we might conclude that those country differences are caused by different welfare regimes. However, there is a missing link. Differences between Sweden and Italy in intergenerational care may go back to supposed regime influences, but they may just as well not. If we find more private intergenerational care in Italy than in Sweden – even after considering individual and family characteristics – we might conclude that this empirical result is rooted in more public expenditure for families in Sweden. However, empirically we simply discovered country differences without proving that these empirical disparities are really the result of welfare policies. Therefore, we need to identify specific country contexts – so-called 'macro indicators' – that potentially influence corresponding human behaviour. Such macro indicators are suggested in the following. Their impact will be assessed by empirical analyses.

Figure 2.3 presents the four macro indicators that are employed throughout this book (details on their sources can be found in Table A3). Social and family expenditure represent the scale of the welfare state in the respective country. Wealth per capita and the poverty rate are indicators of social stratification.

The percentages of *social expenditure* document total public spending (for old age, survivors, incapacity related, families, active labour market programmes, housing, other social policy areas) in per cent of GDP per country. Public expenditure represents welfare conditions that are likely to influence private intergenerational solidarity. The figure shows comparatively strong welfare states in Northern Europe. Sweden and Denmark represent the 'social-democratic' regime and, according to the characteristics of this type of welfare system, more public

Countries	Social 0 10 20 30	Family 0 1 2 3 4	Wealth 0 5 10 15	Poverty 0 10 20 30
Sweden	29	3.3	9	11
Denmark	28	3.6	7	12
Ireland	16	2.7	10	23
Netherlands	21	1.7	13	14
Belgium	27	2.6	9	16
France	30	3.0	10	14
Germany	27	2.1	10	17
Poland	21	1.1	3	21
Czech Rep.	19	1.7	4	12
Austria	27	2.8	8	13
Switzerland	20	1.4	15	15
Italy	25	1.3	13	20
Spain	21	1.2	10	21
Greece	21	1.1	8	20

Figure 2.3 Family in context

Sources: OECD 2012 (social expenditure and family expenditure); Davies et al. 2007 (wealth per capita); OECD 2008 (poverty rate).

means are available to the population in these countries. This is in stark contrast to Eastern and Southern European states. From this perspective, inhabitants of 'post-socialist' countries, such as Poland and the Czech Republic, face overall conditions similar to those confronting residents in the familistic states of Spain and Greece. Conservative welfare states such as France, Germany and Austria are marked by substantial social expenditure, the extent of which is quite similar to that of the northern countries.

Family expenditure offers a closer look at public support for private (intergenerational) relations. Such expenditure consists of family allowances, maternity and parental leave, other cash benefits, day care/home-help services and other benefits in kind in per cent of GDP per country. Midway between the extremes of Denmark and Sweden at one end and Poland and Greece at the other lies Germany. Compared to social expenditure, we find an even more pronounced south-north gradient of family welfare, with particularly high rates in the north and especially low rates in the south. The situation is similar for the east-west gradient: post-socialist countries are less able to offer their citizens sizeable family allowances. This is especially striking when we consider where these countries are coming from, namely from a political system with a wide range of state-run social services. It also shows the importance of successful economies, which are better able to provide social benefits to their inhabitants.

The other two variables represent indicators of social stratification. Figure 2.3 documents per capita *wealth* per country adjusted for purchasing power parity in 10,000 €. Switzerland is the richest country with 150,000 euros (converted) per person. An immense fortune has been accumulated, not least as a result of its strong performance in finance and the economy, and the fact that these gains have not been wiped out by war or inflation. On the opposite side of the spectrum, we find Poland and the Czech Republic. In the former 'socialist' states, private wealth was greatly restricted, and the time after the fall of the Iron Curtain has not been sufficient for the general population to acquire substantial assets. Moreover, the accumulation of wealth is a very long process, including bequeathing fortunes over generations. To a lesser degree, this also applies to East Germany, which somewhat reduces overall wealth in Germany. The figure also shows considerable assets in Ireland, Italy and Spain, which are countries with a comparatively high rate of private home ownership.

Last but not least, *poverty* can be expected to have an influence on intergenerational relations. The figure documents the percentage of people below 60 per cent of the median net equivalent income in a country. Poverty not only means that people are deprived of common goods and living conditions. The rate of poverty in a country may also have an influence on common norms and rules as well as on people's feeling of security with regard to their private lives. The figure indicates that countries with relatively large wealth per capita are not necessarily those with less poverty, and vice versa. With few exceptions, one can identify three groups. In the middle of Europe, wealth and poverty are inversely proportional: the more wealth, the less poverty. This general picture applies neither to the north nor to the south of Europe. In the northern countries, wealth per capita is below the average, yet poverty is especially low in Sweden and Denmark. At the opposite end, we find Italy and Spain, which have considerable mean assets, but at the same time extreme poverty. This also applies to Ireland.

Crowding-out, crowding-in

Obviously, there are weaker and stronger welfare states. But what are the consequences for intergenerational family relations? In principle, there are two basic scenarios:

- Welfare states 'crowd out' intergenerational solidarity. In other words, public welfare displaces the family as the main provider of support. Since the welfare state takes over, families retreat.
- Welfare states 'crowd in' intergenerational solidarity. In other words, public welfare enhances family resources to provide support. Since the welfare state takes over some tasks, family solidarity is stimulated and strengthened.

With reference to 'crowding-out', one can consider the 'traditional' family as the main institution for supporting relatives in need (e.g., Kohli 1999). Absence of welfare state support means, for example, that frail elderly persons have to be cared for by family members, and in the 'traditional' family, it is typically women who are assigned these tasks. 'Crowding-out' also implies that the family loses importance in individuals' lives. From this perspective, family becomes a space with young children. 'The influence of the family is reduced to the period before and during schooling (. . .). The risks of work and of old age are no longer covered by the family but by the newly developed welfare state' (Kohli 1999: 83). Into this picture fits Talcott Parsons' credo that relations between adult children and parents are quite weak, if not non-existent: 'Hence, when the children of a couple have become independent through marriage and occupational status the parental couple is left without attachment to any continuous kinship group' (1942: 615f.).

At first glance, the 'crowding-in' argument seems to be contradictory: why should family members give more to one another when support is provided by other sources? There are several possible answers to this question. *First*, concentrating all efforts and available resources on one dependent relative may lead to reducing support for many others. If one person receives everything, nothing is left for all the others. In other words, the resources spent on one family member in great need can restrict opportunity structures for others. For example, if families are relieved of intense care for a frail elderly person, more time and attention may be available for helping others. *Second*, the strain hypothesis suggests that stressful situations and long-lasting dependence may lead to estrangement and conflict amongst family members, which in turn may reduce future solidarity. *Third*, (need for) support can overburden relatives and thus weaken families in the longer run. For example, intense care of frail elderly family members can be extremely strenuous for the carers, even to a point where they become care-dependent themselves, limiting resources and increasing demands even more (e.g., Colombo et al. 2011: 85ff.).

Furthermore, crowding-in assumes additional stimulation of family solidarity by public services. Here it is helpful to differentiate between basic and further needs. A priori, basic physical needs have to be fulfilled, including eating, personal hygiene etc. In a weak welfare state, these basic tasks mainly fall upon family members, leaving fewer resources for further engagement. However, if those basic needs are fulfilled by outside sources, crowding-in implies that families are able to take over other tasks that go beyond basic physical demands. Relieving family carers of the emotionally and physically most strenuous tasks may free up more time and energy for further help, including attention, emotional devotion as well as coordinating the various carers and care tasks.

Whereas the crowding-out scenario proposes in principle an either/or perspective, crowding-in rather points to a combination of private and public responsibility in terms of a mixed welfare regime, engaging both family and state. Developing this idea even further, one might speak of 'mixed responsibility', 'functional differentiation', 'task-specificity' or 'specialisation' (Litwak 1985; Künemund and Rein 1999; Daatland and Herlofson 2003b; Litwak et al. 2003; Daatland and Lowenstein 2005; Motel-Klingebiel et al. 2005; Igel et al. 2009). In such a mixed welfare regime, family and state complement one another, each fulfilling tasks for which it is particularly well suited. For example, heavy burdens, including intense care, are taken over by professionals, whereas other kinds of help, including sporadic assistance as well as emotional attention, are provided by close relatives. In this way, each partner in the support arrangement does what that person or entity can do best, providing comprehensive help to persons in need that exceeds basic physical demands, and at the same time, preventing an overburdening of families in general and daughters in particular (Haberkern et al. 2015).

Crowding-out and crowding-in arguments assume a vivid connection between welfare regime and family solidarity. Again, we need empirical investigations to address the relevant questions: Does the family really step into the breach in the case of a weak welfare state? Does public expenditure reduce or enhance the provision of private support? Is there, indeed, any indication of a specialisation of private and public solidarity?

Generation and inequality

Connections between family and society go in both directions. Cultural-contextual structures have an impact on intergenerational family relations. At the same time, individuals and families influence societal structures as well. This applies most prominently to connections between intergenerational solidarity and social inequality over the whole life course.

Table 2.1 provides an overview that displays (a) central forms of support provided by parents, (b) their effects on children and (c) their consequences for social inequality. It identifies key stages in the children's life course that represent decisive junctions and differentiates between childhood and youth on the one hand and adulthood on the other (see Szydlik 2012a).

Childhood and youth

Stage one: Home

Immediately after birth and in early childhood, parents provide their small children with a more or less favourable environment. This includes the home as such, for instance, whether the child has a room of his or her own, the size and furnishings of the home and the room, and whether there is a garden. Additionally, the parents, via choice of neighbourhood, determine the social background of their children's first friends, their educational ambitions, and the preschool and other educational facilities that their children will attend. Moreover, parents' financial resources can affect their children's allowances, their access to brand-name clothing, computers, sports equipment and long-distance holidays. All of this may enhance or reduce the children's quality of life as well as the social prestige they receive from their peers. The question is whether parents are able to offer their children a lot, or whether the living conditions are cramped or otherwise unfavourable, perhaps even to the point of poverty.

Of course, money and space are not the only factors to affect early childhood. Parental attention and educational effort, in particular, is a key factor in setting the course for child development. Books play an important role in acquiring skills, particularly as part of reading socialisation in the family, which includes reading children's books aloud and looking at picture books together. Moreover, early access to and attentive supervision of handling information technologies may

Table 2.1 Generation and inequality

	Support of parents →	*Effect on children* →	*Inequality effect*
Childhood/ youth	*Space, money, time:* House, garden, room, city, neighbourhood, books, education	**Home** – *Quality of life and esteem. Friends* (neighbourhood)	*Inequality in the quality of life in (early) childhood*
	Aspirations, time, money: Computer, help with homework, private tutoring	**School** – *Choice of school and school success:* Lower, medium, higher school	*Lifelong inequality:* Education → income, prestige, (un)employment, partner, health, . . .
	Aspirations, information, network, money: Internship, apprenticeship, job	**Work** – *Choice of profession, vocational success*	*Inequality in vocation and career*
Adulthood	*Provision of living space and time*	**Space** – *Saving* money and time. *Investments* in education	*Inequality in living conditions and education*
	Monetary support: Payments, goods, presents, securities. *Passing on of wealth*	**Money** – *Quality of life. Investments* in education and vocation. *Wealth creation*	*Inequality in education and quality of life in adulthood*
	Bequest	**Inheritance** – *Quality of life.* Wealth, security, independence, influence	*Inequality in quality of later life*

contribute to a so-called 'digital divide' (e.g., DiMaggio et al. 2001; Korupp and Szydlik 2005). All in all, parents who place great emphasis on education and fostering their children's abilities intensively early on results in lifelong benefits for these children (e.g., Ermisch et al. 2012).

Conversely, the children of parents with a lower educational background who harbour lower educational aspirations are at a disadvantage their whole life. In this way, unequal living conditions and different parenting styles lead to an unequal quality of life and unequal preconditions for the child generation, thus laying the foundations for lifelong inequality.

Stage two: School

In an education society, one of the most important, if not the most important, junction in life is the type of school attended. Inequality in education contributes to lifelong social differences early on. The better educated achieve higher incomes in more secure employment, receive greater professional prestige, enjoy a more favourable position in partner and marriage 'markets', are in a better state of health and live longer (e.g., Szydlik 1994, 2002; Blossfeld 2009; Mackenbach et al. 2008). The type of school is strongly influenced by the parents (e.g., Becker and Lauterbach 2010; König 2016). In this respect, early parental support, but also the parents' wishes and aspirations, affect the transition to schools offering advanced-track education. As a primary effect of social background, better-educated parents with more resources are more likely to offer their children an encouraging learning environment right from the start. This results in greater educational achievement and thus facilitates the transition to higher education. As a secondary effect of social background, parents with lower education and fewer resources tend to send their children to the lower tracks of education, even if their children perform well in school. By contrast, for better-educated parents it is a matter of course that their children attend advanced schools, all the way to college or university (Boudon 1974). In fact, a major reason for relatively low numbers of university students from a lower social background is choice of school at a very young age.

Parental influence, however, does not stop with the choice of school. Instead, parents continue to promote their children's development throughout their entire school career to a greater or lesser degree. Better-educated parents are better prepared to provide their children with a learning environment at home that is conducive to developing school-related skills (see Bourdieu and Passeron 1971; Buchmann and Kriesi 2010; Angelone and Ramseier 2012). This includes assistance with and supervision of homework as well as providing equipment, such as school materials, computers, musical instruments, language courses and, if necessary, with costly private tutoring. Therefore, it comes as no surprise when empirical studies attest to a significant correlation between parental resources and their children's skills. For example, the PISA study (Programme for International Student Assessment) shows that reading proficiency varies greatly according to parental status. In the OECD (Organisation for Economic Cooperation and Development), the children in the lowest of four status groups scored 451 points, whereas the offspring in the highest status group scored 540 on the reading scale. In other words, youths whose parents fall into the bottom status group score nearly 100 points lower on the reading scale than 15 year olds in the top quarter. Differences related to parental status are much more pronounced compared to those related to gender (female 513, male 474) or migration status (migrants 457, natives 499; OECD 2010a/b; Szydlik 2012a: 63).

Stage three: Work

Besides parents laying the foundations for all vocational prospects because of their immense influence on education, they can also play a direct role in the transition from education to employment. This may involve the contacts they can provide, for instance, to help find an internship, an apprenticeship position or even employment. For example, the children of employees or important customers may have an advantage compared to youths and young adults who cannot draw on parental resources of this kind. It can be helpful when parents own a business or can provide orientation and assist in decision making drawing on their own experience, or that of friends and acquaintances. The taken-for-granted application of cultural rules in the sense of 'subtle distinctions' (Bourdieu 1979) can also be beneficial in the search for employment. Parents' different endowments with various resources are therefore a crucial factor in determining the opportunities that the next generation faces in the course of their lives, thus leading to reinforcing and deepening social disparities. This applies not only to the better chances of already privileged children, but also to the continuous disadvantages of underprivileged offspring. In any case, empirical research shows that 'living conditions during childhood and adolescence structure socio-economic circumstances in midlife' (Bäckman and Nilsson 2011: 107).

Adulthood

Since, in anticipation of the empirical results of this book, intergenerational relationships do not cease once the children have become adults, the question is to what extent parents continue to be a source of intergenerational support, and what consequences this entails for their offspring and for social inequality.

Stage four: Space

When children become adults they do not necessarily move out of their parents' homes. Provision of living space is a valuable form of functional solidarity, which will be addressed in detail in Chapter 6. Adult children still living with their parents are mostly of a younger age (Figure 6.1), which means that they are postponing leaving the parental home rather than staying there forever. Coresident adult daughters and sons save money since they do not have to pay rent for their own place, and they also often receive support in the form of time spent on cooking, cleaning and doing laundry, for example. Thus, when assessing the consequences of coresidence, one should not neglect the time parents spend in supporting their adult children who still live within the same four walls. Furthermore, provision of space can often also be seen as an investment in education. For example, university students still living 'at home' may enjoy a more favourable learning environment than those who have to earn their own living and provide for their own housing.

In any case, there are benefits involved – whether in the form of financial savings, time support or investments in education – to the children of parents who are able to provide living space to their adult children. These benefits, or the absence thereof, can be considered a form of inequality between young adult children whose parents have the opportunity to do so and those who do not. This type of support may comprise coresidence in the strict sense, namely sharing the same household, or near coresidence – that is, living in the same building although in different apartments – as well as supporting adult children financially when moving out and living on their own, at a greater or lesser geographical distance.

In fact, most adult children and parents do not live in the same household anymore, especially when the adult child is beyond the age of thirty. Therefore, when researching adult intergenerational solidarity and its consequences for social inequality, we need to address, in particular, the monetary resources passed on from parents to adult children, while differentiating between inter vivos and mortis causa transfers, i.e., financial support amongst living generations as well as inheritances from deceased parents.

Stage five: Money

Table 2.1 lists payments, goods, presents and securities as monetary support from parents to adult children as well as the passing on of wealth in the form of substantial gifts. All of these are important sources of support. They can take the form of financial assistance for children in higher education, at times of unemployment, when starting or redirecting one's career, during further training, or in establishing self-employment. Such support can involve contributions in the case of family events, such as the birth of a child (grandchild from the parents' perspective), marriage or divorce, as well as loan guarantees or direct transfers to acquire a home or set up a household. Furthermore, presents – for instance, on birthdays, at Christmas, for a wedding etc. – serve an important function. Besides the financial gain, they act as a signal symbolising affection and close bonds, encourage future reciprocity and consolidate intergenerational relationships beyond the boundaries of the household.

Chapter 7 investigates monetary transfers from parents to adult children. One of the questions raised in this context pertains to the connection between these transfers and social inequality. Previous studies show that such transfers are, indeed, often a response to need. When the adult child is (still) in education, this increases the likelihood of transfers considerably (Szydlik 2000: 136; see also Künemund et al. 2005). From this perspective, intergenerational transfers can temporarily reduce social inequality in the children's generation, as such financial support decreases income differentials between students in higher education and young workers *in the short term*. However, graduates of higher education typically earn a significantly higher income, so that the support provided by parents to children in higher education tends to contribute to increasing social inequality *in the long run*. Intergenerational transfers make higher education possible in the first place, and it is much easier to focus on one's studies without having to worry about earning a living. Moreover, according to empirical findings (see above and Chapter 7), parents' financial resources are a tremendously important factor in intergenerational transfers. The more income and financial assets parents have, the more likely they are to give money or goods to their adult children. Parents who have more give more. Parents who have no resources cannot support their descendants financially, no matter how great the need of their adult children may be.

Apart from everyday assistance, inter vivos transfers include extraordinary gifts, which can also involve the transfer of wealth. Previous findings show that these gifts stem mostly from parents. They fall to children at an earlier point in their lifetime than inheritances (Szydlik 2000; see also Leopold and Schneider 2010). However, gifts occur less often than inheritances. Apparently, parents are reluctant to part with the whole of their property too early. After a lifetime of saving to live in their own home, many parents do not want to end up living in their children's house. Besides, along the lines of a 'King Lear effect', prospective testators are perhaps not completely sure that their future heirs will still provide sufficient attention or even care if those heirs have already received everything. Nevertheless, the findings also provide evidence that the upper classes in particular are frequent beneficiaries of substantial gifts, so that those who have already benefited most from intergenerational transfers by parents during childhood and adolescence are at a further advantage.

Stage six: Inheritance

Receiving a sizeable bequest may lead to (more) wealth, financial security and independence as well as greater influence in the family and beyond. Previous studies show that inheritances stem mostly from parents (Szydlik 2004, 2011b). Inheritance research is intergenerational research. However, only fairly small portions of the population are beneficiaries of large bequests. Furthermore, inheritances are less likely to accord with need. Beneficiaries are frequently adult children with more than sufficient income. By contrast, those who could use an inheritance most seem to be the least likely to receive one. This is reinforced further by educational background. Here, the consequences of lifelong intergenerational solidarity are particularly apparent. Parents who are able to offer their children better educational opportunities from the start are also in a position to bequeath larger estates at the end of their lives. Yet it is the lower educational classes that would need such financial gain the most.

Since passing assets from one generation to the next generally occurs along family lines, such transfers do not contribute to changing social inequality when viewed from a family perspective: poor families stay poor, and wealthy families stay wealthy. An argument can also be made that a smaller sum may represent a comparatively larger *relative* gain for people without previous possessions. To a millionaire, an inheritance of a million euros may stand for a lower *relative* gain with regard to the person's previous wealth, compared to a much smaller sum inherited by a person with little or no prior wealth at all. To someone whose previous 'wealth' amounted to one euro, an inheritance worth one hundred euros (e.g., a few used clothes or simple tableware) is mathematically one hundred times greater in relative terms than a million euros is to a millionaire. Thus, one needs to take absolute sums into account in order to assess the usefulness of an inheritance for improving previous living conditions. Moreover, the empirical findings show that heirs are strongly favoured as it is. Before the death of their parents, they will already have received substantially greater support over their entire lifetime compared to what lower-class parents will have been able to provide to their children owing to a lack of resources.

If the analyses in Chapter 9 confirm these findings, we can conclude that, from a life course perspective, inheritances at least stabilise, if not deepen, previously existing social inequality between advantaged and disadvantaged children. The increase in inequality over the life course via lifelong intergenerational support is especially pronounced when it comes to education and choice of school, that is, early in life. However, differentiation between children according to parental resources does not end here but lasts over the parents' entire lifetime – and even beyond in the case of bequests.

Summary

This chapter lays the groundwork for the empirical investigations later on. In a book about generations, the first task is to outline what 'generations' are about. In principle, two concepts are distinguished, namely generations in family and society. Family generations refer to grandparents, parents, children, grandchildren etc. They represent the term 'generation' in the closest and clearest sense. Other concepts – and especially the abundance of generational labels that have been coined on the basis of more or less sound foundations – are much more difficult to grasp. Nevertheless, one can identify social generations, which, in principle, can be further distinguished as political, cultural and economic generations. However, there are several challenges and conditions to be met when trying to identify social generations, in contrast to family generations.

Since this book addresses intergenerational family solidarity, we also need to clarify what is meant by this term. Generally, it refers to bonds and interactions between family members of different generations. Three main dimensions can be distinguished, namely affectual, associational and functional solidarity. Affectual solidarity describes emotional closeness, associational solidarity refers to contact and functional solidarity comprises the giving and taking of money, time and space. Furthermore, one has to note that solidarity is not necessarily 'good', just as conflict is not inevitably 'bad'; these are rather empirical questions. Nor does solidarity imply that these relationships are devoid of controversy. These considerations lead to Figure 2.1 which illustrates the connection between solidarity and conflict that shows that most intergenerational relations can be attributed to 'consensual solidarity'.

To explain intergenerational cohesion, a general theoretical model is proposed, comprising opportunity, need, family and cultural-contextual structures (ONFC). Opportunity structures reflect opportunities or resources. They enable, promote, hinder or prevent social interaction. Need structures indicate the needs for social interaction. They also include desires, goals, interests, motives, wants and wishes of individuals, for themselves or for significant others. The relation between parent and child is embedded in family structures. They include, for example, family size and composition, earlier family events as well as family roles and norms. Cultural-contextual structures represent societal conditions in which intergenerational relations develop. These include social, political, economic and cultural conditions as well as rules and norms of institutions and groups. Furthermore, in continuation of the previous subchapter, the ONFC model is related to the notion of ambivalence.

As a basis for the international comparisons, various general welfare types are distinguished, namely social-democratic, liberal, conservative, familistic and post-socialist regimes. Furthermore, one can identify 'special cases'. Should we thus speak of 'worlds of welfare', or is it more appropriate to consider different states? In between these two opposites, the book pursues a third way: its theoretical reasoning includes arguments connected with the aforementioned welfare types, whereas the empirical investigations will refer to states. Classifications of countries can be helpful orientation points. However, for empirical analyses of intergenerational relations, country-oriented analyses seem to provide a more suitable approach. Furthermore, four macro indicators are suggested, which put family cohesion in context: social and family expenditure, wealth and poverty. The potential impact of weaker and stronger welfare states on intergenerational solidarity is discussed via the 'crowding-out' and 'crowding-in' hypotheses, which provide alternative scenarios for the subsequent international analyses.

Last but not least, the chapter addresses connections between private intergenerational solidarity and social inequality. Applying a life course perspective, it discusses most relevant forms of support from parents to children, spanning from cradle to grave. Six stages are identified: home, school, work, space, money and inheritance. The first three stages refer to childhood and youth. Affluent parents succeed in many ways by ensuring that their offspring enjoy a particularly high quality of life. Of special importance are parental efforts to promote the educational success of their children, leading to lifelong disparities between educational classes, including income, prestige, (un)employment, success in partner and marriage 'markets' as well as lifelong health and even longevity. Further support for adult children comprises space, regular monetary support and extraordinary gifts as well as bequests. Children of affluent parents seem to be advantaged over their entire life course. The precarious connection between solidarity and inequality will also be addressed in more detail in the following chapters of this book.

3   Crisis? What crisis?

Introduction

Many arguments have been made about why families seem to be in crisis: decreasing fertility, increasing longevity of frail elderly relatives, a higher care burden and smaller care capacity, more flexibility demands in the labour market, individualisation, high divorce rates, geographical mobility, unemployment, mounting intergenerational conflict, negative consequences of the retreat of the welfare state, shrinking household sizes, separation of generations due to techno-logical change, a lower degree of family orientation as a consequence of rising female employment, obstinate youth and stubborn elders, egoistic adult children and irresponsible parents who would rather spend their children's inheritance, and so on. The crisis scenario is indeed worrying, since it may easily result in a crisis of society at large.

How true is this so-called crisis? How many families actually experience crisis in reality? This is one of the general questions addressed in this book. In order to find out whether demographic change, flexibilisation, individualisation, welfare state retreat, and so forth, have indeed resulted in alienation between (adult) children and parents, we need empirical investigations on intergenerational cohesion. At the same time, a closer look at these bonds can help assess whether there exists a sound basis to withstand those challenges in the future.

Before investigating contact, conflict, space, money, time and inheritance in detail, this chapter provides a general outline of intergenerational cohesion. This first empirical chapter rests on two pillars. It starts with the identification of basic potentials for intergenerational cohesion, namely the existence and distance of fam-ily generations as well as norms of obligation. Naturally, the first prerequisite of intergenerational solidarity is the existence of generations. If one does not have living parents, it makes no sense to consider current solidarity between adult chil-dren and parents. In the same vein, potential bonds with adult children depend first of all on the existence of an adult daughter or son. The second relevant prerequi-site is close geographical distance, which provides opportunities for direct personal interaction without long-distance travel or technological mediation. A third potential for solidarity are norms of obligation, which provide a framework for intergenera-tional cohesion and support among family members. The first part of this chapter discusses these three prerequisites successively on the basis of empirical results.

The other pillar on which this chapter rests is an empirical overview of intergenerational relationships, which revolves around solidarity and conflict. Is it symbiosis or autonomy, or is it harmony or hostility that prevails? The empirical results are organised into a general typology on the basis of the four categories developed in Chapter 2 (Figure 2.1), namely consensual solidarity, conflictual solidarity, conflictual autonomy and consensual autonomy. Furthermore, it will be shown whether there are differences in the distribution of relevant types among educational classes, income groups, women and men, as well as migrants and natives.

Both parts of the chapter aim to provide a basis for the following in-depth investigations of intergenerational relations between adult children and parents.

Potentials

Existence

Figure 3.1 documents the percentage of respondents who are part of families consisting of one, two, three or (at least) four generations. For example, the notation '4 generations' means that these SHARE participants live in at least a four-generation family, including themselves. Under consideration are parents, children, grandchildren and great-grandchildren (the survey does not provide information on the respondents' grandparents).

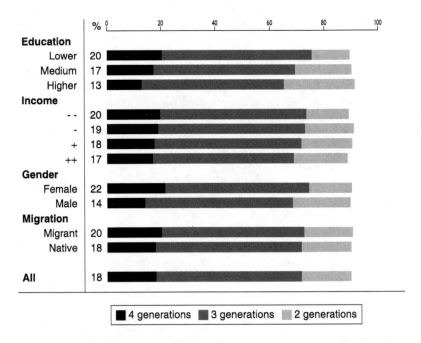

Figure 3.1 Multigenerational families

Source: SHARE (n: 39,045).

First of all, the figure indicates that family generations are indeed very common. The great majority, namely 90 per cent of those aged 50+, have at least one more living generation. In turn, only a tenth report neither a parent, nor a child or a (great-) grandchild. Further differentiation of these 10 per cent (not presented in the figure) shows that people without a partner and sibling account for only 2 per cent. Being without any other family member at all, or having only more distant relatives, such as aunts, uncles, nieces, nephews or cousins, is thus very rare.

There seems to be great potential for intergenerational solidarity. A quite impressive fact is that close to a fifth of the European population of at least 50 years of age even lives in a four-generation family, which means that they have three other living family generations, be they parents, children and grandchildren, or children, grandchildren and great-grandchildren (in the figure, families consisting of five generations are subsumed into this category as well; however, they are almost non-existent). Over half of the respondents live in three-generation families, i.e., with parents and children, children and grandchildren etc. Nearly another fifth have one living family generation, be it at least one parent or one offspring.

What about population groups? Lower education is associated with a higher number of family generations, at least when it comes to four-generation families. One in five of those with relatively low education has a family consisting of three other living generations, whereas this applies to only 13 per cent of the academics. Reasons include timing of childbirth and number of children. Fewer children (Figure 3.2) and later birth over several generations – which is quite typical of the better educated – lead to less (great-)grandparenthood. Further investigations show that over two-thirds of the lower class has at least one grandchild, whereas this 'only' applies to 43 per cent of the academics. Twelve per cent of the former and 3 per cent of the latter group report great-grandchildren. This does not mean that academics are less likely to have any other living generation at all. In fact, the better educated have fewer multigenerational families. They are, however, not less likely to be without any other family generation.

With regard to multigenerational families, income groups show a similar pattern to the educational classes (although the differences are less pronounced). Poorer households have more generations. One possible reason is that this simply reflects educational background. Financial obligations towards more family members may at times also lead to a situation in which making ends meet becomes a difficult task.

Women are much more likely to have more living generations. This applies to grandchildren and great-grandchildren in particular, suggesting a strong influence of longevity on shared lifetime with these younger family members. In this respect, men are at a disadvantage. The difference between migrants and natives is small here and attributable to children, grandchildren and great-grandchildren.

Figure 3.2 provides a more detailed picture of the potential availability of parents and children. The left part focuses on the parental side. The first group consists of those respondents whose parents are both still alive. In total, this applies to 6 per cent of the respondents. At first glance, this percentage may seem to be surprisingly low. However, the survey refers to the population aged 50 years

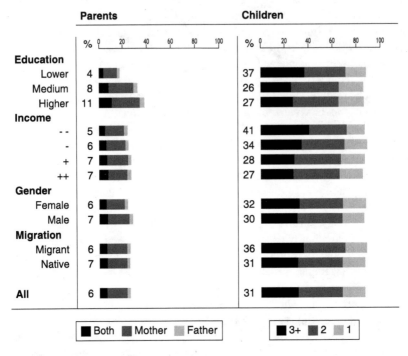

Figure 3.2 Parents and children

Source: SHARE (n: 38,599/39,151).

and older. Furthermore, when one considers respondents with a living mother or father, more than a quarter of those aged 50+ have the potential for intergenerational solidarity with a parent.

Further investigations show that this number depends on age in particular. More than three in five of the 50–55 year olds have at least one living parent. This applies to three in ten of the 56–65 year olds, but only to 3 per cent of the older respondents. This means that upward intergenerational relationships are basically limited to people under the age of 66 years. Unsurprisingly, we find more living mothers than fathers owing to the longer lives of women and their younger age at the time of the child's birth.

When considering relationships with parents, one might also think of parents-in-law (not shown in the figure). Including them adds another 8 per cent to the proportion of respondents with a living relative on the parental side. All in all, a third of the SHARE participants have at least one living mother (-in-law) or father(-in-law). This applies to over seven in ten of the 50–55 year olds, four in ten of the 56–65 year olds and 6 per cent of the older population. For these respondents, the potential for intergenerational relationships with a parent(-in-law) is still intact.

Particularly striking differences between population groups with regard to the potential availability of parents are associated with educational class. The better-educated population is much more likely to have a living parent, which reflects the longer lives of the upper classes (Mackenbach et al. 2008). This also indicates that the small number of upper-class respondents without any other family generation in Figure 3.1 is a result of more academics having living parents. Only 4 per cent of those with a lower educational background still have both parents, whereas this applies to 11 per cent of the academics, 38 per cent of which have at least one parent (48% including parents-in-law) compared to only 18 per cent of the lower educational class (24% including parents-in-law). Due to social immobility, higher-educated children have higher-educated parents (who live longer), and lower-educated children have lower-educated parents (who pass away earlier).

In contrast to class, differences between income groups are less pronounced, and migrants do not differ from natives in this respect. However, we find some gender disparities. Women live longer than men, and are more likely to survive their parents. Four in ten male interviewees are potentially able to experience intergenerational solidarity with the previous generation (including parents-in-law), whereas this applies to fewer than three in ten female respondents.

The right part of Figure 3.2 documents potential relationships with the next generation. Of the European population aged 50 years or more, 87 per cent have at least one child. This means that, when parent-child relationships are investigated, only 13 per cent are excluded from the analyses. More than two-thirds have at least two children, nearly a third three or more descendants, one in eight has at least four offspring and 5 per cent even five or more children. Indeed, there is huge potential for intergenerational solidarity.

The lower educated have fewer living parents but more children. This is primarily a result of parents having more children, and much less owing to different shares of childlessness. A similar thing applies to income groups and migrants compared with the native population.

Further investigations (not shown in the figures) indicate that the potential for intergenerational solidarity reaches beyond the next generation. Three in five respondents have at least one grandchild, nearly half of the interviewees report two or more grandchildren, a third three or more, a quarter four or more, a sixth five or more, and 12 per cent have at least six grandchildren. Moreover, 8 per cent mention at least one great-grandchild. Grandchildren and great-grandchildren are more frequent in the lower classes and income groups as well as amongst female respondents and migrants.

Distance

When it comes to potentials for intergenerational solidarity, one prerequisite is the existence of parents and children. Another is geographical distance. Close distance provides opportunities for personal contact; it allows spontaneous encounters and a range of interaction forms. Meeting in person and talking face to face is likely to foster a different quality of relationship compared to contact by electronic devices such as telephone and computer. Living close by also facilitates quick help, for instance, in times of illness or when there is a need for support with gardening, household chores, running errands and taking care of one another. One might also presume that living in the same city, village or region can contribute to a better mutual understanding since this involves sharing similar living environments. Seeing and meeting each other on a regular basis can be expected to contribute to being informed about the current needs of the other person, and may also foster a stronger sense of responsibility.

Research has indeed shown that distance is a crucial factor for intergenerational support (e.g., Szydlik 2000; Brandt et al. 2009; Haberkern and Szydlik 2010; Igel and Szydlik 2011). This is also supported by the analyses presented in this book. A shorter distance increases the frequency of contact considerably (Chapter 4) as well as the amount of help and care provided (Chapter 8).

Figure 3.3 offers information on geographical distances of those aged 50+ from parents and adult children. Only persons with at least one living parent or adult child, respectively, are surveyed. In the case that both of a respondent's parents or several children live at different distances, the closest one is reported in order to assess the potential for solidarity.

First of all, only a very small fraction (below 1%) of the respondents share the same household with a parent, and a mere 6 per cent reside in the same house.

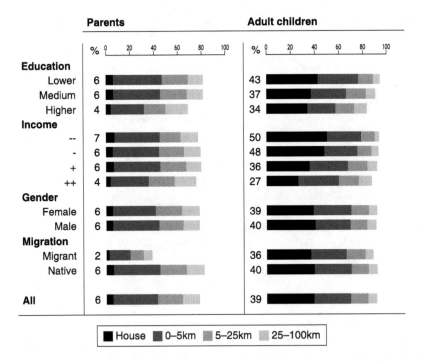

Figure 3.3 Distance

Source: SHARE (n: 10,133/34,483).

However, this does not mean that parents generally live far away. In fact, for 22 per cent the spatial distance is less than 1 kilometre and for 43 per cent up to 5 kilometres. Nearly two-thirds reside at a distance of up to 25 kilometres from a parent, and close to four out of five report a distance of 100 kilometres at the most. Half of the remaining respondents live between 100 and 500 kilometres away, a quarter more than 500 kilometres, and the last quarter (i.e., 5% overall) more than 500 kilometres away in another country.

Nevertheless, there are striking differences between educational classes. Figure 3.3 confirms previous analyses that observed a considerably lower likelihood of geographical proximity for the higher classes (e.g., Szydlik 2000). Academics face flexibility demands in education and employment that result in greater distances from their family of origin. Less spatial proximity can also be found amongst the highest income group. In contrast, there does not seem to be a great difference in geographical distance from parents between daughters and sons. However, as expected, there is an immense disparity between migrants and the native population. Of course, migration very often involves greater distances from mothers and fathers. Two-thirds of the natives live 25 kilometres away from a parent at the most. This applies to less than one-third of migrants. If we consider a range of up to 500 kilometres, the difference is 94 versus 48 per cent.

The right part of Figure 3.3 presents geographical distance from adult children. Close to 40 per cent of the parents aged 50+ live under the same roof with at least one adult child. If we add those parents whose closest child lives a maximum of 1 kilometre away, we arrive at a total of 54 per cent. If we consider a radius of 5 kilometres, we find that seven out of ten parents have at least one adult child who lives in close vicinity. Expanding that distance to 25 kilometres includes 84 per cent of the parents. More than nine out of ten parents live within 100 kilometres of an adult child, 98 per cent within 500 kilometres.

In what way do the distances differ according to education, income, gender and migration? Better-educated parents, who are more likely to have better-educated children, live at a greater spatial distance from their offspring, which reflects the greater geographical mobility of the higher educational classes. The situation is similar for income groups, whereas mothers and fathers do not report notable differences in terms of spatial separation. Although migration seems to lead to fewer children living nearby, the difference from the native population is not very pronounced. The major discrepancy between migrants and natives is rather their geographical detachment from parents.

Further investigations refer to the distance of generations living in separate households (not shown in figures). Since there are very few respondents who live with their parents, the picture is very similar to the one in the left part of Figure 3.3. However, this is not the case for parents living with children. If we only consider parents and adult children in separate households, a third still lives within 1 kilometre, 56 per cent within 5 kilometres, for more than three in four the distance does not exceed 25 kilometres, and nearly 90 per cent live within a maximum distance of 100 kilometres. This means that even after leaving their parents' home, most adult children do not move very far away. In fact, they tend to stay in close proximity.

The results with regard to class confirm the previous findings: again, the lower classes are more likely to live close to their children even after they have left home. This also applies to income groups. Mothers are somewhat more likely to live close to an adult child. This is less probable for migrants, although the difference from the native population is not overwhelming.

Obligations

A third prerequisite of intergenerational solidarity is norms of obligation. General norms about how things ought to be and what one should or should not do may lead to significant acts of solidarity, not least out of a sense of duty. The existence of parents or children and a close distance between family generations are crucial factors. However, if people do not feel obliged to help one another, it may well be that they will not. In fact, family obligations can be seen as normative guidelines that stimulate solidarity behaviour. They are 'stable, but striving to be more adaptive' (Daatland and Herlofson 2003a: 127; see also Finch and Mason 1990; Elmelech 2005; Gans and Silverstein 2006; Merz et al. 2009).

The Survey of Health, Ageing and Retirement in Europe addresses obligations with regard to older people and children in different ways. The left part of Figure 3.4 refers to responsibilities of families as opposed to the state when it comes to older persons. Apart from obligations to provide financial support and/or help with household chores, SHARE asks: 'In your opinion, who – the family or the State – should bear the responsibility for (. . .) [p]ersonal care for older persons who are in need such as nursing or help with bathing or dressing?' Five answers are possible: 'Totally family' – 'Mainly family' – 'Both equally' – 'Mainly state' – 'Totally state'.

The right part of the figure refers to a statement on obligations towards children: 'Parents' duty is to do their best for their children even at the expense of their own well-being'. The five possible answers are: 'Strongly agree' – 'Agree' – 'Neither agree nor disagree' – 'Disagree' – 'Strongly disagree'. Again, the last category is represented in the figure by the empty spaces between the bars and the total of 100 per cent.

First of all, when assessing the overall shares of care obligations regarding older people (not least parents from the respondents' point of view), one notices that the middle category of 'both equally' receives the most approval of all response options: 46 per cent of the respondents agree that family and state are equally responsible. Although this is not the majority, those who see responsibility resting either more with the family or more with the state each represent a smaller group. Further indication of mixed responsibility is that the extreme groups – namely 'totally family' and 'totally state' – are especially underrepresented (5% and 6%, respectively). If we add up those respondents who do not favour one of these extreme groups and lean toward a mix of public and private instead, we arrive at very impressive numbers. Nine out of ten interviewees are in favour of some kind

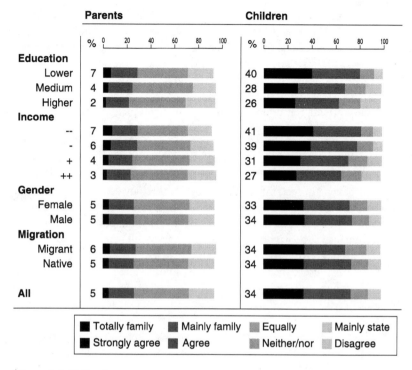

Figure 3.4 Obligations

Source: SHARE (n: 24,048/24,197).

of mixed arrangement between family and state, be the emphasis more on the family or more on the state.

Educational classes, income groups, women and men, migrants and natives – all these groups follow the general pattern overall. However, some differences can be noted regarding education and income. Extreme points of view, such as absolute family or state orientation, as rare as they are in general, are more frequent in the lower educational and income groups, whereas academics especially often favour mixes of family and state. In fact, we find a linear relationship: the more education and income, the less extreme the respondents' opinions. At the same time, higher education and income are associated with fewer family obligations, indicating that since the affluent classes are more able to afford professional care, they are less likely to feel entirely responsible themselves (Finley et al. 1988; Gans and Silverstein 2006).

Further investigations refer to help and money. It is worth comparing where the interviewees see the primary responsibility when it comes to helping with household chores (cleaning, washing etc.), personal care and financial support for the elderly. Whereas help in particular is rated as a family affair, many respondents are in favour of the state when monetary assistance is the issue. More than a third believe that the family is mainly (30%) or even totally (6%) responsible when it comes to providing assistance with household chores for older people in need. The corresponding shares for financial means are only 12% and 3%. While, overall, household help tends to be attributed more to the family and financial transfers more to the state, personal care does not lean one way or the other. Moreover, further country results support the general assumptions on welfare regimes (Chapter 2), showing much greater preference for the state in the north and more family orientation in the east and south. Nevertheless, in all countries, the vast majority agrees to a mix of private and public support.

When considering obligations towards children according to the right part of Figure 3.4, it is impressive how many people (strongly) agree with the statement that '[p]arents' duty is to do their best for their children even at the expense of their own well-being'. In fact, this applies to nearly three-quarters of the respondents (and this even includes the childless). Every third respondent strongly agrees to put children first, even if this involves personal disadvantages. This is an indication of an immense solidarity potential. Only every tenth person disagrees, and just 2 per cent disagree strongly.

Solidarity norms are especially prevalent among the lower social class, which has less opportunity to draw on outside sources (see above). Four out of five respondents with lower education agree to this statement; two in five even strongly. By contrast, this applies to 'only' a quarter of the academics. However, also amongst academics a large majority of 62 per cent agrees to put children first. The situation is similar with regard to income groups. If the household is able to make ends meet easily, less obligation is felt towards the next generation. A difficult income situation, however, is associated with an increased sense of duty toward children. Nevertheless, norms of intergenerational solidarity are strong across all income groups. This is also the case for women and men as well as for migrants and the native population.

High rates in the sense of obligation towards children are found in the familistic south in particular, and it is no surprise that family-oriented Ireland and Poland also show very high shares of approval. Further results indicate that it makes sense to consider individual countries instead of regimes, since several states that are actually attributed to the same regime seem to differ in the populations' point of view on matters of intergenerational obligations.

Types

There are a number of ways to identify types of intergenerational relations, including different analytical and methodological strategies, based on different data sets, resulting in different outcomes with regard to the number and share of types of relationships as well as the labels that they are assigned (e.g., Silverstein et al. 1994; Silverstein and Bengtson 1997; Szydlik 2000; Van Gaalen and Dykstra 2006; Fokkema et al. 2008; Ferring et al. 2009; Nauck 2009; Silverstein et al. 2010; Dykstra and Fokkema 2011). Following the theoretical reasoning illustrated in Figure 2.1, a quite simple procedure is chosen in the context of this analysis.

To provide a general picture of the relationships between family generations, three dimensions are summarised: contact, conflict and support. Solidarity and conflict are related to one another in the process, including associational (contact) and functional solidarity (support). The three dimensions result in eight relationship types; two of each belong to the four categories described in Figure 2.1.

Tight

The generations are in frequent personal contact, there is no or only rare conflict, and they provide support. These parents and adult children have tight relationships.

Close

There is frequent contact and no serious disputes, but also no current support. This does not mean that help is denied. Instead, close contact and few quarrels indicate that help is currently not needed, and that the generations will step in if necessary.

Strained

Contact in this case involves conflicts and support. These are close relations as well, but ones in which controversies emerge, for instance, as a consequence of financial or health-related stresses and strains.

Entangled

There is contact and conflict, but no current support. The generations may refrain from (accepting) transfers, and although quarrelling is quite common, parents and adult children are still in touch with one another on a regular basis.

Obligatory

Here, contact is rare and comes with conflict and transfers. Although family generations provide support, they prefer not to spend too much time together, and if they do, disputes are not far away.

Table 3.1 Generation types

Category	Type	Contact	Conflict	Support
A Consensual solidarity	1 Tight	x		x
	2 Close	x		
B Conflictual solidarity	3 Strained	x	x	x
	4 Entangled	x	x	
C Conflictual autonomy	5 Obligatory		x	x
	6 Divided		x	
D Consensual autonomy	7 Customary			x
	8 Separate			

Divided

Parents and children do not see, write or talk to one another regularly, do not support each other, and if they are in contact, there is often quarrelling.

Customary

There is infrequent contact and disputes, but there is assistance. The generations do not really spend much time with one another, and they do not argue often. However, these relationships are nevertheless supportive.

Separate

There is no or only rare contact, no frequent debate, and there is no support. In fact, these generations lead their own separate lives without much interaction with one another, if at all.

Figure 3.5 provides a general overview of the respondents' relationship with parents and adult children. For the typology, (a) frequent personal contact is defined as occurring at least once a week (more details can be found in Chapter 4), representing associational solidarity; (b) generations are regarded as being in conflict if the respondents state that they often experience conflict with their

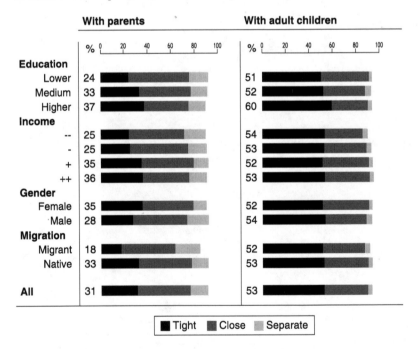

Figure 3.5 Types

Source: SHARE (n: 5,686/20,371).

parents or children (Chapter 5); and (c) support exists if the generations live in the same household (Chapter 6), or give money (Chapter 7), or help or care for one another (Chapter 8). These patterns reflect functional solidarity, i.e., giving or receiving money, time or space. The analyses refer to interviewees who have living parents or adult children, respectively. Since most generations are found to live in tight, close or separate relationships, Figure 3.5 concentrates on these types. The empty spaces between the bars and the total of 100 per cent represent the other relationships. Naturally, the figure documents quite general shares, which will be subject to more detailed analysis throughout this book.

Overall, the vast majority display consensual solidarity consisting of tight and close relations. The main reason is frequent contact. These adult children and parents see, talk or write to one another at least once a week, even when most of them no longer live in the same household. Pronounced conflict is not a frequent phenomenon at all. Although disagreements may occur from time to time, essentially conflictual relationships are quite seldom. This applies particularly to the category of 'conflictual autonomy': disputes of any significance seem more likely to lead to reduced contact, which confirms previous empirical results (Szydlik 2008a). Additionally, one should not neglect separate family generations, which describe the relationship of every seventh person aged 50+ to their parents. Most of these adult children and parents are only loosely connected, if at all.

Relationships with parents seem to be somewhat less tight than those with children. First, there is more support from respondents for their offspring, which results in a higher share of tight relationships. Second, there is a higher rate of no or loose ties to parents than there is to children. These results imply that respondents are more inclined to turn to their children than to their parents. When push comes to shove, people seem to feel even more responsible for the generation that they have brought into the world than for the one from which they originated. In other words, people do everything for their children and nearly everything for their parents. Nevertheless, one should not overinterpret these results: relationships with parents are also impressively strong, and more functional solidarity with regard to children may also reflect differences in current need structures rather than discrepancies in intergenerational devotion.

Belonging to either tight or close relationships depends on intergenerational support. Academics are more likely to have a tight relationship with their parents and adult children than members of the lower educational class. By contrast, the lower educational class has more close relationships, which leads to a balanced overall share of consensual solidarity.

The more money, the more consensual solidarity. If the household is able to make ends meet fairly easily there is a greater likelihood of parents and adult children staying in frequent contact. Money can be used for intergenerational transfers to support relatives, it can cement intergenerational bonds, and sufficient financial resources may also lead to less burdensome relationships with family members. Additionally, a difficult financial situation seems to be associated with fewer tight connections with the respondents' parents.

As expected, women entertain closer intergenerational relationships than men, especially with regard to their parents. Daughters are more likely to fulfil the so-called kinkeeper function (e.g., Rossi and Rossi 1990) in holding the family together. By contrast, sons report a separation from their parents more often than daughters do (19% vs. 11%). However, the figure suggests that gender differences in parent-adult child relationships are rather small. Further analyses in the following chapters will investigate in much more detail to what extent this applies to the diverse forms of intergenerational solidarity.

In contrast to the native population, migrants show considerably fewer intense connections with their parents. This is reflected in the different shares of tight and close relationships as well as in a considerably lower percentage of migrants who experience consensual solidarity with their parents (63% vs. 77%). Moreover, separation from parents is more widespread amongst migrants (22% vs. 15%). Moving to another country often means leaving one's parents behind, which results in less solidarity and more autonomy.

Further investigations reveal that the highest rates of consensual solidarity with parents can be observed in the Southern European countries of Italy, Spain and Greece (see Chapter 4). Nevertheless, tight relations with parents are often found in Northern European countries such as Sweden and Denmark. These results provide a first indication that strong welfare states can indeed show marked intergenerational solidarity. Separation is somewhat more frequent amongst the Eastern countries Poland and the Czech Republic, followed by the Western European countries and is especially rare in the south. However, identifying quite general categories and types neglects valuable insights into implications of cultural-contextual structures for intergenerational relations. It is the task of the following chapters to investigate these patterns in more depth and detail.

Summary

Many arguments have been brought forward to propagate a so-called crisis of the family. One image evoked in this context is that of more or less isolated individuals, who fend for themselves and are preoccupied only with their own advantage. It is suggested that both long-term and recent developments support this kind of 'single (wo)man'. When companies force employees to migrate from one place to another in order to follow jobs, it seems quite unlikely that permanent close connections with other individuals would emerge. At the same time, an argument can be made that a lack of societal solidarity is also not likely to provide stable foundations for interindividual solidarity. In the light of these – and many more – crisis scenarios listed in the introduction to this chapter, it is crucial to subject this view to a reality check with the help of empirical investigations. This first empirical chapter provides initial clues for a more realistic picture of adult child-parent relationships.

The results show that the existence of family generations represents immense potential for solidarity. Nine out of ten Europeans aged 50 years and older have at least one living family member of another generation. More than seven in ten are part of a family consisting of at least three generations. Women are more likely to live in a family with many generations, and so are members of the lower educational class. Nearly nine out of ten respondents have at least one child, close to a third even have three children or more. Inevitably, the likelihood of living parents amongst those aged 50+ is lower and declines further the older the population. Nevertheless, more than three in five 50–55 year olds still have at least one living parent. The lower class has more children, whereas the higher classes tend to have more living parents.

At the same time, most family generations live close by. All in all, the results on geographical distance attest to ample opportunity for many forms of intergenerational solidarity. Most people can meet their parents and adult children face to face without much effort. Nearly two-thirds live a maximum of 25 kilometres away from a parent. Only a fifth report distances of more than 100 kilometres. Geographical proximity to children is even closer. Four in ten parents live in the same building as a child, seven in ten only 5 kilometres away – at the most. If desired or necessary, most family generations can quite easily meet each other personally. However, there are pronounced differences between population groups. Migrants naturally live considerably farther away from their parents and academics are separated by greater distances, both from their parents and offspring.

Besides existence and distance, norms of obligation are likely to be prerequisites of intergenerational cohesion and, again, we find substantial potentials. The results indicate a strong sense of obligation to exercise intergenerational solidarity. Close to three-quarters (strongly) agree that '[p]arents' duty is to do their best for their children even at the expense of their own well-being'. Nevertheless, it is not only the family that is seen to be responsible for intergenerational support. In fact, many claim that the state should at least partly bear responsibility for older persons in need. In general, one finds a response pattern that indicates a demand for a mixed responsibility of family and state. In this respect, higher-educated classes and better-off income groups report a somewhat lower sense of obligation towards parents and children.

Last but not least, a typology is proposed that draws on the solidarity-conflict scheme in the previous chapter (Figure 2.1), consisting of consensual and conflictual solidarity as well as consensual and conflictual autonomy. Each of these four patterns is further differentiated into two relationship types (see Table 3.1), which may be called tight, close, strained, entangled, obligatory, divided, customary and separate. The empirical results indicate that most intergenerational relationships belong to the category of consensual solidarity, showing strong cohesion and few conflicts. Nearly a third of the relationships with parents and over half of the connections with adult children can be classified as being 'tight', involving frequent contact, support and only few disagreements. However, the degree of separation between generations should not be neglected. Nearly every fifth respondent reports a relationship of consensual autonomy with regard to his or her parents; most of these relationships can be characterised as being 'separate'. The corresponding share for the respondents' relationships with their adult children is much lower. In general, connections with adult children seem to be even closer than those with parents.

Overall, the results support the existence of substantial (potential for) intergenerational cohesion. At this point, however, these findings need to be confirmed or rejected by closer investigations. This is the task of the following chapters.

4 Contact

Staying in touch

Introduction

Is Talcott Parsons right? Is it really true that once adult children leave their parents' home, intergenerational attachment is severely weakened, if not suspended altogether? In other words, do we find only rare intergenerational contacts among non-coresident adult children and their parents according to the adage, 'Out of sight, out of mind'?

Of course, this general question leads to: Who is more frequently in contact with one another, and which generations rarely stay in touch? Can we observe distinct patterns, and do they correspond to what theoretical ideas would lead us to expect? Answering these questions requires complex (multivariate multilevel) empirical analyses based on corresponding theoretical reasoning.

Contact is the most general form of intergenerational cohesion. It includes many kinds of interpersonal connections, be it via meeting in person, talking on the phone or writing to one another, with or without a special purpose. Thus, this chapter, devoted to the topic of contact, is the first chapter of this book to apply complex theoretical reasoning and empirical analyses. It is also the first time in this book that the ONFC model is applied to empirical investigations. In what way do individual, family and societal structures play a role in intergenerational cohesion? Can we find significant differences between the rich and poor, women and men, migrants and natives, the healthy and the sick, married and singles? Are there discrepancies between countries, and do welfare states and social stratification matter?

When investigating adult family generations, one of the first decisions concerns the issue of coresidence. Should we include parents and adult children who live together in the analyses, or should we concentrate on those who no longer live in the same household, that is, the 'non-coresidents'? Of course, coresidence is an important form of intergenerational solidarity that must not be neglected. An entire chapter of this book is accordingly devoted to coresidence (Chapter 6). However, when it comes to contact, those relationships between family members who no longer share the same living space provide the acid test for intergenerational bonding. Is it really 'out of sight, out of mind'? When family members live together, it is inevitable that they will see one another regularly. But what about the generations that live in separate homes?

In fact, there are good reasons to consider both views. To gain a general impression, we would like to see both the *overall* contact rates including coresidence and, more specifically, the contact frequency of *non-coresident* adult children and parents. However, for a more refined analysis of intergenerational bonding, the latter case can be expected to be more informative. Therefore, Figure 4.1 gives an overview that provides information on both groups. The more specific focus of this chapter, however, addresses the question of why non-coresident adult children and parents stay in touch. Does there remain a steady bond between adult generations even if they no longer live together, and if so, what are significant reasons for intergenerational contact? In turn, we can also expect to find out more about the family generations who do not spend much time together. What are the typical differences between those with regular or sparing intergenerational contact?

As in all of the following chapters, the first task is to point out what we are actually talking about when investigating a specific form of family solidarity; in this case, intergenerational contact. The next step is to review previous research and develop hypotheses on the basis of the ONFC model. With regard to the empirical analyses, it is documented how the corresponding questions are phrased in the Survey of Health, Ageing and Retirement in Europe, and what the possible answers are that respondents could give. The actual answers given are described in figures that differentiate between population groups with regard to education, income, gender and migration as well as country. The following analyses provide explanations of intergenerational solidarity on the basis of the previous theoretical considerations. Last but not least, the main results are summarised.

Research and hypotheses

What is contact?

Interpersonal contact occurs in various general forms. It includes meeting in person, talking with the help of tools such as telephones and computers, and writing on paper or using electronic devices. Meeting in person can be regarded as the closest form of contact. It involves direct interaction, handshakes, embracement, smell, unmediated eye-to-eye contact, facial expressions and gestures as well as those forms of personal help and care that depend on personal presence. Talking on the phone or via the Internet still provides an opportunity for instantaneous and spontaneous reaction, direct emphatic involvement, and can even lead to more intense personal exchange than meeting in person. This is also possible in writing, though in general it is a less direct form of interpersonal encounter.

Contact may be totally spontaneous or planned well in advance. It may last seconds, minutes, hours, days, weeks, months, years or even decades. Contact may involve a whole range of support, be it one-sided, reciprocal or mutual. It may involve personal help and care, advice and consolation, helping with household chores, gardening, repairing, planning and organising, and sharing local and family gossip. Contact may be totally voluntary or obligatory; it may follow social roles, rituals, customary practices and traditions, including family ceremonies such as birthdays, weddings and funerals. Contact may be conflictual or entirely harmonious; it may come (and go) with love, hate or total indifference. One may like it or not. We may expect something from meeting another person, be it good advice, social bonding, companionship, avoidance of loneliness, emotional assistance, present or future support. We may even pay directly or indirectly, or be paid to engage with the other, or we might just want to enjoy time with the other person and participate in each other's lives.

Since contact may involve many different forms, reasons and consequences, one should be careful not to assume, explicitly or implicitly, that more contact is always positive and less contact always negative in principle. Of course, daily contact with significant others reduces isolation and loneliness, and may come with many other very welcome benefits. However, there can also be too much contact, whether in emotionally strained relationships, because of burdensome situations or due to interpersonal abuse in one way or the other.

Research

Previous studies have shown that frequent contact persists among family generations, even after the children have grown up and left their parents' home. For example, in Germany two out of five 40–85 year olds who have adult children living outside of their household report daily contact with their children. More than two-thirds meet, write or phone several times a week, and 85% at least once a week. Of course, contact rates would be even higher were one to include the coresident generations. Contact of 40–85 year olds with their parents is somewhat less frequent, but still quite impressive: one-quarter report daily contact, more than two-quarters speak of several times a week, and three-quarters stay in touch at least once a week. Only 1 and 2 per cent, respectively, state that there is no intergenerational contact at all (Szydlik 2000: 109ff.).

Tomassini et al. (2004) document weekly contact between elderly parents and children in Finland, Great Britain, the Netherlands and Italy. They find frequent contact in all countries, with higher levels in Italy than in the Northern European countries. Hank (2007: 163) condenses the seven answer categories of the first wave of the Survey of Health, Ageing and Retirement in Europe into three categories, while concentrating on the most frequently contacted non-coresident child: two-fifths of these respondents speak of daily contacts with the child, half report having contact at least once a week, and only one in ten meets, talks or writes less than once a week. Even more frequent contact can be found in the Mediterranean countries, particularly in contrast to the Northern European states.

Several studies provide further clues about the determinants of frequent intergenerational contact. Obviously, distance is found to be crucial: the larger the geographical distance, the less intergenerational contact (Frankel and DeWit 1986; DeWit and Frankel 1988). A study in the United States (Sarkisian and Gerstel 2008) suggests that marriage of adult children leads to less intense relations with parents, implying that married adult children are more strongly oriented towards their partners. Cohabiting or married 18–34 year old adults in the Netherlands also engage in less frequent face-to-face contact with their parents; yet having children of their own (i.e., grandchildren from their parents' perspective) increases intergenerational contact with (grand)parents (Bucx et al. 2008). In closing their paper, the authors nevertheless concede that '[i]t is not clear to what extent our results can be generalized to countries with different structural characteristics'.

Divorce also seems to lead to less frequent intergenerational contact, especially for fathers. Studies show that marital dissolution has negative effects on intergenerational relations with adult children (Aquilino 1994a; Shapiro 2003; Tomassini et al. 2004; De Graaf and Fokkema 2007; Kalmijn 2015). Less research, though, has been conducted in the opposite direction, namely on whether the divorce of adult children affects the relationship with their parents.

Further empirical analyses on contact amongst adult family generations, employing different data sets and analytical foci, have been conducted for several countries, for example: Grundy and Shelton (2001) for Great Britain; Bordone (2009) for Italy and Sweden; Treas and Gubernskaya (2012) for Australia, Austria, Germany (West), Great Britain, Hungary, Italy and the United States; Steinbach (2013) for Germany and Ward et al. (2014) for the United States.

Hypotheses

Throughout this book, the ONFC model (Figure 2.2) is applied to analyse intergenerational relations. In this chapter, the aim is to explain (the frequency of) contact between adult children and parents living in separate households. Thus, the theoretical reasoning in this chapter aims to develop corresponding, empirically testable hypotheses, differentiating opportunity, need, family and society.

First, contact is likely to depend on *opportunity structures*. The question is not only whether generations would like to meet, but also whether conditions are such that they can do so. In this respect, staying in touch may involve costs in order to bridge geographical distances between households. A similar thing applies when sharing common activities. The better-educated classes are in a better position to cover these costs, and they are also more likely to use modern communication technologies (Korupp and Szydlik 2005). Similarly, higher income may be a relevant prerequisite of more frequent intergenerational contact. Furthermore, financial resources not only facilitate the ability to bear current contact costs, but may also serve as a 'motivator' for family generations to stay in touch. In this perspective, it is another empirical question whether adult children keep closer contact with their parents when they can expect a larger inheritance.

Health may play a role as well if poor health restricts opportunities for contact. However, there is also reason to assume the opposite relationship when family members help relatives in poor health. From this perspective, it would be need rather than opportunity that defines the connection between contact and health.

Although contact includes telephoning and writing, the obvious hypothesis in accordance with previous studies is that geographical proximity is one of the most crucial factors for staying in frequent touch.

Need structures include financial needs. The demand for intergenerational monetary transfers may lead to more frequent contact. On the one hand, financial need may enhance the willingness of dependent relatives to stay in touch. On the other hand, awareness of a close family member in need may increase contact as a form of support.

Age is another factor that may potentially influence contact behaviour. An obvious hypothesis here is that the elderly are in greater need of closer contact with their offspring, for example, to prevent loneliness in old age. Again, it is an empirical question whether adult children actually meet these contact needs of the elderly.

The situation is similar for health. Having a frail parent who is in need of support may lead to more frequent contact with this parent. However, as mentioned above, poor health may also restrict opportunities for common activities, and it is not only need that defines a relationship.

Relationships between parents and their adult children are embedded in *family structures*. First of all, gender combination is likely to play an important role. A substantial body of research has shown that women are families' kin-keepers (e.g., Rossi and Rossi 1990), involving activities ranging from full-scale care, through mutual practical help in many areas, and on many occasions all the way to frequent telephone conversations and 'enjoyable visits' (Fingerman 2000). Although one should not neglect men's role in this respect, they fall behind when it comes to ensuring family cohesion. Thus, the most contact can be expected amongst mothers and daughters, and the least frequent contact between fathers and sons. The question here is whether it is the mother-son (son-mother) or father-daughter (daughter-father) relationships that are marked by more intergenerational contact.

Apart from gender combination, previous research indicates that partnership status is another factor that plays a considerable role in accounting for differences in contact (see above). Marriage might strengthen family bonds overall, including connections between parents and adult children. However, other arguments treat (married) couples and adult intergenerational relationships as more distinct spheres, implying that spouses have less frequent intergenerational contact (Parsons 1942: 615f.; Parsons and Bales 1956: 19f.; Sarkisian and Gerstel 2008: 360f.). In other words, when adult children marry or enter a steady partnership, this may weaken the connections with their parents.

In this respect, it makes sense to differentiate between relationships with parents and adult children. The previous argument suggests that being single might result in more frequent contact with parents. However, this does not mean that separated or divorced parents show closer bonds to their offspring than parents who still live together. Previous research has shown that being an absent parent (mostly fathers) in childhood and youth has long-lasting, even lifelong negative consequences on closeness to adult children (Szydlik 2000: 197ff.; see also

Bertogg and Szydlik 2016). This even applies to later-life divorce, for instance, due to the influences of parental conflict on parent-child relationships, the geographical mobility of a divorced parent, the division of time between separated parents and the discontinuation of common family activities. By contrast, a deceased parent (i.e., widowhood) is likely to have a different effect on intergenerational contact, not least since common grief and need for support may even intensify bonding between the surviving family members (Pett et al. 1992; Aquilino 1994b: 909; Shapiro 2003: 266; De Graaf and Fokkema 2007).

Further assumptions with regard to family structures refer to the number of children and siblings as well as to the existence of grandchildren. The presence of more relatives may, in general, lead to forming stronger family bonds. However, family members may also become 'competitors' with respect to time and attention. The empirical analyses will show which of the contrasting hypotheses is closer to reality.

Last but not least, *cultural-contextual structures* are to be considered as well, including the effects of migration, the welfare state and social stratification. Naturally, migrants tend to live at greater geographical distances, particularly from their parents (Figure 3.3), and frequently command fewer financial resources, which should result in less intergenerational contact overall. However, according to the 'safe haven' hypothesis, migrants are likely to maintain stronger family bonds. Since living in a new country often comes with cultural discrepancies between home and host countries as well as huge challenges, insecurities and even discrimination, migrants may have a more pronounced need for a close family circle as a 'safe haven' in an unfamiliar environment. This may well result in more frequent contact amongst family generations, at least net of geographical distance. Also, remittances, feelings of connectedness with the country and family of origin, and the need for emotional support due to the migration experience may foster bonds between relatives across country borders.

According to the theoretical reasoning on welfare states discussed in Chapter 2, we are again faced with contradictory assumptions. The crowding-out hypothesis would suggest that a well-developed welfare state is likely to result in quite loose intergenerational connections. Since the welfare state takes over, family members are thought to withdraw from one another. By contrast, the crowding-in hypothesis would even assume more frequent contact between adult family generations. Since a strong welfare state relieves family members of obligations and burdens, they are believed to develop strong voluntary mutual bonds. If this is the case, more social and family expenditure should result in more frequent intergenerational contact.

Finally, influences of social stratification on intergenerational cohesion may play a relevant role. If considerable financial resources provide a basis for intense intergenerational bonds, living in a rich country should increase the frequency of contact. When it comes to poverty, the picture is less clear. There may be reason to expect less contact owing to family members retreating from burdensome situations. However, more intense family solidarity in a difficult environment is conceivable as well.

Explaining contact

Questions

The Survey of Health, Ageing and Retirement in Europe asks about the frequency of contact in the following way:

> During the past twelve months, how often did you have contact with your [mother/father], either personally, by phone or mail?

The interviewers were also instructed to remind the respondents to think about 'any kind of contact, including for example E-mail, SMS or MMS'. The corresponding question with regard to children reads as follows:

> During the past twelve months, how often did you [or your husband/wife/ partner] have contact with [child name], either personally, by phone or mail?

The survey gathered information on up to four children. However, respondents living with their parents or children were not asked these contact questions. In these cases, we assume daily contact (Tomassini al. 2004; Hank 2007: 161). The possible answers to both questions are as follows:

1. Daily
2. Several times a week
3. About once a week
4. About every two weeks
5. About once a month
6. Less than once a month
7. Never.

The multivariate analyses consist of multilevel ordered probit models. Since only a few dyads have monthly or even less contact, those cases are allocated to the fourth category. Additionally, the order of the values in the questionnaire is reversed so that the coefficients refer to increasing contact. Therefore, the four values of the dependent variable are 'less often', 'about once a week', 'several times a week' and 'daily' (see Table A2). As mentioned above, the multivariate analyses are based on dyads (the relation of a mother with the first child is one dyad, whereas the mother's relationship with the second child represents another dyad and so on). The figures refer to a respondent's most frequent contact in cases in which there is more than one relative of the other generation.

Description

As discussed in the introduction to this chapter, it makes a difference for contact whether the generations live together in the same household or not. Therefore, the first step is to examine the frequency of contact with the other generation for all respondents with living parents or adult children, whether they coreside or not. Figure 4.1 gives an overview. The lower two bars refer 'only' to the adult generations who no longer share the same household.

The contact rates are in fact very pronounced. If we include coresidence, three in five of the respondents even have daily contact with at least one adult child. It is striking that more than four out of five meet, talk or write at least several times a week, and 93 per cent every week. The connections with parents are somewhat looser, but still extraordinarily frequent: 27, 56, 78, 86 and 92 per cent report daily, at least several times a week, weekly, fortnightly and monthly contact, respectively.

Since these numbers include generations living together, the contact rates amongst non-coresident parents and adult children are somewhat smaller, albeit still very high. Although they no longer share the same household, 44 per cent still report daily contact with an adult child. Three-quarters meet, talk or write at least several times a week, and nine out of ten report at least weekly contact. Again, contact with parents is somewhat less frequent, but the relationships are still very intense (one-quarter daily, 56 per cent at least several times a week, 78 per cent weekly, 86 per cent at least every second week).

Figure 4.2 documents the rates of daily and weekly contact of *non-coresident* respondents with parents and adult children. Obviously, coresidence entails very frequent contact. Living together in the same household means seeing one another on a regular, usually a daily basis. Thus, the crucial question of this chapter is not whether coresident generations regularly stay in touch. Instead, when analysing reasons for more or less contact, it makes sense to concentrate on adult children and parents living separately (see also Hank 2007). In addition, coresidence is addressed in its own right in Chapter 6.

The figure shows that daily contact is especially widespread in the lower classes. Nearly a third of the respondents with lower education have daily contact with a parent, and over half with an adult child. For academics, the rates are 'only' 22 and 30 per cent, respectively. However, these considerable discrepancies disappear by and large once we also include weekly contacts.

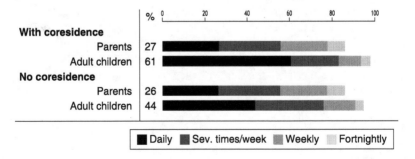

Figure 4.1 Contact: Overview

Source: SHARE (n: 10,129/34,472/10,053/24,826).

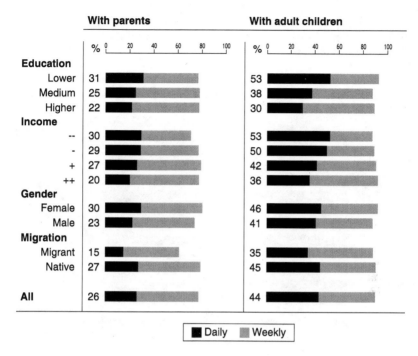

Figure 4.2 Contact: People

Source: SHARE (n: 10,053/24,826). No coresidence.

A similar picture emerges with regard to income groups. Over half of the respondents from the lowest income group report daily contact with an adult child; this applies to 'only' 36 per cent of the most affluent population. However, the survey results for weekly contact reverse the picture. This difference speaks of the strong effect of short geographical distance for the lower classes (Figure 3.3) as well as a combination of monetary resources and needs, which will be addressed more specifically by the multivariate analyses.

The hypotheses section of this chapter suggests more frequent intergenerational contact of women. This assumption is supported by the empirical findings. Women are more likely to stay in touch with their parents and children. Yet one should not neglect the fact that close to a quarter of sons also report daily contact with parents, and this applies to two in five fathers with regard to a non-coresident adult child as well.

It is also not surprising that migrants are considerably less able to be in daily contact with their parents. Migrants also show less daily contact with their adult children. However, if we consider at least weekly contact with offspring, the discrepancy between migrants and the native population diminishes substantially.

What about intergenerational contact in different countries? The results documented in Figure 4.3 show impressive discrepancies. With regard to daily and

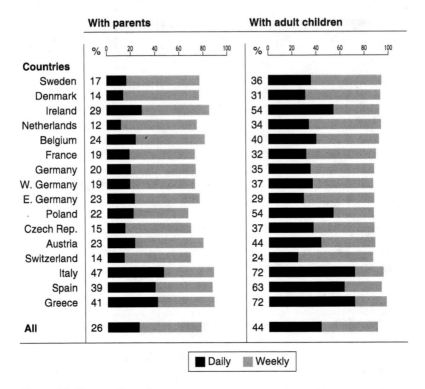

Figure 4.3 Contact: Countries

Source: SHARE (n: 10,053/24,826). No coresidence.

weekly contact, one can identify roughly two groups of countries: the south and the other countries. The three Southern European countries display extraordinarily high rates of respondents who stay in frequent touch with their parents and offspring. Nearly half of the Italian respondents report daily contact with their parents, whereas at the other end of Europe, this applies to only a sixth of the Swedes. Regarding adult children, the corresponding figure is twice as high in Italy and Greece as in Sweden (72% vs. 36%). To a lesser degree, but still existent, are country differences in at least weekly contact, which again point to more frequent intergenerational contact in the south of Europe.

These findings are a first indication in support of the so-called 'crowding-out' hypothesis, since strong welfare states seem to be associated with a lower frequency of contact. Conversely, private intergenerational contact is more widespread in weak welfare states, which suggests more family coherence in countries where public services provide less support.

If we include coresident generations, the frequency of contact with *parents* still remains much the same (this result is not reported in a figure). Since only a few of the respondents live with a parent, it suffices to refer to the numbers presented in Figures 4.2 and 4.3. As shown in Figure 4.1, daily contact increases from 44 to 61 per cent if we include coresident *adult children*. Nevertheless, the proportions between the population groups and countries in general stay the same. Greater increases in contact rates are observed for population groups and countries with particularly high coresidence rates (Chapter 6). The highest shares by far of daily contact including coresidence with adult children can be found in the Southern European countries Italy (85%), Greece (84%) and Spain (81%), whereas Sweden (43%) and Denmark (37%) display particularly low rates. However, gender differences in daily contact disappear owing to the higher rate of coresidence among sons.

At this point, one must bear in mind that the figures represent simple descriptions and not a thorough analysis of the possible factors for intergenerational contact. For example, we do not know whether descriptive country differences are really due to country characteristics, or rather to different shares of population groups in those countries. To really get to the bottom of the various factors that explain greater or lesser intergenerational cohesion, we have to conduct multivariate analyses. Moreover, in the next step, the focus will no longer be limited to the parents and adult children who have the most frequent contact. Instead, the analyses will explore all non-coresident child-parent and parent-child relationships in much more detail.

Explanation

Why do family generations stay in touch? Figure 4.4 refers to the net coefficients of Table A4.2 (see Appendix for more information): '+' signifies more contact, '–' indicates fewer contacts with regard to the corresponding factor.

The first factors represent *opportunity structures*. With regard to contact with their adult children, the multivariate analysis shows no class differences. Yet the higher-educated respondents seem to have more frequent contact with elderly parents, indicating the relevance of resources (see also Chapter 8). At first glance, income increases the frequency of contact, at least according to the corresponding gross models in Table A4.2 (see Appendix). However, when one takes a future inheritance into consideration, the current income situation no longer seems to have an impact, which points to the special relevance of family wealth and the prospects of receiving it.

Indeed, when the respondents expect an inheritance, they are much more likely to stay in touch with their parents. Since bequests stem largely from parents (Chapter 9), one may presume that wealth is an opportunity for elderly parents for closer contact with their offspring. This effect is not restricted only to the respondents' relationship with their parents, but also applies to their connection with their adult children. If the respondent or his or her partner is likely to *leave* an inheritance, this increases the frequency of contact with the adult child significantly. The smaller bequest effect that contact with children has in comparison to contact with parents might be due to less immediate expectations of receiving wealth.

The respondents' health does not seem to have a particular influence on intergenerational contacts, be it with parents or adult children. However, it might also be the case that the abovementioned hypotheses offset one another.

		With parents	With children
Opportunity Structures	Education: Lower (ref.)		
	Medium	+	
	Higher	+ +	
	Income		
	Future inheritance	+ +	+
	Health		
	Distance	− − −	− − −
Need Structures	Money transfer	+ + +	+
	Age	+ + +	−
	Health parent	−	
Family Structures	Daughter-mother (ref.)		
	Daughter-father	− −	−
	Son-mother	− − −	− −
	Son-father	− − −	− −
	Married (ref.)		
	Partner		−
	Widowed		−
	Divorced		− −
	Single	+ +	− −
	Partner parent/child	−	−
	Number of children	−	− − −
	Grandchild		
	Number of siblings	− − −	+
Cultural-contextual Structures	Migrant	+ + +	+
	Social expenditure	−	−
	Family expenditure	−	−
	Wealth per capita	+	+
	Poverty rate	+ + +	+

Figure 4.4 Explaining contact

Source: SHARE, Table A4.2, see Appendix (net). '+': more, '−': less contact with parents/adult children. No coresidence.

The most important factor is geographical distance: the greater the distance, the less intergenerational contact. This attests to the fact that even modern communication technologies do not compensate for remoteness. Additionally, this is an indication that many adult children and parents would like to spend more time together – if they could. However, some adult children are more inclined to move farther away from their parents' home. In this case, looser intergenerational ties may play a part in greater spatial distance. Nevertheless, it is fair to say that this alternative relation of distance and cohesion is much less prevalent (see Greenwell and Bengtson 1997; Engstler and Huxhold 2010; Isengard 2015).

When considering individual characteristics, one must not neglect differences in *need structures*. First of all, there is a connection between economic support and staying in touch: the giving and taking of money is associated with more frequent contact. This is an indication that meeting financial needs, in fact, contributes to family generations spending more time together. It is the actual transfer of money rather than the availability of resources via a higher income that plays a crucial role. The findings support Simmel's (1908) assumption that gifts and the resulting feelings of gratitude stabilise interpersonal relationships (see Chapter 7). This applies in both directions of the intergenerational lineage.

The age of the respondents shows opposite effects in terms of contact with their parents and their adult children. When it comes to parents, age increases intergenerational cohesion. This is in accordance with the assumption that elderly people – both the respondents and their older parents – are in greater need of interpersonal attention in later life. However, when it comes to the relationship with their adult children, it is the younger respondents who report more frequent contact. This again speaks to the relevance of needs. When younger adult children have just moved out of their parents' home, they still have a greater need for intergenerational advice and support. The older the children become, the more they are able to stand on their own feet.

Needs are not always met by intergenerational solidarity. For example, the health-related needs of elderly parents do not necessarily lead to a higher intensity of contact with their adult children. This does not at all mean that adult children would refrain from providing help and care to their frail elderly parents (Chapter 8). However, the overall frequency of contact seems to be reduced in these cases, be it due to physical impairments restricting common activities and interpersonal exchange, or due to emotional strain. At the same time, contact with the middle generation's adult children is not affected when those middle-generation respondents have parents with poor health.

Family structures include a number of relevant contact factors. As expected, gender plays a crucial role. The results prove that women are indeed families' kin-keepers; it is the women who maintain close contact with their parents. Daughters and mothers report the most frequent contact with one another. In second place are daughters and fathers. By contrast, son-mother and especially son-father relationships are definitely weaker. The parent-adult child relationship mostly corresponds to the same pattern. Again, it is the mothers and daughters who meet, talk or write most frequently, followed by contact between fathers and daughters. The connections with sons are generally less intense, at least in terms of frequency of contact.

Married parents have the closest bonds with their adult children. The strongest effects can be observed for divorced and single parents. Further analyses show that this applies especially to fathers. This is again evidence of the long-term consequences of parental separation, particularly on father-child relationships. Rare contact is a phenomenon that is associated with parents – mostly fathers – who are absent after family break-ups. By contrast, the widowhood of a parent results in only a modest overall decrease in contact with adult children (less parent-child contact applies particularly to widowed fathers).

It makes sense to distinguish between the family status of the parent and that of the adult child. In general, being married is less significant when it comes to the relationship of the respondents with their parents. Yet there still is a weakly significant divorce effect inasmuch as divorced children seem to report less contact with their parents. Most interestingly, single children meet or talk to their parents more frequently, which is an indication that the children's marriage in fact directs their focus away from their parents to some extent, whereas children (especially sons) remaining single may result in more opportunities (e.g., time) and a greater need for close contact with parents.

This interpretation is also supported by the findings for partnerships of the corresponding parent or adult child. If a parent or adult child has a partner, the frequency of contact between the family generations is significantly lower. The situation is similar as the number of children increases. The more offspring the respondents have, the less often they stay in touch with their parents. Having more children decreases the frequency of contact with each child even more, which is an indication of parents splitting time between their offspring. The existence of grandchildren does not show a significant effect, yet having more siblings leads to considerably less contact with parents. This again indicates that parents divide their time between their offspring. Moreover, if there are more siblings, each child is less likely to help elderly parents, as other siblings are also potential support providers (Chapter 8). With regard to contact with adult children, the number of siblings shows a rather weak positive effect, suggesting somewhat stronger bonds within larger families, including more occasions for contact such as birthdays and family events.

Cultural-contextual structures have a strong impact, too. The previous figures and gross results of Table A4.2 (see Appendix) indicate that migrants have less frequent contact with their parents. This is not surprising since migration often results in leaving parents – and sometimes even children – behind in their home countries, which results in particularly large geographical distances, and thus reduces opportunities for frequent personal contact. However, when we control for geographical distance, migrants show even more intergenerational contact. This is an empirical indication of the 'safe haven' hypothesis, suggesting that the migrant population turns to the close family circle in response to cultural differences and the challenges faced in an often unfamiliar environment.

Furthermore, considerable country effects emerge. The figures and the country analyses (see Appendix, Table A4.1) show especially high contact rates in the Southern European countries. The macro indicators also attest to this: the higher the social and family expenditure in a country, the fewer intergenerational contacts. Conversely, adult family generations in weaker welfare states meet, talk or write to each other more often. These results support the assumption that welfare states actually 'crowd out' family solidarity. The effect is even stronger for the relationship of the respondents with their parents than for their relationship with their adult children.

More wealth per capita is associated with more frequent contact, which testifies to the significance of resources and closer family bonds in affluent societies.

Additionally, high poverty in a society goes hand in hand with generations staying in closer contact as well. In the latter case, a difficult environment may lead family members to stand together. These results make it particularly interesting to see the more detailed analyses of the different forms of contact, especially those distinguishing between help and care (Chapter 8).

Summary

Individuals can count on close intergenerational bonds. Staying in touch is definitely not always an easy task. Sometimes one might prefer more privacy, and some encounters or telephone conversations might even be discomforting. With this in mind, one should refrain from automatically painting too positive a picture when observing intergenerational contact. Nevertheless, the empirical results definitely contradict the idea of the prevalence of isolated adults without any contact with significant others, including family members. If one defines 'individualisation' as a process geared towards autonomous individuals without close human bonds, then the empirical results come to the opposite conclusion. Moreover, frequent contact supports the conclusion of the previous chapter, contradicting the idea of families in permanent and unsolvable crisis. This applies particularly to adult family generations who no longer live in the same household. 'Out of sight, out of mind' in no way reflects the reality of contemporary family generations.

Nearly 80 per cent of the respondents have at least weekly contact with a parent, and over 90 per cent stay in touch with an adult child on a weekly basis at the least. The corresponding shares for having even daily contact are 27 and 61 per cent, respectively. These numbers include coresident generations, who naturally meet on a daily basis. When excluding those cases, the percentages for contact with parents stay the same, whereas the rate of daily and at least weekly contact with non-coresident adult children is still 44 and 91 per cent, respectively. These are impressive numbers. Even in adulthood, family generations stay in close touch; even when living apart, adult children and parents do not lose contact; and even in modern times, family bonds persist over a lifetime.

Apart from these global figures, we find considerable differences between population groups and countries. Moreover, opportunities and needs, family and cultural structures all play a prominent role. When it comes to money, it is the actual transfers that increase the frequency of contact, and less the current income situation. Expected wealth in the form of a future inheritance is also associated with staying in touch more frequently. Obviously, money appears to be a binding agent for human bonding. However, respondents reporting poor health of parents speak of less frequent contact. Reduced opportunities for common activities could play a relevant role here. In this context, geographical distance between households proves to be the most important factor of all.

In general, as expected, the analyses demonstrate much closer bonds of women, who can rightly be called the families' 'kinkeepers'. The relationships between sons and fathers are considerably looser. Moreover, parental divorce and separation reduces parents' contact with adult children, whereas further analyses show that this result goes back to fathers in particular, indicating the long-term, even lifelong effects of absent fathers in childhood and youth. Additionally, having more close family members seems to reduce the time spent with each parent and adult child overall.

At first glance, migrants have fewer close relationships with their parents, which is not surprising considering that migration from one country to another often leaves parents behind. However, if we consider geographical distance, migrants report even closer intergenerational bonds, supporting the hypothesis that the close family circle acts as a 'safe haven' in an unfamiliar environment.

Regarding the consequences of welfare states, the findings support the crowding-out hypothesis. More social and family expenditure is associated with less intergenerational family contact. The most frequent contact between adult family generations is found in Southern Europe.

Last but not least, social stratification plays a crucial role as well. Interestingly, both wealth and poverty seem to enhance cohesion between adult family generations. Affluent societies are likely to offer a basis for intense bonds, whereas living in a difficult environment also seems to increase intergenerational solidarity.

5 Conflict
Quarrels and fights?

Introduction

Intergenerational conflict comes in many forms. First of all, the specifics and patterns of controversies depend on the corresponding concept of 'generations' (Chapter 2). Different concepts make different assumptions about the causes and patterns of conflict. Political generations clash in political arenas, for example, via political parties, media or civic engagement in various forms. Cultural generations, as vague as they may be, quarrel about the interpretational sovereignty over cultural norms and values, orientations and lifestyles. Economic generations can be in dispute over economic opportunities and risks, whether they are related to the labour market, economy or welfare state regulations, for instance, (dis)advantages of cohorts concerning contributions to and the receipt of welfare state benefits, such as public pensions and health support. 'Generations' in the sense of age groups are placed in a conflict setting when a 'young generation' is assumed to quarrel with an 'old generation' over political influence, cultural expressions and economic opportunities.

These and other conflict scenarios are not surprising given that societal and colloquial 'generations' are, in general, defined or implicitly assumed as being social entities with specific abilities, opportunities, behaviours and outcomes – which are set against other social entities of a similar kind. One can hardly think of the specifics of one social generation without at least contrasting them implicitly with the corresponding features of another generation or cohort. Often these 'generations' are even defined in essence by clashes with another 'generation' of the same kind.

This is not the case with family generations. Of course, when referring to parents and children, conflict is, in principle, not out of the question. However, at the same time controversies are not an integral part of being a parent or a child per se. (Adult) children and parents can get along with one another quite well, and the advantage of one family generation does not have to come at the expense of the other. Instead, from a family perspective, one generation supporting the other may be a win-win situation for both, whether this involves parents and children, or grandparents and grandchildren.

In any case, conflict between family generations is quite specific since, in contrast to other generation concepts that are based on cohorts or age groups, it principally involves direct personal interaction. When cohorts are in conflict, there is not necessarily a direct encounter of specific individuals, including persons who have known each other for a very long time. Of course, this is precisely the case when referring to discord between family generations, especially in the case of adults. Whereas clashes of cohorts and age groups are structural in general, family strife is personal. Over 100 years ago, Georg Simmel stated:

> [. . .] just the closeness of life together, the social and economic compatibility, the rather monumental presumption of unity – all this directly brings about friction, tension, and opposition especially easily; indeed, family conflict is a form of conflict *sui generis*. Its cause, its intensity, its expansion to those uninvolved, the form of the fight as that of the reconciliation is, by its course on the basis of an organic unity matured by thousands of internal and external ties, fully idiosyncratic, comparable to no other conflict.
>
> (Simmel 2009: 266; 1908)

Recent research has produced a number of studies on the extent of intergenerational cohesion and the factors that have an impact on solidarity between adult family generations. In comparison, the investigation of intergenerational conflicts still lags behind. This is all the more surprising given that the mass media often report on – alleged – substantial conflict between generations from young to old. From this perspective, daily conflicts are a regular feature of the relationships between adult children and their parents, and conflict is seen as an indicator of a crisis of the family and the dissolution of family bonds. It may be argued further that permanent conflict prevents generations from helping and taking care of each other, which may ultimately lead to isolation and deprivation not only in old age.

These assumptions and arguments give rise to a number of important research questions: To what extent are intergenerational relations between parents and adult children characterised by conflicts? What are the reasons for, and the consequences of intergenerational controversy? What is the relation between conflict and solidarity on the one hand, and family conflict and societal context on the other?

The present chapter will address these questions. First, drawing on Figure 2.1, conflict and solidarity will not be treated as opposites in principle. Second, intergenerational conflicts will be compared with controversies with other people, such as partners, other relatives and friends. Additionally, it will be investigated whether people are more likely to report conflict with their children or parents. Third, the chapter will explore reasons for and consequences of conflict. It will examine individual and family factors as well as connections between intergenerational conflicts within families and societal contexts, including welfare state characteristics and social stratification.

Research and hypotheses

What is conflict?

Conflicts can range from minor, brief differences regarding trivial details, through heated arguments over issues of some significance, all the way to severe physical violence. Controversies can arise once, sporadically, episodically or constantly; they can be destructive or constructive (see Canary et al. 1995; Segrin and Flora 2011: 87).

According to interaction theory, conflict means:

> [. . .] dual enforcement of independence and autonomy of action in the mutual dealing of two subjects. (. . .) Conflict is, therefore, dual or reciprocal action against the will of the other when two people deal with each other; it is interaction in the sense of a series of alternating 'acts of contravention' and therefore 'estrangement'.
>
> (Tyrell 1976: 258f.).

In fact, there has to be some kind of bond between people in order to ignite controversies, and the dispute itself ties one person to the other. '[C]onflict is a mutual activity' (Hocker and Wilmot 2014: 15; see also Braiker and Kelley 1979: 137) – unless the consequences of conflict, including emotional strain, appear unbearable. Controversies may destroy a relationship. Severe conflicts can be so pronounced and irreconcilable that the relationship ultimately comes to an end. However, respectful arguments between individuals may, in turn, offer a chance to clarify different opinions and wishes. People who argue with each other at least show some interest in the other person and possibly the wish to continue the relationship. Stierlin (1974: 181) even speaks of a 'loving fight' that can lead to 'mutual liberation (. . .) in the context of this conflict of generations'.

In general, intergenerational family conflict can be seen as a form of inter-active behaviour of family generations based on different interests, feelings or opinions (see Sev'er and Trost 2011: 9). Conflict can contradict solidarity, while both can also occur at the same time (Figure 2.1). Discord may even be associated with support, for example, when parents give money and, implicitly or explicitly, expect something in return (e.g., specific behaviour or attention). With regard to relationships with parents, care for frail elderly may also come with controversy. Whatever the case may be, family members have conflicts of a special kind. To quote Simmel once again: 'It is [. . .] presumed, without more ado, as a reality of experience that a stronger antagonism is found on grounds of familial commonalities than among strangers' (2009: 248; 1908).

Research

In comparison to solidarity, research on intergenerational conflict in adulthood is relatively rare (e.g., Suitor and Pillemer 1991; Clarke et al. 1999; Van Gaalen and Dykstra 2006; Lowenstein 2007; Szydlik 2008a; Buhl 2009; Schwarz 2013; for a number of case studies on family conflict, see also Sev'er and Trost 2011). This applies especially to conflict in middle age. The lack of conflict research regarding adult children and parents may not least be due to the lack of corresponding data. Conflict is a sensitive topic, which is not easily addressed in (representative) surveys.

Existing empirical studies do not find much notable intergenerational discord amongst adults. The low rates of conflict between family generations are documented by Lowenstein (2007) for the urban population aged 75 years and older in England, Germany, Israel, Norway and Spain. Van Gaalen and Dykstra (2006) find low rates among 18–79 year olds in the Netherlands. Furthermore, in a qualitative study for the United States, Clarke et al. (1999) identify six themes of conflict between older parents and adult children. In order of appearance they are: habits and lifestyles; communication and interaction style; child-rearing practices and values; politics, religion and ideology; work orientation; and household maintenance (see also Usita 2001; Usita and Du Bois 2005; Gapp 2007).

The German Ageing Survey, which observes 40–85 year olds, focuses on pronounced conflicts that clearly go beyond differences on topics of little significance and minor episodic quarrelling. The respondents are asked:

> There are, time and again, situations in life in which one's view of important issues is completely different from that of people one is close to, which causes conflicts. Does this apply to you? Is there a person or are there people in your life with whom you are in conflict?

Almost one-quarter agree with this statement, a fifth state that they have conflict with family members, a good tenth report intergenerational family conflict, and only 8 per cent talk about conflict with considerably older or younger members of the family, i.e., parents and children (Szydlik 2008a).

The German Ageing Survey also asks about the consequences of conflict, allowing for multiple responses. Of those 8 per cent who experience intergenerational family discord, only 14 per cent claim to be working on a solution. Over 40 per cent of them see no end to the controversy. These generations quarrel a great deal, and they fail to resolve their differences. A little over 30 per cent avoid the topic of controversy, and almost half of the 8 per cent who experience conflict between family generations avoid the other person or break off contact altogether.

Further multivariate analyses on the basis of this study indicate that discord between adult family generations is associated particularly with less frequent contact and weaker emotional closeness. Additionally, adult children who have health problems, financial debts or receive transfers from their parents clash with them more often; so do respondents with higher education, and women. Divorced or separated parents as well as West Germans are also more likely to be in conflict with their descendants.

Hypotheses

In view of previous studies (and Figure 3.5), it would be a big surprise to find huge numbers of family generations in fierce conflict. Nevertheless, controversies between adult children and parents should not be downplayed, or even neglected. They are evidence of the complex interactions of family generations as well as their multifaceted causes and consequences.

Although the theoretical model illustrated in Figure 2.2 focuses on family solidarity, it can also be applied to intergenerational conflict. Therefore, besides developing hypotheses for the empirical analyses, the following theoretical discussion also aims to expand the ONFC model.

First, controversies require *opportunities* to engage in this type of interaction. Education, income and the prospects of inheriting may have an influence on inter-generational dispute. Education can be seen as a valuable resource that provides considerable opportunities. With regard to conflict, one might assume that people with a higher education are in a better position to risk discord with other family generations since they can rely on their own 'human capital' in potentially dif-ficult situations. By contrast, owing to their more vulnerable position, the lower educational classes might be more inclined to refrain from risking discord and thus current and future family solidarity. If dependence restricts (open) contro-versy, the lower classes can be expected to show less intergenerational conflict. These class-specific resources may also be associated with different communica-tion, discussion and thus conflict styles.

It will be especially interesting to see whether current income and prospective wealth transfers have an influence on disputes between adult generations. Several effects are conceivable here: people with more monetary resources may face less opposition from other family members; relatives expecting financial contribu-tions or even wealth may be more likely to refrain from quarrelling with potential transfer givers; financial difficulties may give reason for dispute, whereas affluent family members are also in a better position to risk controversy.

Without so much as minimal contact, personal disputes are quite unlikely. In turn, more frequent contact may be associated with more conflict on the one hand. This is in accordance with the assumption that especially close relationships are likely to involve more discord. Thus, family generations who see each other on a daily basis may be more likely to display some degree of dispute. On the other hand, the previous analyses indicate that bitter controversies can result in less contact and even in the termination of the relationship. Following both strands, there seems to be a paradox involved in the contact-conflict relation: more contact may come with more conflict, but more conflict may also result in less contact. In other words, personal controversies may be associated with close bonds, yet fierce disputes are also likely to put the relationship at risk.

Needs may cause conflict as well. If parents or adult children are in finan-cial need, the corresponding 'negotiations' about transfers as well as the difficult situation itself may lead to controversies. This situation may involve accusations about the reasons for needing monetary support, and there may be conflicting ideas about 'payback', be it financial, or in terms of attention, compliant behav-iour or subordination.

It can be assumed that intergenerational family conflicts decrease over time. In young adulthood, children have greater need to distance themselves from their parents, whereas this need may play a lesser role in later years, leading to less conflict. However, poor health is likely to create stressful situations, which bear the potential for discord between generations. As well as reducing life satisfac-tion and thus increasing the potential for dispute amongst close family members, poor health can involve experiences of stress and strain, and also divergent expectations as to how to handle the difficult situation. In this regard, help and care may also be a source of intergenerational discord in adulthood. The needs of the frail elderly may come up against the needs of adult children for autonomy. Role reversals of parent and child, new dependencies, contrasting definitions of the situation, its causes and consequences may all lead to family conflict.

Regarding *family structures*, gender, partnership, (grand)children and siblings can be assumed to have an effect on intergenerational conflict. In accordance with the German study on family conflict mentioned above, daughters in particular could be expected to have disputes with parents more often, owing to their stronger involvement in family duties.

Previous analyses have also shown long-term effects of parental divorce on intergenerational relationships with children in adulthood (e.g., Aquilino 1994a; Szydlik 2000, 2008a; Ahrons and Tanner 2003; Frank 2007; Bertogg and Szydlik 2016). Divorcees may experience more discord even with parents, not least since 'habits and lifestyles' seem to be a prominent conflict theme (Clarke et al. 1999). It also cannot be ruled out that greater demands for support to or from singles might put more strain on intergenerational relations.

Having more children may increase the likelihood of disputes with one of them. The existence of grandchildren leads to contrasting hypotheses. On the one hand, grandchildren may lessen discord between parents and adult children since the middle generation is a likely 'gatekeeper' who grants or bars grandparents from access to their grandchildren. This may reduce grandparents' readiness to engage in conflict with their adult children. The alleviating effect of grandchildren on conflict between parents and grandparents may even be enhanced by the adult children's need for their parents to care for their children, especially in order to reconcile parenthood and employment (Igel and Szydlik 2011; Igel 2012). On the other hand, grandchildren may be a reason for dispute between parents and grandparents with regard to different educational styles or different wishes as to the length of time grandparents and grandchildren are allowed or required to spend together.

More siblings may reduce stress and strain with elderly parents, thus leading to less intergenerational dispute. However, competition amongst siblings may also enhance conflict. Again, it is an empirical question which of these divergent hypotheses dominates in reality.

Last but not least, *cultural-contextual structures* are likely to affect intergenerational controversy. Here, the special situation of migrants should not be neglected, including cultural norms and different adaptation, integration, assimilation, language skills, discrepancies in education and divergent lifestyles of migrant parents and children as well as disputes over staying in the host country or returning to the country of origin.

Considerable effects of different welfare states cannot be ruled out either. It is one of the main assumptions of this book that welfare state regulations have strong consequences for intergenerational family bonds. The hypothesis reads as follows: Stronger welfare states that support families in many ways relieve parents and adult children of strenuous tasks and corresponding tension. Therefore, the Northern European countries should show less family conflict, and this should also hold true for higher public expenditure.

What about social stratification? The contrasting hypotheses regarding the impact of income and prospective wealth on conflict can be extended to the general situation, in terms of wealth and poverty in a country. Rich societies can generally be expected to offer more financial security and thus less reason for discord. However, greater wealth might also trigger more dispute within society and families. This could be particularly true in the case of widespread poverty (see Wilkinson and Pickett 2010).

Explaining conflict

Questions

International investigations of intergenerational family conflict are particularly scarce. It is difficult, if not impossible, to compare the empirical results of research on conflict that have been collected using different samples, procedures and survey questions. It is fortunate that the Survey of Health, Ageing and Retirement in Europe asks the same questions in all countries participating in the survey. SHARE collects information about conflict via a self-administered questionnaire (drop-off). After the interview, respondents are asked to fill out a paper-and-pencil questionnaire on their own. The two conflict questions read as follows:

> There are sometimes important questions about which we have a disagreement with persons close to us, and which therefore may lead to conflicts. Please tell us how often, if at all, you experience conflict with each of the following persons. (Please tick one box in each row).

Six (groups of) persons are named:

a) Parents
b) Parents-in-law
c) Partner/spouse
d) Children
e) Other family members
f) Friends, coworkers, acquaintances.

The boxes for each of these are: Often – Sometimes – Rarely – Never – Does not apply. The next question follows the same logic:

> How often do you experience conflicts with your children or children-in-law over the education and bringing up of your grandchild(ren)? (Please tick one box).

With regard to intergenerational conflict with parents, only respondents with at least one living parent are considered. Correspondingly, in order to assess controversy with adult children, these analyses focus on SHARE participants whose youngest child is at least 18 years old.

Description

Figure 5.1 offers a first overview of the answers of the respondents. Overall, 11 per cent report frequent conflict, 43 per cent occasional and 34 per cent rare disputes with at least one of the six groups of people. This already shows that frequent conflicts with another person are actually not very frequent. When one compares the six groups of people, most controversies occur with partners. However, only 6 per cent of couples report continual disagreements, even if only respondents with partners are considered.

What about family generations? Only 5 per cent of the adult children and parents speak of frequent conflict (the percentages for all parents with adult or underage children are the same). This is one of the most important results of this chapter. It shows that substantial intergenerational controversies are exceptionally rare. On the whole, generations do not quarrel and fight extensively. This result on the basis of SHARE is also supported by the previously mentioned analyses for Germany, according to which only 8 per cent of the 40–85 year olds report frequent conflict with older or younger family members.

Figure 5.1 documents that there are more disagreements with adult children than with parents, which corresponds with the findings for contact and coresidence (Chapters 4 and 6). Spending a lot of time together could provide more opportunity for disagreements, and older age may generally come with less inclination to engage in controversy; these hypotheses will be tested by further analyses.

Common belief as well as jokes about parents-in-law seem to have only a weak foundation in reality, at least when considering the very low rate of 5 per cent of the respondents reporting frequent conflict (here, only SHARE participants with at

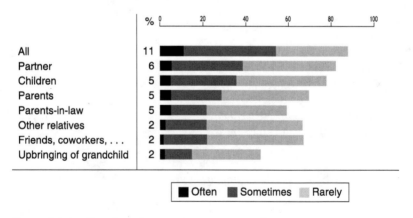

Figure 5.1 Conflict: Overview

Source: SHARE (n: 23,870).

least one parent-in-law are included). All in all, there is more discord with parents than with parents-in-law.

Interpersonal conflicts seem to emerge especially between close family members. This supports the abovementioned interconnectedness between closeness and conflict (closeness-conflict hypothesis). 'Other relatives' can be avoided more easily, and there are presumably fewer occasions for dispute. In particular, quarrels with friends, coworkers and acquaintances occur less often than conflicts with partners, children and parents, and this is even more the case if we consider the number of people with whom a person could have conflict.

The degree of discord with children or children-in-law over the education and upbringing of grandchildren is assessed for respondents with at least one grandchild. Obviously, these conflicts are especially rare. As mentioned above, the gatekeeper position of the middle generation may lead grandparents to refrain from open arguments about educational styles, and dependence on grandparents in order to reconcile parenthood and employment may play a role as well.

Figure 5.2 documents conflict frequencies with regard to education, income, gender and migration. The bars suggest no class-specific differences regarding frequent or occasional controversy with parents, whereas the results on rare conflict point to somewhat more disputes among the higher classes. The better

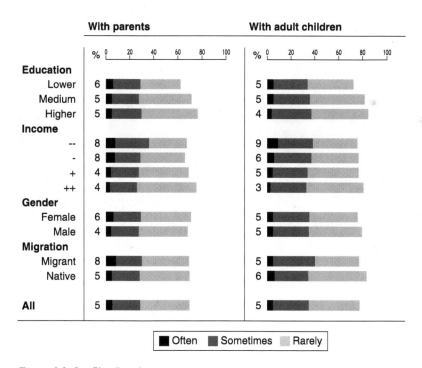

Figure 5.2 Conflict: People

Source: SHARE (n: 5,686/20,371).

educated also report more occasional and rare discord with their offspring. One cannot rule out that these response patterns might be a result of members of the higher classes being somewhat more at ease in admitting disputes. Nonetheless, the results support the abovementioned hypothesis.

Income shows a different picture. When the household is able to make ends meet (fairly) easily, there is considerably less intergenerational conflict. Nine per cent of the parents with low income speak of frequent disagreements with their adult children; the corresponding share for affluent parents is only 3 per cent. These results support the hypothesis that money reduces family arguments, or correspondingly, financial shortage puts a strain on intergenerational relations.

The results on quarrels with parents tend to support the assumed gender differences, not least due to the kinkeeper role of women. However, these differences are not substantial, and the figure shows no gender gap in frequent or occasional disputes between the respondents and their children.

Migrants show more frequent conflict with parents and more occasional disputes with adult children. These results indicate an influence of transnational mobility on intergenerational family conflicts. According to Figure 5.2, moving to another country may increase discord between generations. Some of the possible reasons are different norms and lifestyles, difficult integration processes, and divergent prospects and goals between the generations.

Figure 5.3 documents frequent, occasional and rare discord with parents and children in Northern, Western, Eastern and Southern Europe. The figure shows substantial differences. Overall, most controversies seem to occur in Western Europe. Considerably less conflict can be found in the north and the east. Only 13 per cent of the Swedish and Danish respondents experience frequent or occasional disputes with their parents. This applies to nearly every third respondent in Germany, which is even exceeded by Austria, Switzerland and Italy.

A similar pattern exists with regard to the relationship of the respondents with their adult children: Swedish and Danish parents again have the lead when it comes to 'harmonious' intergenerational relations, and at least occasional conflict is especially pronounced in Austria, Switzerland and Italy.

It is also noteworthy that the Eastern European generations seem to be exceptional in terms of intergenerational discord. This finding could be a consequence of close private relationships in former 'socialist' countries, where there was a comparatively large discrepancy between trusted family members and a suspect outside environment. The rapid changes in Eastern Europe may have also emphasised the importance of conflict-free family bonds.

Furthermore, the results suggest influences of welfare states. Northern European countries with stronger welfare states seem to successfully unburden family members of conflict-provoking stresses and strains. It is quite impressive that in those countries that offer relatively generous social benefits, clashes between parents and children are kept within even closer bounds. There may also be considerable effects associated with social stratification.

However, it is quite a risky endeavour to engage in extensive interpretations on the basis of the descriptive results considered so far. It has to be assessed

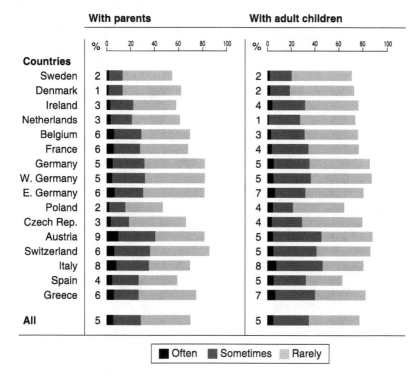

Figure 5.3 Conflict: Countries

Source: SHARE (n: 5,686/20,371).

whether a whole number of possible factors, reflecting individual opportunities and needs as well as family and cultural structures, have a significant impact on intergenerational controversy. This also applies to the question of whether education, income, gender and migration differences still hold under simultaneous consideration of other relevant factors. Moreover, we need to conduct further examinations employing suitable macro indicators.

Explanation

Figure 5.4, which draws on Table A5.2 (see Appendix), provides a summary of the corresponding multilevel multivariate analyses: '+' signifies higher conflict rates, whereas the '−' sign indicates fewer controversies between adult family generations. As in the other chapters of this book, the signs refer to the net effects including the first macro indicator.

Clearly, *opportunity structures* play a relevant role when it comes to family conflict. The higher-educated classes report more intergenerational controversy with adult children, and this holds even after controlling for factors such as

		With parents	With children
Opportunity Structures	Education: Lower (ref.)		
	Medium		+
	Higher		+ +,
	Income		− −
	Future inheritance	+ +	+
	Contact: Day	+	+ +
	Week (ref.)		
	Month		+
	Year	+ + +	+ + +
Need Structures	Money transfer		+ +
	Age	− − −	− − −
	Health	+ + +	+
	Time transfer	+ +	
Family Structures	Women	+	
	Married (ref.)		
	Partner		
	Widowed		
	Divorced		
	Single	+ + +	
	Number of children		+ + +
	Grandchild	− −	− − −
	Number of siblings	− − −	
Cultural-contextual Structures	Migrant		+ +
	Social expenditure	− − −	+ +
	Family expenditure	− −	−
	Wealth per capita	+ + +	+ + +
	Poverty rate	+ +	+ +

Figure 5.4 Explaining conflict

Source: SHARE, Table A5.2, see Appendix (net). '+': more, '−': less conflict with parents / adult children.

income, contact and financial support. These results support the hypothesis that a better education, which is associated with less dependence on intergenerational solidarity, offers more opportunity to risk discord. This may also lead to divergent discussion and conflict styles between educational classes.

In comparison with educational class, the current income situation shows a different pattern. Here it is not affluent parents who report more conflict with children, but the other way around: a difficult financial situation leads to more dispute, indicating the impact of stresses and strains. If the household has difficulty in making ends meet, we observe more intergenerational controversy. A favourable financial situation gives less reason for quarrels and fights, and parents with money might also restrict their children's wish for opposition and dispute.

Interestingly, income- and education-related differences in intergenerational controversy pertain to relationships with (younger) adult children and not to relationships with (elderly) parents.

Respondents who are more likely to receive a future inheritance report more quarrels with their parents. The situation is similar with regard to controversy with their children if the respondents perceive a good chance of leaving an inheritance, including property and other valuables. This result is again more in line with the effect of education, indicating that people with more resources are rather more likely to risk dispute and engage in controversy.

The contact-conflict hypothesis is confirmed by the multivariate analyses. The empirical results suggest a twofold picture. Daily contact leads to more discord. However, frequent strife diminishes intergenerational cohesion. On the one hand, especially close relationships, which are marked by daily contact, are associated with a significantly higher degree of controversy. On the other hand, being in significant conflict with one another often leads to less contact. The conflicting parties seem to reduce their time together. In fact, this is one of the most notable effects found by the empirical investigation.

Regarding *need structures*, four potential factors are investigated: money, age, health and time. There are no significant conflicts in cases in which the respondents have given their parents financial support of at least 250 € during the previous year. However, when their children are the recipients, intergenerational tension increases considerably. This finding underlines the argument that monetary independence is a prerequisite of less conflict-laden relationships. When children are in lesser need of money, there is less discord with parents.

Conversely, age decreases clashes with other generations. This is an indication that people have less desire to engage in controversy as they become older. The results suggest that younger people are more conflict-prone. However, poor health increases intergenerational controversy. Respondents with good or excellent health report less conflict with parents and children. This finding suggests that the greater needs of family members who are in poor health often inflict stress and strain on intergenerational relationships. This becomes especially apparent when the respondents provide help or care to their elderly parents. There is a wide range of possible conflict themes, including ensuring that the elderly take medication, elderly parents who do not want to accept support or demand attention day and night, intimate care, the needs of the helpers and carers, overstressing and reversal of roles (i.e., when children have to take responsibility for their parents).

The results regarding *family structures* also support this interpretation. The frequency of quarrelling with adult children does not seem to be different for mothers and fathers. However, when we turn to the relationships with elderly parents, it is daughters in particular who talk of controversies. Women's greater involvement in family tasks, including serving as kinkeeper and caregiver, is understandably associated with somewhat more frequent conflict.

In contrast to married couples, singles are more often in dispute with their parents (the corresponding effect for singles with regard to their children is only weakly significant). Possible explanations are, amongst other things, parents' disapproval of their child's lifestyle and adult children's or parents' greater demands towards the other generation. This may also apply to some divorcees, at least according to a weakly significant effect for conflict with parents (see Appendix, Table A5.2).

Furthermore, the number of children, grandchildren and siblings plays a significant role in the level of intergenerational discord. The more children the respondents have, the more likely they are to be in conflict with at least one of them. In contrast, the existence of grandchildren significantly decreases quarrels between family generations. Having a grandchild (and thus living in a four-generation family) seems to reduce disputes between respondents and their parents, possibly via focusing on the (great-)grandchild. This applies even more so to the respondents' relationship with their adult children. It is possible that grandparents refrain from starting arguments with their adult children in view of the gatekeeper position of the middle generation. Conversely, potential dependence on (grand) parents caring for grandchildren in order to help their children reconcile parenthood and employment might reduce the middle generation's willingness to argue with their parents as well. Beyond that, having more siblings also reduces the probability of discord with parents. One possible reason is a less stressful individual adult child-parent relationship due to the shared responsibility of siblings for their elderly parents.

Of further importance are *cultural-contextual structures*. Migrants do not seem to differ from the native population with regard to controversies with parents. However, there are considerable discrepancies when it comes to their relationship with their adult children. The analyses show that migrants report discord with their offspring relatively often. The conflict themes may be different norms, lifestyles and integration into the host society, which may separate migrant parents from the 'second generation'. Moreover, disadvantages in education, the labour market and societal participation, including discrimination, may also put stresses and strains on intergenerational family relationships.

Last but not least, the investigation addresses influences of the four macro indicators (Figure 2.3), considering differences in welfare state regulation and social stratification. On the whole, the analyses support the hypothesis that stronger welfare states lead to less intergenerational controversy. This is not the case when observing the respondents' relationships with their adult children in the light of social expenditure. However, this macro indicator only provides a rather general view of welfare states that comprises many different forms of social support (see Appendix, Table A3), and it also shows considerably less discord with regard to parents. More importantly, both for parents and children, the more specific indicator of family expenditure is clearly associated with fewer disputes. Higher public expenditure on families corresponds with less intergenerational quarrel. This is an empirical indication of strong welfare states relieving families of the intense burdens that fuel conflict.

Most interestingly, both macro indicators of social stratification point to more conflict. Greater wealth per capita is associated with more intergenerational discord, with regard to both parents and children. This result supports the assumption that rich societies offer more reason for intergenerational dispute. This line of reasoning could lead us to expect that a huge poverty rate would result in less conflict between family members. Yet the opposite is the case. More poverty is associated with more discord. An obvious explanation is that living in difficult circumstances puts more stress and strain on family members, which again leads to more intergenerational conflict.

Summary

Audiences – and thus the media, publishing houses and the film industry – prefer stories involving conflict. It is therefore not surprising to find a wealth of news-paper articles, books and films that paint a picture of discord and dispute. The general topic of generations is no exception in this respect. In fact, some generation concepts are actually based on controversy among age groups, cohorts or social generations – even to the point of propagating a 'battle' or a 'war of generations'.

Against this background, one of the main findings of this chapter might be disappointing. In fact, all over Europe only a fraction of adult family generations mention frequent struggle with one another. Five per cent speak of frequent con-flict with their parents or adult children, whereas 95 per cent do not. Obviously, pronounced conflicts are rare. Only if we add occasional discord do we find that a little more than one-third of the respondents are often or sometimes in dispute with an adult child, and nearly three in ten frequently or occasionally quarrel with a parent. Moreover, when it comes to considerable controversy, it is mainly amongst close family members. After disputes with partners, conflict with chil-dren and parents comes in second and third place.

Figure 2.1 and Table 3.1 have already indicated that solidarity and conflict are not necessarily opposites. In fact, particularly strong solidarity amongst adult fam-ily generations is also associated with relatively frequent discord: generations with daily contact experience more conflict. Also, disputes within (intergenerational) relationships are not necessarily negative. It is possible that candid discussions contribute more to sustaining than destroying the relationship. However, it also has to be noted that more discord often results in less cohesion. More contact may mean more conflict, but more conflict may also lead to less contact.

What are reasons for disputes and fights? Again, opportunities and needs as well as family and cultural-contextual structures play a crucial role. On the one hand, more resources come with more disputes. This applies especially to education and wealth. Better-educated parents and those who expect to leave an inheritance report more frequent controversy with their offspring. Economic power, via the independence it offers, seems to increase the readiness to risk dis-cord. On the other hand, intergenerational conflict is often based on stresses and strains. Low income leads to more dispute. Financial transfers to adult children are likely to come with more controversy, too. This also applies to help and care for elderly parents. In other words, when adult children need money and parents need time, intergenerational conflict is much more likely to occur.

Poor health also tends to increase the frequency of discord with both parents and children. Singles mention having more frequent arguments with parents.

One explanation for this is greater strain due to heightened demands for intergenerational support. Migrants experience more conflict with their adult children, suggesting some degree of 'drifting apart' between migrant parents and their children due to different contexts in the home and host countries as well as the impact of the strains that come with migration.

Consistent with these results is that intergenerational family discord is especially prominent in weak welfare states. The more public expenditure is spent on families, the less frequent are quarrels and fights between family generations. This leads to the conclusion that welfare states relieve families of excessive burdens, which in turn reduces intergenerational conflict.

Wealth and poverty in a society have a huge influence, too. More wealth per capita is associated with more family discord. Apparently, richer societies offer more reason for intergenerational controversy. A greater abundance of material resources in a country does not generally lead to more harmony between family members. However, poverty also increases discord. Stresses and strains on individuals, families and societies at large contribute to more conflict between adult children and parents.

6 Space
Living together

Introduction

Living within the same four walls is an especially intense form of relationship for adult family generations. Living together means seeing and talking to one another every day, sharing the same bathroom and kitchen, negotiating basic tasks such as shopping for groceries, cooking, doing the laundry or repair work and possibly paying bills. Adult children and parents living together ultimately also means that it is *adult individuals* who are living together. These individuals typically have a (life)long history with one another – a history that is characterised by a formerly great responsibility and dominance on one side of this relationship and total dependency on the other. In the present, the adult children encounter parents who once cared for them in infancy, whose authority they were subject to whilst they were young, and with whom they probably have not only shared many pleasurable moments but also less harmonious times, for instance, during puberty.

This special situation of still living in the same household as adults is embedded in a societal context that harbours other expectations. At some point in life, adult children are supposed to move out of their parents' home ('Hotel Mum') and find their own space. This general norm is also accompanied by the desire of grown-ups to stand on their own feet and no longer live in their old children's room in adulthood. Moreover, as we have just seen in the previous chapter, daily contact of adult family generations tends to increase intergenerational conflict. Living in the same household, sharing space and hence being in a situation that contradicts general norms might fuel dispute and motivate both parties to consider changing the situation. At least with a twinkle in the eye, authors of guidebooks aim at this potential target audience by offering titles such as *Still in Their Children's Room at Thirty – How to Get Rid of Nestlings Before It Is Too Late* (Meinert 1996).

Considering people's preferences and social norms, one might expect very low numbers of adult children and parents to be sharing the same household. However, coresidence also has its advantages. It helps with pooling resources and saving costs; it provides opportunities for (mutual) intergenerational help and contact within close reach and without having to spend time bridging spatial distances; it offers young adult children the opportunity to continue to receive attention and support and gives parents the chance to remain in close contact with their offspring.

It is therefore, first and foremost, an empirical question whether generations live together or run separate households instead. Another question that needs to be addressed is the reasons for coresidence and whether there are significant differences in the individual opportunities and needs, family contexts and societal conditions that account for sharing space. Why do adult generations live together? Who does and who does not? In the event that parents and adult children do live together, do they typically live in the parental home, or is it the other way around? Do adult children and parents really choose to coreside, or is it out of necessity? From an international perspective it is furthermore crucial to learn more about country-specific differences in terms of welfare states and social stratification.

In addition, there is good reason to also consider 'near coresidence'. This pertains to generations who do not live in the same household but in the same house. Here the question is whether these adult children and parents are similar to coresident generations, or whether they resemble those who live in separate places.

This chapter is structured in the same way as the other empirical chapters comprising multivariate analyses. First, different forms of (near) coresidence are discussed, arguing additionally for the benefits of distinguishing between individuals and dyads. The next step is to briefly review previous research. In order to link theoretical reasoning, previous research and the empirical investigations presented below, a number of hypotheses will be developed. After documenting the wording of the corresponding questions in the Survey of Health, Ageing and Retirement in Europe, the chapter goes on to give descriptive information on (near) coresidence. Since this is the first chapter to address functional solidarity, it provides some additional comparative information on space, money and time. A differentiation is made between population groups and countries, coresidence and near coresidence as well as between individuals and dyads. The analyses performed to explain (near) coresidence are presented, and the main results summarised.

Research and hypotheses

What is (near) coresidence?

Coresidence of parents and adult children comprises various forms according to whether the generations have stayed or moved. There are adult children who have never left their parents' home, and who might be called 'stay-at-homes' or 'nestlings'. 'Boomerang kids', for example, return to their parents' home after job loss or divorce. Elderly parents, for instance, may move into their adult children's home when caring for grandchildren or when needing care due to old age. After living in separate places, offspring and parents may both decide to move into a shared home.

Furthermore, it is helpful to distinguish between coresidence in the strict sense, meaning sharing the same household, and near coresidence, which refers to living in separate apartments in the same house (Kohli et al. 2000b: 186; Isengard and Szydlik 2012). Near coresidence provides an additional perspective to consider family generations who live under the same roof without sharing the same rooms. Such an arrangement can take a number of different forms within a fam-ily-, owner-occupied or tenant-occupied house, which to a greater or lesser extent reflect a similar situation as the case of strict coresidence. For example, adult children can just move from their former children's room into a small flat in their parents' house (e.g., in the attic), or into a rented apartment of their own within the same tenant-occupied house. An adult child can also return to a sepa-rate apartment in the parents' house after having lived independently somewhere else for a period of time. Conversely, elderly parents might move into a child's house, including cases in which an adult child has built a new family home with a 'granny flat'. Near coresidence can also occur when adult children and parents move into separate rental or owner-occupied units within the same building.

Whatever the case may be, for empirical investigations it is necessary to clearly define what is meant by (near) coresidence. The coresidence rates observed will depend on this definition. Including near coresidence will obviously result in higher rates. At the same time, one might not necessarily find the same patterns when looking at parents and adult children living within the same four walls ver-sus living in separate apartments under the same roof.

It also makes sense to clearly distinguish coresidence rates for respondents and dyads since parents might have both coresident and non-coresident children. Asking how many parents live together with at least one adult child results in higher rates than asking how many parent-adult child relationships are marked by coresidence. Having one child at home and another child elsewhere amounts to a coresidence rate of 100 per cent at the individual level but only to a 50 per cent rate if we refer to parent-child dyads. Figures 6.2 and 6.3 consider both perspec-tives, whereas the multivariate analyses are based on dyads.

Research

The first public release of SHARE data (the first wave in ten countries) shows 42 per cent of parents with at least one child living in the same building (Hank 2007). The highest rates (around 60%) are found in Italy, Greece and Spain, the lowest shares in Denmark and Sweden (17%). In a study on living distances in Europe, Isengard (2013: 249) documents, on the basis of the second SHARE wave, that around a fifth of parent-adult child relationships (dyads) are marked by coresidence in the sense of living in the same household – with large discrep-ancies between countries. Coresidence is much more prevalent in Southern and Eastern Europe, whereas relatively few adult generations live together in the north (for similar results on the basis of the first SHARE wave, see also Isengard and Szydlik 2012).

In regard to resources, Fingerman et al. (2015) find for Philadelphia (United States) that adult children of higher-educated parents are less likely to coreside with them. This is in line with Goldscheider and DaVanzo (1989), who document that a high family income is more likely to lead to young adult children moving out of the parental home, suggesting that the financial resources of parents might be a factor that supports adult generations living within their own four walls.

Nevertheless, Angelini and Laferrère (2013: 417) also show that '[a] more comfortable, less crowded home or which provides more privacy is left later.'

Previous investigations indicate that in many cases adult children and parents sharing the same space is the result of the economic needs of the child, for example, a difficult income or employment situation (e.g., Norris and Tindale 1994; Aassve et al. 2002; Blanc and Wolff 2006; Sandberg-Thoma et al. 2015). Ward et al. (1992) find for the United States that the needs of adult children are primarily crucial here. This is in line with the finding that coresidence applies to young adult children in particular, which speaks in favour of adopting a life course perspective with regard to crucial transitions such as moving out of the parents' home (e.g., White 1994; König 2016). Research also suggests that not only the needs of children, but also those of parents, such as needs related to health issues, can motivate intergenerational coresidence (e.g., Lee and Dwyer 1996; Choi 2003; Smits et al. 2010; Seltzer and Friedman 2014).

In contrast to daughters, sons tend to stay longer in their parents' home (e.g., Billari et al. 2001: 345), indicating more frequent intergenerational coresidence among parents with male offspring. Aquilino (1990) points out that most coresident adult generations live in the parents' home and the marital status of children is the most important factor to account for this. Similarly, White and Peterson (1995) report that divorced and, in particular, never-married children are much more likely to live with their parents.

The aforementioned differences between European regions are also found in other studies. Cordón (1997) documents that young adults in Southern European countries (Spain, Italy and Greece) are considerably more likely to still live with their parents than their counterparts in France, Germany and the United Kingdom. This is in accordance with Billari et al. (2001), who report a substantial share of early move-outs among young adults in Northern Europe, in contrast to the rather late leavers of the parental home in the south (for a thorough analysis on home-leaving patterns of young adults in West Germany and Italy, see Rusconi 2006 and Rossi 1997). In a qualitative study of Italian and German university students and their parents (43 participants), Luetzelberger (2014) finds divergent normative patterns: Italians seem to adhere to *interdependence* of family members, whereas the German participants in this study favour *independence* of young adults (for a qualitative study on delayed home-leaving in Spain, see Holdsworth 2005).

Further investigations (Isengard and Szydlik 2012) indicate that country-specific characteristics play a crucial role: greater public expenditure is associated with fewer adult generations sharing the same space. By contrast, the higher the poverty rate in a country, the more coresidence.

Hypotheses

Again, the hypotheses are developed on the basis of the ONFC model, which differentiates between characteristics of individuals, families and societies (Figure 2.2).

Regarding *opportunity structures*, education is likely to be a relevant factor, even though there might be opposite influences at work here. On the one hand, upper-class parents are likely to have adult children with longer educational phases – not least due to university studies – which postpones moving out and thus increases intergenerational coresidence. On the other hand, the higher educational classes have better opportunities in the labour and housing market (for example, better-off parents can grant a guarantee for their children) and display greater geographical mobility, both of which favour less coresidence. Here again, empirical investigations need to establish which of the hypotheses is a more accurate account of reality.

Income can be a crucial resource for fulfilling people's wishes and desires. If parents would like to keep their children at home as long as possible, they might provide financial support to prevent their offspring from moving out. However, if parents and adult children would prefer to live in their own places, we might observe the opposite resource effect. In this case, more money could lead to less coresidence, for instance, when parents use their money to find – and pay for – a separate place for their adult children. According to the results on conflict in the case of daily contact and in line with notions of 'intimacy at a distance' (Rosenmayr and Köckeis 1961, 1963) and 'inner closeness through outer distance' (Tartler 1961), one can assume that adult generations rather prefer to live within their own four walls, which in turn would mean that money offers the opportunity to fulfil that wish.

Parents living in a large home have more available space that they can offer to an adult child. At the very least, there is less pressure to find space elsewhere, be it within the same or in a different house.

In line with the abovementioned studies, one can expect the following investigations to attest to the (great) relevance of *need structures*. This applies particularly to the needs of the adult children with regard to their vocational situation. Still being in education is likely to be associated with a higher rate of young adults still living in their parents' home. Unemployment might be another factor implying the need for parental support in terms of providing living space. Also, age of the child could play a role inasmuch as younger adult children, in general, are still in greater need of functional solidarity from their parents.

However, when observing needs, we should not direct our attention to children only. Parents may also find themselves in situations where they need support from their offspring. This applies particularly to health problems. Thus, it should be especially interesting to see whether parents reporting poor health are more likely to live together – or at least within the same house – with an adult child.

Family structures are likely to influence intergenerational (near) coresidence as well. On the one hand, one might assume that mothers and daughters are more inclined to live together, since they show the closest intergenerational bonds. On the other hand, the research cited above suggests that it is sons in particular who tend to be stay-at-homes. If gender differences in coresidence reflect certain time patterns of moving out of the parental home, one can in fact expect later home-leaving to be a matter for male adults, especially in light of gendered age differences in partnership. Since women tend to enter into a partnership at a younger age, they are likely to move out of the parental home at an earlier point in time, which should reduce the rate of daughters still living with their parents in comparison to sons.

The aforementioned research further suggests that single children are more likely to live with their parents. Conversely, living with a partner, and especially marriage, should entail a higher rate of moving out of the parental home. Another interesting case is divorced children. Do divorced children really tend to become boomerang kids once their marriage is over?

From the point of view of parents, the number of children may have an influence too. The obvious hypothesis is that having more children tends to reduce the likelihood of intergenerational coresidence with each child. Their children having children could be another significant factor. Here we could expect to find two opposite influences. On the one hand, starting a family of their own should increase the willingness of adult children to leave their parents' home. On the other hand, adult children who are parents themselves might be interested in having their own parents around, especially to provide grandchild care and thereby ease the burden of raising a child, not least in order to reconcile parenthood and employment (Igel and Szydlik 2011; Igel 2012). Once more, it should be interesting to compare coresidence and near coresidence.

When considering *cultural-contextual structures*, migration is likely to play a relevant role (e.g., Smits et al. 2010; Isengard and Szydlik 2012). Cultural background may lead to more intergenerational (near) coresidence among migrant parents and their adult children. Discrepancies between home and host countries as well as difficult integration processes – according to the 'safe haven' hypothesis – also suggest that migrant families show more (near) coresidence (see Chapter 4).

In accordance with previous results, the following analyses are likely to attest to considerably higher rates of coresidence in the south and east of Europe. If adult generations prefer to live close by, albeit in different homes, a stronger welfare state could result in fewer parents and adult children living together. In this perspective, lower social and family expenditure is likely to be associated with more intergenerational coresidence.

What impact does social stratification have here? If the general hypothesis turns out to be true, namely that the generations would prefer not to share the same four walls, more wealth should be associated with less coresidence – and more poverty should result in more adult children living with their parents.

Explaining space

Questions

SHARE asks the respondents a considerable number of questions about their offspring, including the number of children, whether they are natural/step/adopted/foster children, their gender, year of birth, geographical distance, marital and partnership status, the frequency of contact with their children, their year of moving

out of the parental household, their employment status, education and the existence of grandchildren. This set of questions begins by asking the following:

> Now I will ask some questions about your children. How many children do
> you have that are still alive? (. . .)

> We would like to know more about [this child/these children]. Let us begin
> with the oldest child. What is the first name of your [1st/2nd/3rd . . .] child?

Later on, the survey enquires about geographical proximity in the following way:

> Where does [{child name}] live?
> 1. In the same household
> 2. In the same building
>   (. . .)

Since this chapter investigates (near) coresidence, the focus is on the first two categories of this latter SHARE question, differentiating between parents (respondents)
with adult children in the same household, or in different units within the same
building. The other categories of this question refer to the distance of children living
further away (1, 5, 25, 100 and 500 kilometres), ranging from 'Less than 1 kilometre
away' to 'More than 500 kilometres away in another country'. More information on
geographical distance can be found in Figure 3.3 as well as in Isengard 2013.

Description

First, one needs to bear in mind that coresidence of the respondents with their
parents is very rare. Less than 1 per cent of those aged 50+ with at least one living
parent share the same household, and no more than 6 per cent reside in the same
building (Figure 3.3). Were we to take all SHARE participants as the baseline,
including those with deceased parents, we would arrive at even much smaller
numbers. Instead, the following analyses refer to respondents living with adult
children. Among this group, one finds impressively high rates of sharing the same
household or building.

    Since this is the first chapter investigating factors of functional solidarity,
Figure 6.1 provides a first summarised comparison of space, money and time.
The figure documents how many parent-adult child relationships are marked by
sharing the same household, transferring money or providing help or care during
the last twelve months – in reference to the age of the adult child.

    The figure suggests that the needs of adult children play a prominent role,
and this applies particularly to intergenerational coresidence. From age 33
onwards, the space curve approximates the curves for money and time, and
shows no distinct amplitudes thereafter. However, when the child is between
the ages of 18 and 25, no other form of functional solidarity is as frequent as the
provision of living space by the child's parents. This result also shows that it is

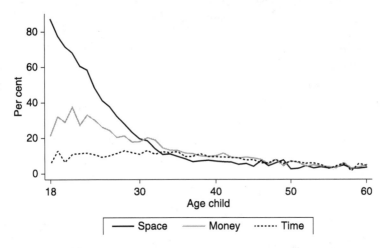

Figure 6.1 Space: Overview

Source: SHARE (n: 76,847). Parent (respondent)-adult child dyads. Space: coresidence. Money and time: no coresidence.

in fact primarily adult children living with their parents and not vice versa. The older the young adults become, the more likely they are to leave their parents' home and move into their own places.

The money curve shows a somewhat similar pattern – however, on a much lower scale. Nevertheless, looking ahead to the chapter on money, we can expect monetary transfers from parents to adult children to reflect the children's economic needs, at least to a considerable extent. As offspring grow older, intergenerational transfers stabilise at a lower, although still relevant, level. According to the figure, time transfers between parents and non-coresident adult children do not seem to follow a pattern related to the age of the offspring.

As mentioned above, Figures 6.2 and 6.3 distinguish between two perspectives. The first perspective centres on parents (respondents) who have at least one adult child living in the same house(hold). Such a focus leads to fewer cases but higher shares of (near) coresidence, since siblings of (near) coresident adult children who have left their parents' house(hold) are not considered. The second perspective takes all adult children into account, which leads to more observations but relatively fewer (near) coresident parent-adult child dyads.

Figure 6.2 illustrates that nearly a third of the parents live with at least one adult child. If we include near coresidence, 39 per cent have a daughter or a son in the same building (see Figure 3.3). These percentages attest to the great relevance of intergenerational coresidence in Europe. In fact, the rates are impressively high, especially considering the general norm that adult children should move out of their parents' home sooner rather than later.

The figure also provides first insights into reasons for sharing the same living space, which are related to differences in terms of education, income, gender

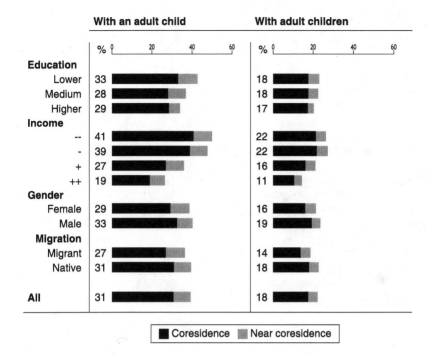

Figure 6.2 Space: People

Source: SHARE (n: 34,483/76,909).

and migration. Better-educated parents show somewhat lower rates of (near) coresidence with adult children, indicating higher mobility rates of the upper-educational classes. Larger discrepancies exist between income groups, suggesting that economic necessity is a crucial reason for adult family generations to share the same household. Less than a fifth of well-to-do parents live with an adult child, whereas this applies to more than twice as many of those whose household has great difficulty in making ends meet. As opposed to income, differences related to parents' gender or to parents having migrated, or not, are rather small.

As expected, the percentages in the right part of Figure 6.2 are lower than those considering (near) coresidence with at least one adult child. Nevertheless, they are still impressive: 18 per cent of adult generations share a household, and 23 per cent live under the same roof. All in all, the differences between population groups point in the same direction as in the left part of the figure. This applies especially to the relation between financial resources and space, which is reflected in the coresidence patterns of income groups. If the parental household is able to make ends meet (fairly) easily, adult children seem to move out considerably earlier. Poorer parents have more stay-at-homes. The descriptive results also suggest that sons tend to move out later than daughters, and there seems to be a somewhat higher rate of coresidence among the native population.

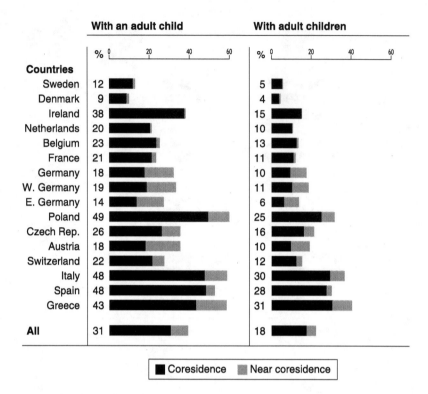

Figure 6.3 Space: Countries

Source: SHARE (n: 34,483/76,909).

Figure 6.3 gives information on countries. The discrepancies are even more pronounced than those between the population groups. The focus on parents living with at least one adult child produces the following results: in Northern Europe the coresidence rate is about one in ten; whereas in Poland, Italy and Spain it nearly reaches an extraordinary 50 per cent. Adult generations living together varies extremely according to country and region.

Focusing on the relationships of the respondents with all their adult children confirms that the most striking differences are observed when comparing countries. In Northern Europe, (near) coresidence is extremely rare, but it is very frequent in the south and in Poland. The share of adult generations living within the same four walls in Italy, Spain and Greece is around 30 per cent. This applies only to one in twenty dyads in Sweden and Denmark.

Furthermore, Figures 6.2 and 6.3 demonstrate that sharing the same household is much more widespread than living in different units in the same building. Near coresidence is considerably more pronounced in Central and Southern Europe. In the north, by contrast, it is nearly non-existent. There, adult children not only seem to leave the parental household quite early, but are also less likely to live in very close proximity to their parents.

Explanation

Figure 6.4 summarises the net coefficients of Table A6.2 (see Appendix), where '+' signifies higher probabilities of (near) coresidence and '−' indicates fewer adult generations living in the same household or house. All three alternatives will be considered, namely coresidence, near coresidence and living in separate buildings, of which the latter category represents the reference group.

With regard to *opportunity structures*, the higher educational classes show less (near) coresidence when the children's age is taken into account. This supports the hypothesis that adult generations prefer to live in separate households, if resources permit. Since more education generally leads to better opportunities in the labour

		Coresidence	Near coresidence
Opportunity Structures	Education: Lower (ref.)		
	Medium	− −	−
	Higher	− − −	− −
	Income	−	
	Number of rooms	+ + +	−
Need Structures	Child: Education (ref.)		
	Full-time	− − −	− −
	Part-time	− − −	− −
	Unemployed		
	Not in workforce	−	
	Age child	− − −	− − −
	Health	+	+
Family Structures	Mother-daughter (ref.)		
	Father-daughter	−	
	Mother-son	+ +	+
	Father-son	+ +	+
	Child: Single (ref.)		
	Divorced	− − −	− − −
	Widowed	− − −	− − −
	Partner	− − −	− − −
	Married	− − −	− − −
	Number of children	− − −	− − −
	Grandchild	−	+
Cultural-contextual Structures	Migrant	+	+
	Social expenditure	−	+
	Family expenditure	− − −	− − −
	Wealth per capita	− − −	− −
	Poverty rate	+ + +	+ + +

Figure 6.4 Explaining space

Source: SHARE, Table A6.2, see Appendix (net). '+': more, '−': less (near) coresidence with adult children.

and housing market, these resources are used to support the preferred way of living; this includes parents helping their adult children to live in a place of their own. Furthermore, higher education is often associated with greater geographical mobility, which in turn significantly increases spatial separation of family generations, and thus entails less opportunity for living in the same building, let alone the same household (see Figure 3.3).

The negative income effect is another sign that adult family generations do not really prefer to coreside. When the household is able to make ends meet (fairly) easily, parents and adult children are less likely to live within the same four walls. This is a further indication that resourceful parents support their children in moving out and finding their own place. In any case, since separate housing is more expensive than living together, parents' financial resources can play an important role when it comes to securing the means for adult offspring to live in a place of their own. Accordingly, financial transfers from parents to non-coresident children will be addressed in the next chapter.

The number of rooms in the parental household offers more or less opportunity for parents and adult children to live in the same residence: the more rooms, the more coresidence. Restricted space naturally reduces the opportunity for adult generations to share the same four walls. With regard to near coresidence, the results point in the opposite direction. There are a number of possible reasons for this. If there is sufficient room, parents and adult children might choose to live together in order to minimise costs. Another factor could be that a larger household might leave less available space for a second apartment in the same (single-family) house, which reduces the opportunity for near coresidence. Living in a spacious home might also be an indication of parental wealth, which provides the opportunity for adult children to live in a place of their own outside the parental house. Conversely, near coresidence is more likely when the parents' residence is too small to house both generations.

When assessing *need structures*, it is of the utmost importance to address the employment situation and age of the adult child. In accordance with previous research, the analyses show that still being in education leads many adult children to live with their parent(s). This applies to both coresidence and near coresidence. Obviously, the children's needs are especially relevant here. Once the adult child has gained employment, that child is likely to move out of the parental home. The discrepancy between being in education and being unemployed or not in the workforce is much less pronounced. An explanation for this is that once adult children have moved out upon entering full-time or part-time employment, a return to the parental home in the case of no employment is not the rule but is still possible, which indicates some support for 'boomerang kids'.

At the same time, the adult child's age is of great significance too. Intergenerational coresidence is mostly a matter for young adults, as illustrated in Figure 6.1. Once children grow older, they tend to find their own place.

Of course, the need for solidarity is not limited to children. Parents in poor health are frequently in need of support as well. The analyses show that these parents are significantly more likely to live under the same roof with an adult child, be it in the form of coresidence (controlling for children's age) or near coresidence. Either the children of parents in poor health refrain from moving away, or the child takes in (or moves to) the frail elderly parent.

Family structures: Although the women in the family tend to have the closest bonds, this does not extend to intergenerational coresidence. More frequently, nestlings are male. When observing family generations still living in the same house(hold), we are more often looking at sons. A reason for this is the different age of women and men when entering a partnership and thus leaving the parental home.

This explanation corresponds with the finding that the child's family status is even more important in explaining intergenerational coresidence than employment. Again, we observe that intergenerational coresidence is mainly due to the situation of the adult child. Being single increases the likelihood of living with one's parents immensely, whereas living with a partner or spouse decreases intergenerational coresidence dramatically. Most interestingly, the discrepancies between singles on the one hand, and divorced or widowed children on the other, are rather less pronounced, though still very clear. Once an adult child has left the parental home in the wake of marriage, returning does not seem to be the general rule. However, the smaller effect does support the notion that after the dissolution of marriage – be it due to divorce or widowhood – some children indeed become boomerang kids. The results for near coresidence are again less pronounced, but clearly point in the same direction.

From the parent's perspective, the number of children (i.e., siblings from their adult children's standpoint) plays a significant role, too. Parents with more children reduces the likelihood for each child of living with their parents, especially considering the general trend and cultural norm to leave the parental home at some point in time, and also taking into account that once children have become adults, they are likely to need more space.

Coresidence is also less likely once the adult child has become a parent (i.e., grandparent from the respondent's perspective). That said, it is an interesting observation that this does not apply to living in separate apartments within the same building. The presence of a third generation even leads to more instances of the first and second generations living under the same roof, after the child's family status is taken into consideration. Living in close proximity enhances the opportunity for frequent contact, which benefits grandparents who are drawn to their grandchildren, and vice versa. The middle generation may also profit from grandparents living close by and looking after their (grand)children, not least in order to successfully reconcile the demands of parenthood and employment. Possibly, the existence of grandchildren initially motivates grandparents to move into the close vicinity of their adult children, and later on, some of these (grand) parents will be cared for by their offspring as their health deteriorates.

Cultural-contextual structures are of great significance as well. Migrants show more (near) coresidence, which underlines the importance of cultural background and of facing an often difficult situation in the host country, including in terms of education, employment and housing. The results support the 'safe haven' hypothesis insofar as close family members serve as a refuge in the face of a difficult environment.

The macro indicators assess the importance of welfare states and social stratification. The stronger the welfare state, the less coresidence. Higher social and family expenditure is associated with considerably fewer parents and adult children living in the same household. When the child's family status is taken into consideration, the result for social expenditure with regard to near coresidence does not support this same relationship. However, near coresidence is a less intense form of living together, and 'social expenditure' reflects total public spending over a whole range of social policy areas, for example, support in old age, for survivors, disability, families, active labour market programmes and housing (see Appendix, Table A3). By contrast, the expenditure that specifically addresses families is associated with considerably less (near) coresidence.

This result supports the so-called 'crowding-out' hypothesis, which predicts that more public expenditure will lead to a 'retreat' of the family. However, the empirical evidence also confirms the necessity hypothesis: given that adult family members would generally prefer to live in their own households, a weak welfare state leads people to forgo or at least delay their wish for spatial independence.

This interpretation is also supported by the two following results. The more wealth in a country, the less (near) coresidence. When considerable resources are available, fewer parents and adult children need to share the same place. By contrast, a huge poverty rate significantly increases the rates of adult family generations living in the same household or building.

Additional analyses with a further macro indicator also show that high youth unemployment rates are associated with more adult children and parents living together, which again underlines that (a) in societies characterised by difficult economic situations, family solidarity steps in, and (b) that, for a majority of the population, permanent coresidence of adult family generations is a living arrangement born out of necessity rather than preference.

Summary

Living together in the same home is a special form of family life. Parents and children sleeping next door, using the same bathroom and kitchen, sharing the same dining room, seeing and talking to one another several times every day – all this is a scenario that tends to represent a living arrangement of families with young children and adolescents. This setting, however, is no longer the norm once the children have grown up and become adults. The relationship with their parents changes, and staying in one's former children's room becomes increasingly obsolete. At some point in time, adult children are generally expected to move out of their parents' home and stand on their own feet.

In the light of this general rule, the empirical findings are indeed remarkable. Over 30 per cent of the parents share a household with at least one adult child. Nearly 40 per cent live in the same building. In some countries, the coresidence rate even reaches nearly 50 per cent, whereas (near) coresidence peaks at 60 per cent. Of course, when we consider all parent-adult child relationships, these four rates are lower, but still impressive, namely 18, 23, 30 and 40 per cent, respectively.

Coresidence of adult family generations is mostly a matter of adult children not (yet) having left the parental home. Beyond the age of 33, coresidence rates resemble those of exercising solidarity via money and time. Up to the age of 25, sharing space is the most frequent form of functional intergenerational solidarity. There is a sharp decrease in joint living with parents as their adult children become older, and only very few of those aged 50+ have a parent in the same household.

Again, individual and family characteristics have proven to be very important for intergenerational relations. In the short run, prolonged education leads adult children to become nestlings. In the long run, the better educated display greater spatial distance between the generations' homes, including much less (near) coresidence. One cause for this is greater geographical mobility in the pursuit of vocational careers. Another reason is resources. Higher education is more likely to provide the necessary means to establish the preferred independent household. Correspondingly, a better income situation is associated with fewer parents and adult children living together. Having more resources obviously reduces coresidence.

Adult family generations sharing the same home can be attributed to the needs of offspring in particular. Being in education is a major factor in adult children still living with their parents. Conversely, poor health of parents increases the likelihood of living with an adult child. In comparison with daughters, who enter a partnership at a younger age, sons are more likely to be stay-at-homes. Singles also (still) live with their parents much more often. When parents have more children, they are less likely to live with any one child. Having a grandchild reduces coresidence with the adult child, but increases the likelihood of grandparents staying in the same house, hence facilitating grandchild care and, in so doing, helping the middle generation reconcile parenthood and employment.

Migrants have higher rates of (near) coresidence with adult children, indicating the significance of cultural background. This is also another finding in support of the 'safe haven' hypothesis, according to which a difficult environment can contribute to family members staying together.

In comparison with other forms of intergenerational cohesion, the disparities in coresidence between countries are especially pronounced. In Northern Europe, it is unusual for adult family generations to share the same household, whereas this form of living is widespread in the south. In the north, every tenth parent lives with an adult child. In Southern Europe, it is nearly every second parent. Cultural-contextual structures are of great significance. Here, the extent of welfare state provision is a major factor. In countries where it is primarily the family that is expected to provide support, coresidence of adult generations is very common. By contrast, countries that spend much more money on public family expenditure have relatively low rates of parents and adult children sharing the same household or building.

This finding can be read in different ways. Strong welfare states can be perceived to 'crowd out' functional solidarity. By the same token, we can view more generous public support as helping adults pursue their preferred living arrangement, namely living close but not too close to the other adult family generations. This latter interpretation is also supported by the results for social stratification: the wealthier a country, the less coresidence. In the same vein, greater poverty is associated with many more adult generations sharing space. Although living together may bring benefits to all generations, the empirical evidence suggests that in many cases it is a reaction to economic pressure and necessity.

7 Money

Financial support

Introduction

Financial transfers can have a number of forms, motives and functions. This chapter addresses inter vivos transfers, which is to say that the focus is on monetary transmissions from living parents, be it in form of a one-time gift or providing financial means on a regular basis. These transfers can be cash or transferrals, meaning money in the strict sense of the word. However, quasi-monetary gifts in the form of objects are included, too. These can range from small occasional presents, through more or less sizeable birthday and Christmas gifts, on to temporary or regular support for basic needs, all the way to the transmission of large property.

Family members giving money or quasi-monetary items can involve various motives. Altruism implies that transfer givers have no other motive than doing something good for the other person. In the case of exchange or reciprocity, however, some kind of return is expected (e.g., Cox 1987). This 'return' may be appreciation and attention, it may involve exchanges of money and time, and it may even come with implicit or explicit conditions that the potential transfer receiver is not ready to accept – for example, when a financial transfer from parents to adult children is seen as a form of 'payment' or even 'bribe' to receive attention (Kotlikoff and Morris 1989). Reciprocity can also be of indirect nature, for example, when parents provide financial support to adult children pursuing higher education as a form of 'investment' in status reproduction (e.g., Albertini and Radl 2012). Another indirect form is also described by the so-called 'demonstration effect', which refers to the middle generation supporting their elderly parents in order to show the young generation how they themselves would like to be treated once they become old (Stark 1995; Cox and Stark 2005).

Further motives are affection and obligation. Affection may play a role when transfer givers (e.g., parents) prefer one recipient (e.g., one adult child) over another on the basis of emotional fondness. However, parents may also be inclined to give a present to one child because of supporting another child who is in financial need, in order to show equal affection to both children. Last but not least, some monetary transmissions go back to obligations, whether they are rooted in law or common norms. Alimony is one example of a legally binding transfer, statutory support for adult children in education is another. Also, general norms and traditions that define 'customary' presents (e.g., for birthdays, celebrating an educational degree or marriage, birth of a grandchild etc.) or a call for support for family members in need, may enhance the willingness to give money to significant others. Whatever the case may be, research suggests that it is not only one specific motive that triggers financial transfers, but rather a combination of altruism, exchange, affection and obligation (Künemund and Motel 2000).

The various motives are intertwined with the various functions of transfers. From the giver's point of view, transfers can be investments – in attention, time transfers, status attainment etc. Being on the receiving end of financial transfers often represents a most welcome position in times of need (although this may not apply if this money comes with excessive implicit or explicit demands, or dependence).

From a family point of view, money can serve as a form of glue for human bonding. This applies particularly to adult children and parents who live in separate households. Giving and receiving presents shows connectedness and belonging (e.g., Cheal 1987). Gifts are signs of thinking of one another, of feeling close, and they even give a signal of assurance of mutual support in difficult times. Blau (1964: 88ff.) argued early on that an essential function of social exchange is the creation of obligations that stabilise human relations. Even earlier, Simmel (2009, 1908) considered feelings of gratitude as being a binding force between people (see also the results on intergenerational contact in Chapter 4). In his seminal work, Mauss (1950) showed for archaic societies that presents are an important factor in strengthening social relations. In this sense, monetary transfers enhance cohesion and intergenerational solidarity (see Motel and Szydlik 1999; Szydlik 2000: 123ff.).

This chapter addresses a number of relevant questions. In what way are adult generations connected by money? Who gives, who receives? Can we detect linkages between private and public transfers? Do monetary transmissions between family generations follow the same or a different route as in the so-called public 'intergenerational contract', in which young and middle-aged employees support elderly pensioners? Are there connections between financial support and other forms of intergenerational solidarity? In what ways do individual, familial and societal factors influence private flows of money?

Research and hypotheses

What is money?

First, financial transfers between family generations can be differentiated in inter vivos and mortis causa transfers. Inter vivos means that both parties, transfer givers and recipients, are alive at the time of the transaction. This is not the case with mortis causa transfers, i.e., bequests or inheritances. The current chapter addresses inter vivos transfers, whereas Chapter 9 explores inheritances.

Monetary transfers are not restricted to money, let alone cash. In fact, there is a great variety of material transmissions between generations, ranging from smaller presents to large endowments. Examples of such quasi-monetary transfers are goods such as books, clothes, tools and kitchen appliances – as well as a car, an apartment or a house. Others are gift vouchers, loans and securities. When parents lend money to their offspring, this generally amounts to receipt of a monetary advantage. Providing security for a bank loan may enable adult children to buy their own home. Coresidence can also be seen as a financial gift or support when family members are not required to pay (market-based) rent. Helping another person in various ways (i.e., giving time) may represent a quasi-monetary transfer as well, especially when such a time transfer means saving money (e.g., since the recipient does not have to pay someone else for the same service).

This variety of (quasi-)monetary transfers also makes it necessary to be cautious when interpreting empirical results from different sources. Various studies may include or exclude different forms of monetary transfers. Also, divergent time frames, varying lower or upper limits as well as different survey groups are likely to have a notable effect on empirical outcomes. For instance, asking about large payments from an individual child to an individual parent during the previous week would register very few transfers – but considering the smallest present from all parents to all children within the last decade would yield an extraordinarily high transfer rate. Therefore, it is crucial to employ the same survey strategy, including the same wording of the questions about transfers, when conducting comparative studies.

In the following, monetary transfers are defined as financial or material gifts or support of at least 250 euros per person and year, excluding benefits derived from coresidence or time transfers. Thus, first, the definition does not only refer to cash but also includes quasi-monetary transfers. Second, the focus is not only on support in the strict sense of the word, but also on gifts without immediate support character, to avoid a too narrow definition – and empirical investigation – of private intergenerational transfers. Third, a lower boundary is set: concentrating on 250 euros or more per year neglects smaller gifts of only minor material benefit. Fourth, neither shared housing nor personal help and care are addressed here, so as not to confound various forms of functional solidarity. Instead, coresidence is investigated in the previous chapter and time transfers are examined in the next chapter.

Research

As mentioned above, transfer rates greatly depend on the empirical setting (e.g., form of transfer, time frame, limits, survey groups). Thus, disparate findings generally reflect different perspectives on intergenerational transfers.

On the basis of the second SHARE wave, Deindl and Brandt (2011) report that in Europe 4 per cent of children aged 50 years or older received at least 250 euros from a parent within the last twelve months, or since the last interview. Alt (1994: 205f.) conducted a non-representative multigenerational study in Germany, according to which 9 per cent of parents supported their children financially on a regular or sporadic basis within a one-year period. With regard to personal payments and support, the German Socio-Economic Panel states that 11 per cent of parents gave money to a child living outside their household in the past twelve months. The German Ageing Survey finds that 30 per cent of the 40–85-year-old parents gave money, larger non-cash gifts or regular financial support to a non-coresident adult child in the last year (Szydlik 2000: 215, 130; Motel and Szydlik 1999: 12).

On the basis of the first SHARE wave, Deindl (2011) finds that 24 per cent of parents provided financial transfers to a child in the last twelve months before the interview. Drawing on the Health and Retirement Study (HRS) for the United States, McGarry and Schoeni (1995; see also Soldo and Hill 1995) determine a rate of 29 per cent for annual financial transfers of at least $500 from 51–61-year-old parents to non-coresident children. The rate for transfers of at least $100 is of course higher, namely 40 per cent (Berry 2008).

Last but not least, Attias-Donfut (1995) reports a transfer rate of nearly two-thirds. This quite impressive result is based on a French three-generational study that surveyed 49–53-year-old respondents who have both adult children and living parents. A third of this middle generation received money or non-cash gifts from their parents, and 64 per cent gave something to their adult children – within a five-year period. Obviously, a longer time frame leads to considerably higher percentages.

In addition to transfer rates, previous studies also offer a variety of information on transfer patterns. A number of studies point out that parents' resources and their children's needs are crucial factors for monetary transfers from parents to children (e.g., Motel and Szydlik 1999; Szydlik 2000; Fritzell and Lennartsson 2005; Schenk et al. 2010; König 2016). Albertini and Radl's (2012) analyses of the first SHARE wave (eleven countries) show that parents of higher social classes are more likely to give money to their children, even when considering income and wealth discrepancies. Majamaa (2013) finds for Finland that especially parents with a higher education provide money to adult children who are studying. Berry (2008) suggests that parents favour children who are in particular need; this finding is also supported by McGarry (1999). Hartnett et al. (2012) document that parents are more likely to give money to younger adult children.

Emery (2013) points out that the number of siblings is a crucial factor for financial transfers from parents. The multilevel analyses on the basis of the second SHARE wave show that the existence of siblings considerably decreases the chances of receiving monetary means from one's parents.

Previous studies based on the first SHARE wave suggest an overall trend reflecting a north-south gradient, visible in more frequent financial support from parents to adult children in Northern Europe and fewer transfers in the south. However, this pattern is not confirmed when looking at transfer sums (Albertini et al. 2007; Deindl 2011; Zissimopoulos and Smith 2011).

Hypotheses

With the help of the ONFC model, a number of theoretical arguments and hypotheses can be developed that provide the basis for the empirical analyses presented below.

The first hypothesis, referring to *opportunity structures*, is quite obvious: higher-class parents have more opportunities and can be seen as a resource for adult children to receive money. Inter vivos transfers from parents to children can serve as a means of status reproduction (e.g., Albertini and Radl 2012). From this perspective, higher-class parents will provide more intergenerational transfers in order to help their children become members of the higher classes, too; at the very least, the parents' aim is to avoid downward intergenerational mobility of their offspring (Attias-Donfut and Wolff 2000: 43; Majamaa 2013). By doing so, parental financial support can be seen as a direct 'investment' in their children and an indirect one in their own social prestige via the successful child. Additionally, parents with an academic background are more inclined to accept higher and longer education costs for their children than parents with a lower education level. Therefore, it is likely that the higher classes have higher rates of financial transfers than population groups with a lower educational background.

Moreover, giving money or material gifts presupposes that the giver has sufficient material resources to do so. For the empirical analyses, one can expect that having parents with better income and more money in the bank enhances the opportunities of their children receiving monetary transfers. Financial resources may also play a role when it comes to assessing the 'appropriate' value of gifts. A higher transfer rate of better-off parents is also in line with the idea of showing affection via money. How should an adult child interpret a birthday gift of ten euros from a millionaire parent? Thus, better-off parents are expected to spend more money in order to show their affection, and should thus be more likely to report giving items or sums that surpass the threshold of 250 euros per year.

Parents who know the financial situation of their offspring quite well might be more inclined to support them. More intergenerational contact may also give adult children a better opportunity to 'persuade' their parents to pass on resources. Furthermore, according to the 'intergenerational stake' hypothesis (Bengtson and Kuypers 1971; Giarrusso et al. 1995), parents are somewhat more interested in spending time with their children than vice versa, leading to parents providing 'rewards' for intergenerational contact. This idea is put forward by Lennartsson et al. (2010), who find in Sweden that intergenerational transfers are linked to more frequent contact. From this viewpoint, adult children who receive financial means are more likely to stay in close contact with their parents. In any case, the analyses of intergenerational contact (Chapter 4) show that the prospects of a future inheritance as well as current financial transfers are associated with closer bonds between parents and adult children.

Need structures are likely to play an important role as well. When it comes to potential monetary transfers from parents to adult children, it is especially promising to investigate the employment situation of the child. This applies in particular to education, which involves a need situation that requires 'investments' in order to permanently improve the child's life situation (Table 2.1). Here, the needs of adult children may correspond with the needs or wishes of their parents. Also, parents may react to a child's unemployment by helping with money. One can further assume that younger adult children in general are still in more financial need and are thus more likely to receive support from their parents.

However, needs are not only a matter of children. Parents may find themselves in a situation in which their needs call for time support from their adult children, which may be 'induced' or 'reimbursed' via monetary 'incentives' or 'rewards'. Thus, it will be relevant to find out empirically whether help or care *from* their adult children is associated with (reciprocal) financial flows *to* their offspring.

Family structures are likely to be of importance, too. If resources – in the sense of providing opportunities and the lack thereof constituting need – are the major factor, mothers could be expected to give less and daughters to receive more. However, closer connections may come with more transfers, in particular gifts, not least in order to show affection, appreciation and caring. In this case, mothers might give more, especially to their daughters.

The potential transfer giver having a partner may also have various influences. Being single may lead a parent to seek closer intergenerational connectedness via gifts. However, it is also quite possible that spouses and partners 'remind' one another to think of their offspring when it comes to presents and monetary support. Again, it is an empirical question as to which of these alternative assumptions is more in line with reality.

What about the impact of an adult child living in a partnership? On the one hand, parents might be inclined to give special attention to children in partnerships in order to show affection and the wish to stay in close contact with a child who could turn to the partner instead. On the other hand, less contact with adult children in a partnership (Chapter 4) as well as a different (perception of their) need situation might be associated with fewer monetary transfers to that child.

According to previous research (see above), family size is likely to be of relevance. In general, one can argue that more family members on the receiving end means that fewer resources are available for each individual child. In the case of transfers that take the form of giving presents (e.g., for birthdays), having more children may lead to each child receiving a relatively smaller amount. In cases of money as a means of support, siblings may become transfer 'competitors', and parents have to decide whether and, if so, which adult child should receive more considering their current need situation. Another potential factor reflecting family structures is the existence of grandchildren. Adult children who have kept the family line going might be 'rewarded' by their parents, and being the gatekeeper for access to grandchildren may point in the same direction. However, having a grandchild may lead to skipping the middle generation to the direct benefit of the grandchild.

Last but not least, *cultural-contextual* structures should not be neglected. Net of individual opportunities and needs, parents who migrated might give more to their adult children due to closer family bonds, which is supported by the results for contact and space in Chapters 4 and 6. However, growing up in different countries as well as migration experiences may also lead to some degree of 'drifting apart' of parents and their offspring, suggesting fewer transfers.

With regard to welfare states, there are the contrasting hypotheses of crowding-out versus crowding-in (Chapter 2): Does the welfare state reduce or enhance family solidarity? In view of the following analyses for money, crowding-out would imply lower transfer rates in countries with well-developed welfare states, whereas crowding-in would suggest even more private support in these countries.

Wealth and poverty in a society are also likely factors. Aside from resources, cultural contexts might additionally influence the general extent of monetary flows between family generations. In this respect, differentiating between gifts as glue for human bonding and support for family members in need is helpful for theoretical reasoning. Respondents living in a rich country can be expected to give more and higher-value gifts owing to the general cultural norm governing how much one ought to give to show affection, appreciation and connectedness. However, more wealth may also mean that less financial support is necessary, which would have the opposite effect. Correspondingly, the general availability of fewer resources may limit the frequency and value of expected gifts. At the same time, more support would be highly appreciated in such circumstances. Again, multivariate empirical investigations are necessary to assess the validity of the various assumptions.

Explaining money

Questions

Fortunately, the Survey of Health, Ageing and Retirement in Europe provides information for all countries included, employing the same survey strategy and the same wording of the same questions for the same population. SHARE asks:

> Many people provide financial or material gifts, or support to others such as parents, children, grandchildren, some other kin, or friends or neighbours. Now please think of the last twelve months. Not counting any shared housing or shared food, have you [or your husband/wife/partner] given any financial or material gift or support to any person inside or outside this household amounting to 250 euro (in local currency) or more?

Additionally, the interviewers are told:

> By financial gift we mean giving money, or covering specific types of costs such as those for medical care or insurance, schooling, down payment for a home. Do not include loans, only gifts and support.

The following questions are:

> To whom [else] did you [or your husband/wife/partner] provide such financial assistance or gift in the last twelve months?

> About how much did you [or your husband/wife/partner] give to this person altogether in the last twelve months?

Furthermore, SHARE enquires about the main reason for financial assistance or gifts. In the same manner, respondents are asked about the receipt of monetary means, again with regard to the giver, the amount and the reason.

In the following, as in the next chapter on time, the focus is on family generations who no longer live in the same household. Coresidence is another form of functional solidarity that also includes monetary transfers. However, it cannot always be assessed without doubt who the transfer giver is and who is the receiver, whether the coresident generations share rent and living expenses and which amount of money is actually transferred from one generation to the other. Therefore, this book addresses coresidence in a chapter of its own. Also, since SHARE focuses on transfers of at least 250 euros per year, sums below this threshold are not considered here.

Description

Who gives, who receives? Europeans aged 50 years and older report giving considerably more transfers than they receive. One in four gave a gift or financial assistance of at least 250 euros in the last twelve months. Only one in twenty received such monetary means.

The other shares in Figure 7.1 refer to those respondents who stated that they have given or received money. For example, 4 per cent of the total of 26 per cent gave money to their parents. The figure shows that nearly all transfers stay within the family, and the great majority follow the generational line. Two-thirds of the monetary gifts or support from respondents go to adult children, and a sixth go to grandchildren. In turn, it is rare that parents are the beneficiaries. The intergenerational flow of money is reflected by the shares of transfers received. Most of these stem from adult children and parents. However, the low overall share shows that only a small fraction of the respondents actually receive such financial means.

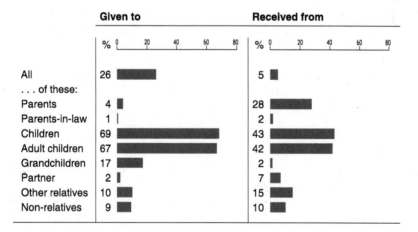

Figure 7.1 Money: Overview

Source: SHARE (n: 39,023/39,352).

The figure confirms the 'cascade model' of intergenerational monetary transfers: money flows downwards from one family generation to the next, from parents to children. Parents do not only support their offspring when they are very young and live in their parents' homes. What we find instead is lifelong functional solidarity that involves supporting adult children by way of gifts and payments even in adulthood and even when living in separate households. By contrast, upward financial transfers are rarely to be found.

Further investigations, not documented in detail here, refer to reasons for transfers stated by the respondents. A fifth of parents provide monetary means to adult children in order 'to meet basic needs', whereas another fifth give 'no specific reason'. Other noteworthy reasons are 'to buy or furnish a house or apartment', 'to help with a large item of expenditure (other than buying a house)' and 'for a major family event (birth, marriage, other celebration)'. By contrast, reasons such as 'to help with a divorce', 'to help following a bereavement or illness', 'to help with unemployment' or 'to meet a legal obligation (e.g., alimony or compulsory payments for parents' care)' do not seem to be of particular relevance. As far as money from adult children is concerned, basic needs and family events play the major role.

Since most intergenerational monetary presents and payments are passed on from parents (respondents) to adult children, Figures 7.2 and 7.3 focus on these transfers to at least one non-coresident adult child. The left parts of the figures document sums of at least 250 euros, whereas the right parts refer to at least 2,000 euros per year. A fifth of the parents give at least 250 euros to an adult child outside the household, and close to a tenth transfer at least 2,000 euros within one year.

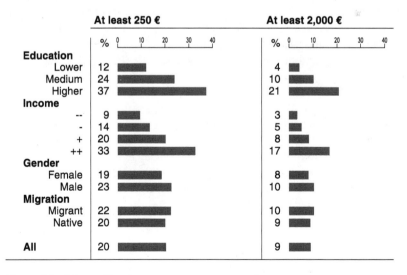

Figure 7.2 Money: People

Source: SHARE (n: 24,751/24,285). Transfers to adult children, no coresidence.

Parents' education and income play an extraordinary role. The more financial resources are available, the better the opportunities for giving money. The discrepancies are impressive. The likelihood of monetary transfers is three times as high for academics as for the lower educational class. A better education results in higher earnings, but it is also more likely that parents with an academic background have children who attend institutions of higher education and therefore need financial help during their studies.

Moreover, only one in ten members of the lowest income group gave money or material gifts of at least 250 euros to an adult child in the last twelve months. The same applies to one in three members of the highest income group. Besides resources, different living standards may also play a role, which leads higher-class parents to support their higher-class children with higher sums, thus exceeding the 250-euro threshold of the SHARE survey. Another factor that may be of relevance is implicit norms about the size of a present. A gift can also serve as a vehicle by which parents show their affection for their child and demonstrate how important the daughter or son is to them. It is fair to assume that this importance is also estimated in relation to the wealth of the giver. A sum of 100 euros from a millionaire carries quite a different weight than 100 euros from a parent living below the poverty line.

In contrast, the differences between women and men (the latter have more resources) are much less impressive, and no notable migration effects are observed.

The major relevance of education and income becomes even more apparent when considering sums of at least 2,000 euros per year. The likelihood of large monetary transfers to adult children is more than five times higher for upper-class parents than for their lower-class counterparts.

Furthermore, Figure 7.3 documents striking international differences: Sweden, Denmark and Germany show the highest rates of parental transfers to adult children outside the household, whereas the rate for Germany roughly matches previous results on the basis of the German Ageing Survey (Szydlik 2000). The lowest shares are found in Poland, the Czech Republic, Italy and Spain, which applies to both parts of the figure, comprising transfers of at least 250 euros and 2,000 euros per year, respectively. This is a further indication of the importance of financial resources, but is also in line with the assumption that family-oriented countries with high coresidence rates in turn show less support for offspring who have left the parental home.

Further investigations refer to the amounts of money transferred (not shown in the figures). A little over half of the transfers to adult children are between 250 and 2,000 euros within one year, including most helpful support to meet basic needs (in times of financial difficulties, even 'merely' filling the fridge or helping with the electricity bill can be of invaluable importance). Moreover, a tenth of the parents gave even more than 10,000 euros to their adult children in the past twelve months. A longer time span would of course have resulted in much larger amounts of money exchanging hands.

Differentiating between population groups and countries confirms the previous results on transfer shares. The lower classes do not only give less often, they also

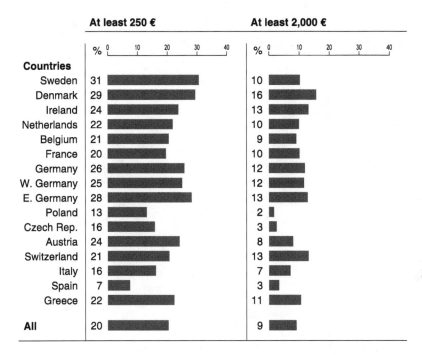

Figure 7.3 Money: Countries

Source: SHARE (n: 24,751/24,285). Transfers to adult children, no coresidence.

give smaller sums. The better-educated and higher-income groups show especially low shares of smaller gifts and assistance. In turn, nearly a third of transfers by academics amount to at least 5,000 euros per year, whereas this applies to less than a fifth of parents with a lower education. Gender differences appear to be quite small, although men report somewhat higher amounts, whereas the native population is in a much better position to give very large sums than migrants. It is also noteworthy that the great majority of transfers in Poland and the Czech Republic fall below the threshold of 2,000 euros.

Explanation

Figure 7.4 summarises the net results of Table A7.2 (see Appendix). The left column of the table lists the findings for all transfers of at least 250 euros per year from parents (respondents) to their non-coresident adult children. The right column refers 'only' to more sizeable financial means, starting at 2,000 euros in the last year. The symbol '+' stands for higher transfer rates, and '–' indicates fewer respondents giving money to adult children outside their household.

First, *opportunity structures* play an extraordinary role. Higher-class parents are indeed a valuable resource to adult children. Parents with higher education can

		At least 250 €	At least 2,000 €
Opportunity Structures	Education: Lower (ref.)		
	Medium	+	+ +
	Higher	+ + +	+ + +
	Income	+ + +	+ + +
	Money in bank	+ + +	+ + +
	Contact: Day		
	Week (ref.)		
	Month	–	–
	Year	– – –	– – –
Need Structures	Child: Education (ref.)		
	Full-time	– – –	– – –
	Part-time	– – –	– – –
	Unemployed	– –	– – –
	Not in workforce	– – –	– – –
	Age child	– – –	– – –
	Time transfer	+ +	
Family Structures	Mother-daughter (ref.)		
	Father-daughter		
	Mother-son	–	
	Father-son	–	
	Partner	+	
	Partner child	– –	– –
	Number of children	– – –	– – –
	Grandchild	–	– – –
Cultural-contextual Structures	Migrant		
	Social expenditure	+	– –
	Family expenditure	+ +	
	Wealth per capita		+ +
	Poverty rate		– –

Figure 7.4 Explaining money

Source: SHARE, Table A7.2, see Appendix (net). '+': more, '–': less money to adult children. No coresidence.

be expected to give more to their offspring because they have more resources at their disposal. However, there are still impressive differences between the educational classes even when considering income and savings. These results suggest a proclivity of higher-class parents to 'invest' in higher education for their offspring as a means of status reproduction, and a willingness to accept the longer period of time that this involves.

If parents have (more than) enough money, it is much easier for them to give some of it to their children. The empirical results clearly support this presumption.

If the parental household is able to make ends meet (fairly) easily, intergenerational transfers are likely. This is not the case if the household only gets by with some or even great difficulty. Money in the bank is another important prerequisite. The more money parents have, the more likely they are to give gifts or support. Also, the results suggest that parents choose 'appropriate' presents on the basis of their financial background as a sign of affection and to strengthen family bonds.

A closer relationship with one's parents seems to enhance monetary gifts and support. Parents who have contact with their child at least several times a week are much more likely to give compared to those who have less contact. If parents and their adult child meet, talk or write less than once a month, financial transfers are particularly unlikely. More contact provides better opportunity to give and receive, whereas one cannot rule out that some offspring maintain close contact with parents who give gifts and assistance.

Second, *need structures* are relevant for receiving financial support from parents. Here, the employment status of their adult children is a crucial factor. Most importantly, adult children who are in education (e.g., university students) are much more likely to receive money from their parents. If the child is employed, he or she is distinctly in lesser need of financial assistance. At the same time, parents may consider support for children in (higher) education as an 'investment' in future benefits, whether such benefits involve an improved job situation of the child, or the enhanced satisfaction of the parents when their child acquires the qualifications for a successful career. Financial support for adult children in education seems to be considerable since its effect is even more pronounced for higher transfers of at least 2,000 euros per year. Apart from education, the results indicate that parents are somewhat more likely to support their adult children financially in the case of unemployment; at least, one finds smaller discrepancies between assistance provided to children in education and those who are unemployed compared to employed children.

Parents are more likely to help their children when they are in need – even if those children are adults and do not live in the parental home anymore. This observation is also supported by the finding that older children receive less. Younger adults generally tend to be in greater financial need, which leads parents to give them more money.

However, it is not only the needs of children that count. Upward support for parents in need via help or care is often accompanied by a downward flow of money from one generation to the next. This does not mean that practical support by adult children is generally reimbursed by *huge* financial rewards: the lack of a significant relationship between time spent to support parents and a larger sum of money indicates the importance of relatively smaller presents for showing gratitude.

Third, *family structures* comprise a range of determinants. The least important one is gender. Sons seem to receive fewer transfers from parents, which suggests the relevance of greater financial needs of female offspring and closer intergenerational connections of parents with daughters. Yet, when it comes to larger sums of money, no significant gender effects can be found. This is an indication that daughters receiving more monetary transfers is rather a reflection of more frequent smaller gifts as a means of showing affection, appreciation and caring.

If the parent has a partner, adult children are more likely to receive financial transfers. This might be due to parents encouraging and helping one another to give gifts to their offspring. However, if the child has a partner, monetary transfers from parents are significantly less frequent. An explanation is the different (perception of the) need situation of children who are single in contrast to those with a partner.

Family size matters. Having more children greatly reduces transfers to each child, and this also applies if there is a grandchild. Siblings (i.e., other children from the respondent's point of view) and (grand)children represent potential competitors for transfers from parents. Faced with limited resources, parents may have to decide to give money to a specific child or grandchild at the expense of another. However, supporting a grandchild often also benefits the middle generation.

Fourth, *cultural-contextual structures* are investigated by considering migration and the four macro indicators. The empirical results do not show significant differences between migrants and the native population when it comes to intergenerational transfers to adult children. Either the divergent patterns suggested in the hypotheses section of this chapter offset one another, or neither of these assumptions are an appropriate account of reality.

What about influences related to welfare states and social stratification? The analyses indicate that more social and family expenditure is associated with higher incidences of monetary transfers from parents to non-coresident adult children. Welfare state expenditure seems to increase the likelihood of private intergenerational transfers. The more money a state spends, the more parents give money to their adult children. Again, this is a sign of crowding-in: strong welfare states relieve potential transfer givers from having to provide intense support to relatives in need, which leaves more resources for gifts and financial help to more offspring. When the number of children is taken into consideration, the analysis shows that social expenditure is associated with fewer transfers of at least 2,000 euros per year, indicating fewer particularly large payments to adult children in countries with more public spending. In this respect, the results for money resemble those for time in the next chapter.

When the child's partner and employment status, respectively, are taken into account, societal wealth and poverty do not have a general effect on material transfers from parents to adult children. However, when investigating higher transfers, we find considerably more frequent transfers in rich countries and fewer intergenerational transmissions in countries with a high poverty rate. This is another indication of the immense importance of resources: more wealth offers more opportunity to give money, and living in a wealthy country might also involve a general norm about the appropriate value of personal gifts in order to show affection, appreciation and connectedness. The opposite applies in the case of poverty.

Summary

Generations are connected in many ways. It is not 'only' contact and space that link adult family generations, as shown in the previous chapters, but also money. On the one hand, even small presents connect family members. Giving something shows affection, caring and belonging. Gifts act as bonding glue for family cohesion, quite in the way Georg Simmel (2009, 1908) suggested over a hundred years ago. On the other hand, monetary assistance represents invaluable support for relatives in times of financial need.

Private transfers follow a cascade model along the generational line. It is mainly the older generations who give and the younger ones who receive. This stands in contrast to both the typical flow of time within families and money within society. Giving money is a form of intergenerational solidarity from parents to children, whereas time tends to take the opposite route – as does money in the realm of the so-called public 'intergenerational contract' with its transfers from the working population to pensioners.

How should one interpret a transfer rate of 20 per cent? Previous research has shown that this number depends heavily on the empirical setting. For example, a French study (Attias-Donfut 1995) arrives at 64 per cent of 49–53-year-old parents giving financial transfers to their adult children over a five-year span. The study at hand counts transfers by parents of at least 50 years of age over a period of one year and observes a rate of 20 per cent for France, which matches the overall European percentage. The same applies to the monetary value of the transmissions. Were we to count transfers across the entire joint lifetime of parents and (adult) children, this would add up to immensely higher rates and sums.

Family solidarity is distributed unequally between population groups. There are huge discrepancies between educational classes: 12 per cent of the lower class has given at least 250 euros to an adult child in the last year – the corresponding share of parents with an academic background is three times as high. The situation is even more pronounced in the case of income groups and, in particular, when focusing on higher transfers of at least 2,000 euros per year. Some parents give much more than others. The main reason is opportunity. The more resources parents have, the more money they are able to pass on to their children.

Needs play an important role as well. Adult children in education are much more likely to receive financial support. Situations of obvious need trigger intergenerational solidarity – especially when linked to an 'investment' in higher education. An argument can be made that this reduces inequality in the children's generation. At least in the short run, such transfers lessen current income discrepancies to employed children. However, investments in education are likely to result in a better economic situation later on, and some of their offspring's success may even reflect positively on the parents, for example, in the form of prestige via status reproduction. Seen from this perspective, current financial help to adult children in education does not lead to lower, but ultimately even to greater social inequality.

Giving money from one generation to the next does not depend on individual factors only. At the meso level, family structures are important, too. Partners, children and grandchildren all have a significant influence on financial transfers from parents to adult children. Parents having a partner seems to enhance financial intergenerational solidarity, whereas other children (siblings) and grandchildren seem to be transfer competitors, potentially leaving less money for the single relative, particularly in large families.

Societal structures must not be ignored either. International comparisons are especially helpful to identify the respective influences. A particularly relevant macro factor is the welfare state. A strong welfare state does not crowd out all family solidarity. On the contrary, more social and family expenditure even comes with more overall private transfers. Another factor is general wealth and poverty in a country. Greater wealth leads to more larger transmissions, whereas poverty reduces sizeable gifts and assistance.

8 Time

Who helps, who cares?

Introduction

Demographic change asserts mounting pressure on welfare states. Increasing life expectancy of the elderly and decreasing fertility shifts the relation of younger contributors and older pensioners. At the same time, expenses for pensions and health already account for a considerable part of public spending. This constellation poses substantial challenges to welfare states – with likely consequences for family relations: 'The state may have a direct influence on the quality of intergenerational relations within the family by the sorts of welfare policies it adopts' (Pfau-Effinger 2005: 28; see also Walker 1996; Kaufmann 2003).

The situation is especially dramatic for the elderly. Being in need of help or care is becoming a widespread phenomenon: the number of frail elderly is increasing considerably (Schulz et al. 2001; Colombo et al. 2011; Lipszyc et al. 2012), while the greater need for support faces fewer available resources. One reason is the so-called flexibilisation of labour and employment (Szydlik 2008b). In fact, we find a conflicting situation: the demands for flexibility in the workplace stand in contrast to the demands of the family for stability and reliability. This contradiction not only affects the compatibility of work and care for children, but increasing flexibility demands in working life can also have negative consequences on support for parents in need. Giving care often involves shouldering a huge burden, at times even too much of a burden (e.g., Perrig-Chiello and Hutchison 2010; Colombo et al. 2011: 85ff.). When working life demands ever-greater flexibility, this reduces the ability of adult children to provide sufficient care for their parents, which again threatens the compatibility of family and employment.

This situation is aggravated further by the fact that work-related demands for flexibility frequently come with increasing pressure for geographical mobility. However, personal help and care depend greatly on proximity. The contact chapter (Chapter 4) shows that closer distance is associated with much stronger intergenerational cohesion, and we would obviously expect the following analyses to show that adult children living far away are substantially less likely to provide personal help and care for their parents. Furthermore, demographic change also implies having fewer children, which will eventually lead to fewer siblings to share the care burden. Thus, demographic change also shifts the relation between fewer middle-aged adult children as potential caregivers and more frail elderly as care recipients. Again, increasing demands face decreasing resources.

In this perspective, connections between family solidarity and welfare state regulations are especially important. This suggests that one should examine support for older parents in different welfare state contexts, not least for best-practice examples. Are family members likely to step in when welfare states retreat, or does less public spending also reduce private support? The first alternative is consistent with the crowding-out hypothesis, suggesting a displacement of the family by the state. In this case, a retreat of the welfare state owing to tight public budgets would result in more family solidarity, which in sum would not reduce the quantity and quality of support for persons in need. The second alternative – namely the crowding-in hypothesis – suggests that more welfare state would lead to more family solidarity. Less public spending in times of demographic change could thus be expected to reduce family support even further, with corresponding negative consequences for people in need (Chapter 2).

Which of these hypotheses – or even a specific combination thereof – is more in line with reality is an empirical question. The aim of this chapter is to investigate the extent to which adult children give time to their elderly parents and the factors that account for this, including the determinants at individual, family and societal level. As usual, the chapter begins by providing information on the issue at stake and goes on to review previous research and discuss hypotheses before documenting the empirical results and closing with a summary.

Research and hypotheses

What is help, what is care?

There are many ways of helping and caring. Help and care may be sporadic or regular, spontaneous or organised, voluntary or mandatory, reciprocal or unilateral, quite easy or extremely demanding. Furthermore, it is important to note that the term 'help' has both a general and a more specific meaning. At a more general level, 'help' includes all kinds of support, ranging from very small favours, such as opening a door for a stranger or giving a small amount of money, all the way to permanent long-term care, 24 hours a day, 7 days a week, 365 days a year. From this perspective, 'help' is an umbrella term, covering the whole range of functional solidarity: space, money and time, and referring to any kind of support.

However, in order to engage in theoretical reasoning about and to conduct empirical studies on time transfers, it is essential to have a closer look at various kinds of support. Lumping together diverse aspects of functional solidarity is likely to ignore relevant, possibly diverse patterns. This is no less so when it comes to practical support that spans from small occasional favours to long-term intense care. It makes a huge difference whether someone helps another person with shopping for groceries from time to time, or provides intense care around the clock. Even if the same amount of time is spent on various kinds of support, it makes a difference whether this time is spent on mowing the lawn or helping a parent with eating and bathing.

In this book, 'help' is therefore defined in a more narrow sense, albeit still encompassing a range of activities. 'Help' means practical support below the threshold of intense care. More specifically, and in accordance with SHARE (see below), 'help' refers to practical support with household chores, repairs, gardening, transportation and shopping etc. as well as providing assistance with bureaucratic matters including filling out forms or addressing financial or legal issues. By contrast, 'care' will refer to personal care; meaning dressing, bathing and assisting someone with eating, getting in or out of bed and using the toilet etc. Both kinds of support are of great importance to the recipients, yet 'care' comprises more intense and demanding tasks.

Research

Previous research has shown considerable time transfers between family generations in many countries and identified a number of factors for practical support, including characteristics of individuals, families and societies (e.g., Attias-Donfut et al. 2005; Albertini et al. 2007; Haberkern and Szydlik 2008, 2010; Brandt et al. 2009; Igel et al. 2009; Schmid et al. 2012).

For example, studies have shown that practical support is particularly provided to close relatives, and that geographical distance between the households of caregivers and care recipients is a key factor in this respect (e.g., Qureshi and Walker 1989; Gruber and Heady 2010). This points to the importance of opportunities for personal support. In this regard, the financial resources of receivers seem to play a role as well, indicating that relatives are more willing to help and provide care if they can expect something in return. In fact, inheritance research suggests the relevance of reciprocity. People are more likely to anticipate the receipt of a future inheritance when they provide household help and care (Szydlik 2004: 39). Previous research has also observed the existence of short-term reciprocity in parent-adult child relationships in terms of the exchange of time and money. Help and care of adult children for parents is often associated with financial transfers from those parents to their helping offspring (Leopold and Raab 2011). On the basis of a pre-study for Germany, Klaus documents that 'the amount of resources and support flowing from parents to adult children is the most decisive predictor of the help they gain in return' (2009: 238).

With regard to family structures, gender is of special importance. The previous studies consistently find women to be the primary providers of time support. It would be a great surprise if the present study were to come to a different conclusion. There is also evidence that adults in late mid-life or early old age are inclined to reduce their help to parents if they have several children (Grundy and Henretta 2006), which indicates that time support for parents at least partly depends on further obligations of the middle generation to their own offspring.

Several international studies do not confirm the crowding-out hypothesis (e.g., Motel-Klingebiel et al. 2005; Keck 2008; Künemund 2008); rather, there seems to be more evidence of crowding-in (Künemund and Rein 1999; Kohli et al. 2000a; Daatland and Herlofson 2003b). Empirical studies that differentiate between help and care tend to observe both: crowding-in for help and crowding-out for care (Brandt et al. 2009). This would imply that public support offers families the chance to specialise in domains for which they are especially capable. If the following study were to come to a similar conclusion, this would provide further empirical evidence in support of the task-specificity model (Litwak 1985; Litwak et al. 2003), of mixed responsibility (Daatland and Lowenstein 2005; Motel-Klingebiel and Tesch-Römer 2006), and of the specialisation hypothesis (see Brandt et al. 2009; Igel et al. 2009).

Hypotheses

It is assumed that intergenerational solidarity – in this case help and care – is determined by factors at the individual, family and societal level (Figure 2.2).

As concerns *opportunity structures*, higher education can be a resource, for instance, in coming to terms with demanding bureaucratic tasks. In the same vein, helping another person may also cost money, and a favourable financial situation is likely to facilitate covering such costs and tolerating forgone income whilst supporting a relative. Conversely, higher income provides more opportunities to hand over demanding care tasks to professionals.

However, the issue at stake here is not only the opportunities for helpers and carers but also those of the recipients. Reciprocity suggests that if dependent family members possess financial resources, this can lead to enhanced efforts on the part of their support providers. For the following empirical analyses, it is important to investigate the prospects of financial gain. In other words, are adult children who have reason to expect a considerable inheritance in the future more likely to provide help and care to their parents in the present?

Additionally, one can expect the health situation of the potential support provider to be relevant. The assumption is that good health is another prerequisite for giving personal assistance, whereas poor health of the adult child would lead to less support for parents.

When it comes to personal help and care, geographical distance is very likely to be an especially important opportunity structure. Living far apart from each other should diminish help and care considerably.

With regard to *need structures*, monetary transfers, age and health of parents are likely to be crucial factors. According to previous studies, it will be important to find out whether current intergenerational monetary transfers play a role. On the one hand, parental resources can be used to encourage the giving of help and care. On the other hand, financial transfers can be assessed from the adult child's perspective inasmuch as accepting money when giving time – and especially when providing strenuous care – might also indicate some dependence of children on receiving monetary support from parents.

The assumption concerning parents' age is obvious: older parents are more likely to be in need of support in the form of time from their children.

Furthermore, it would be very surprising if the health status of the recipients would not play a crucial role, especially in the need for care.

Empirical studies prove that women are families' kinkeepers (e.g., Rossi and Rossi 1990; Szydlik 2000; Haberkern et al. 2015). Since gender roles play an essential part in *family structures*, it is safe to predict that women are the main providers of help and care. The question is therefore not whether but to what extent there are gender discrepancies in this respect.

Children without a partner might be more likely to support an elderly parent owing to more available time resources. Conversely, in the light of the hypothesis that partners are the first ones responsible for helping and caring, one might expect parents who have a partner to receive less practical assistance from their adult children.

The existence of children, grandchildren and siblings might play a role as well. Having both parents and (grand)children is of special interest here. It can be assumed that the middle generation is less involved in helping and caring for their parents if (grand)children need attention too. From the point of view of potential support providers, siblings may serve as alternative sources that can limit one's own obligations and efforts.

Regarding *cultural-contextual structures,* migrants can be expected to show closer family bonds (Chapters 4 and 6). However, adult children who left their home country are less likely to be able to help or care for their parents personally. Another factor that may come into play here is some form of generations 'drifting apart' owing to exposure to different cultural contexts. Once again, multivariate analyses that control for geographical distance should be especially instructive in addressing these questions.

What about country differences in help and care? As a starting point, it is helpful to assign countries to a care typology that differentiates between (a) legal obligations to care for parents (no/minor or yes) and (b) the level of professional ambulant care in a country (high, medium or low), which indicates opportunities to leave demanding and stressful care to professional services. On this basis, the countries under investigation can be assigned to five groups (the typology is an extension of Haberkern and Szydlik 2008; Haberkern 2009: 34 and includes information from Millar and Warman 1996; Daatland 2001; Pinelli 2001; Huber et al. 2009; Saraceno and Keck 2010): (a) no or a minor legal obligation and a high level of professional care (Denmark, the Netherlands, Sweden, Switzerland); (b) no or a minor legal obligation and a medium level of professional care (Czech Republic); (c) no or a minor legal obligation and a low level of professional care (Ireland); (d) a legal obligation and a medium level of professional care (Austria, Belgium, France, Germany) and (e) a legal obligation and a low level of professional care (Greece, Italy, Poland, Spain).

Accordingly, adult children in Denmark, the Netherlands, Sweden and Switzerland are expected to take over personal care to a much lesser degree (e.g., Howse 2007: 6), since this legal situation is accompanied by greater opportunities for professional services. In contrast, Greece, Italy, Poland and Spain should show the highest care percentages owing to a combination of legal obligation and a low level of professional ambulant care. Austria, Belgium, the Czech Republic, France and Germany are likely to be in between, indicating a medium position in country-specific intergenerational care.

Of special interest is the Irish case. Ireland shows low legal obligation and a low level of public care as well. Since one could argue that even in cases of lower legal obligation it is quite unlikely that children will really leave their dependent parents alone, one might assume higher private care levels in Ireland, too. In any case, the results for Ireland will indicate whether it is legal obligation or ambulant care that is of greater importance.

However, this typology focuses on care. Again, it is argued that it makes sense not to lump help and care together. This can be exemplified in particular when discussing possible links between private intergenerational relations in families and public policies. In fact, one can identify four contrasting hypotheses, which empirical research needs to address:

a) The crowding-out hypothesis would lead us to expect less help and care in well-developed welfare states such as the Northern European countries and more family support in the south.
b) Following a general crowding-in approach, the reverse pattern should emerge.
c) The mixed-responsibility or specialisation hypothesis would claim that an easing of the intense care burden through public services would release (time) resources of relatives for other tasks. This implies a divergent ranking of countries in terms of help on the one hand and care on the other: less care in strong welfare states, more care in the south – accompanied by less help in Southern European countries and more help in the north.
d) Welfare states do not affect intergenerational practical support at all.

Last but not least, as in the corresponding chapters of this book, the analyses will refer to social stratification in the form of wealth and poverty. Since help often requires financial means (see above), greater wealth may result in more help, and it may also serve as an incentive to provide care. However, wealth also offers the means for engaging professional services, which in turn may reduce intergenerational family care. As poverty implies considerably fewer resources being available for personal help and external care, it can be expected to have the opposite effect.

Explaining time

Questions

Since help and care include many aspects and types, it is crucial for comparative research to ask about them in the same manner. SHARE does precisely that and thus provides an ideal basis for this empirical investigation. The respondents are asked:

We are interested in how people support one another. The next set of questions are about the help that you may have given to people you know or that you may have received from people you know.

After first addressing received help, the following question is raised:

Now I would like to ask you about the help you have given to others. In the last twelve months, have you personally given any kind of help [. . .] to a family member from outside the household, a friend or neighbor?

Subsequent to enquiring about whom the support was given to, the respondents are offered response options referring to three different types of assistance:

Which types of help have you given to this person in the last twelve months?

1. personal care, e.g. dressing, bathing or showering, eating, getting in or out of bed, using the toilet
2. practical household help, e.g. with home repairs, gardening, transportation, shopping, household chores
3. help with paperwork, such as filling out forms, settling financial or legal matters

In the following analyses, the first type reflects 'care', the second and third types are together defined as 'help', meaning help in the more narrow sense of time transfers below the threshold of emotionally and physically intense personal care. A number of respondents report both help and care. People who care often also provide help to the person in need. However, when reflecting on help, one would prefer to concentrate on people providing help only, focusing on time support below the threshold of intense care. In the following, 'help' therefore only refers to cases without care.

Further SHARE questions gather information on the frequency of and time spent providing support:

In the last twelve months, how often altogether have you given such help to this person? Was it . . .

1. Almost daily
2. Almost every week
3. Almost every month
4. Less often

About how many hours altogether did you give such help [on a typical day/in a typical week/in a typical month/in the last twelve months]?

These SHARE questions refer to help and care in separate homes, and accordingly, the following analyses focus on intergenerational relations between households.

In addition, coresidence of respondents with their parents is extremely rare (below 1 per cent).

Description

Figure 8.1 documents givers and receivers of help (upper part) and care (lower part). All in all, 16 per cent of the respondents have *given* practical household help or assistance with paperwork to somebody outside the household during the last twelve months (for a comparison of household and bureaucratic help, see Brandt and Szydlik 2008: 311; most help is household help, and the second group provides both household and bureaucratic help). In comparison, 14 per cent have *received* help during that time. The care rates show that 6 and 3 per cent, respectively, of those aged 50+ provide and receive care. An argument might be made that these are quite low shares. However, focusing on a longer time period would

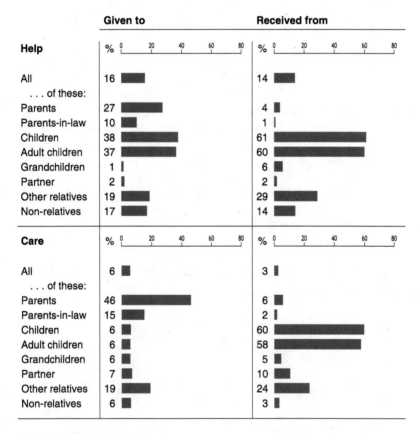

Figure 8.1 Time: Overview

Source: SHARE (n: 39,196/39,145). No coresidence.

have yielded higher percentages (e.g., Attias-Donfut 1995). Furthermore, help and care are generally a response to corresponding needs, and if those needs are non-existent during the period under observation, there will likely be no such support (Figure 8.4 below; Table A8.2 in Appendix).

The figure also gives the shares of persons who received support or spent time providing support. For example, 27 per cent of the helpers provide support to a parent. It is mostly family members who are responsible for help and care. (A little) help – and especially care – from non-relatives is relatively rare. In most cases, both help and care are, furthermore, a matter of family *generations*; more specifically of adult children and parents. When it comes to providing help, the respondents support their children in particular, while they also help their parents. When it comes to receiving help, it is foremost from their adult children that the respondents benefit, although one should not forget other relatives such as siblings, cousins, uncles and aunts.

More strenuous and time-consuming care is often carried out by partners, but this occurs within the same home (Haberkern 2009; Haberkern and Szydlik 2010). Care between households is mostly a matter of family generations. In contrast to help, it is the respondents' parents in particular who benefit, indicating corresponding age-related needs. Similar to help, *received* care is mainly in the hands of adult children. In other words, personal support for older relatives across households is typically the responsibility of their offspring. There is an upward flow of time transfers along the generational line, which testifies to the benefits of lifelong intergenerational solidarity to parents that are in need of help or care.

Since help and care between households is mostly a matter of adult children supporting their parents, from here on this chapter will concentrate on these relationships. Figure 8.2 documents that 16 per cent of adult children aged 50+ have given help to a parent in the last twelve months. Nearly a tenth have provided care – with this lower rate not least due to the fact that intense personal care presupposes corresponding needs of parents. The figure further illustrates that the higher educational classes and income groups give more help. This corresponds with the assumptions that providing personal help quite often involves financial costs, and that the better-educated classes are generally in a better position to help with bureaucratic matters.

Daughters are more likely to provide help – and particularly care – than sons. Obviously, traditional patterns still persist. According to the figure, no difference is as pronounced as the one between daughters and sons with regard to intense personal care. Nevertheless, one should not neglect support by sons. As far as help is concerned, the difference is relatively small.

Migrants are less likely to provide help or care to their parents than the native population. Household help and care depend on personal attendance, which is even more difficult in cases of large geographical distances owing to migration. Although parents of children who migrated may benefit from financial remittances, they are disadvantaged in terms of receiving personal intergenerational help and care from those children.

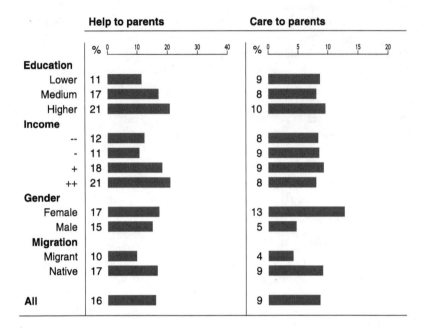

Figure 8.2 Time: People

Source: SHARE (n: 10,041/10,041). No coresidence.

Figure 8.3 shows the country shares. Most interestingly, more help is provided in countries with strong welfare states. By contrast, weaker welfare states are associated with less private intergenerational help. This is an indication of the 'crowding-in' hypothesis. Strong welfare states do not seem to diminish private support: quite the contrary. Three in ten adult children in Sweden and Denmark have given practical household help or assistance with paperwork in the last twelve months. By comparison, this applies, at the most, to only one in ten adult children in Italy, Spain and Greece.

The results for care show a different picture. In Sweden and Denmark remarkably few adult children provide personal care, whereas Italy and Spain exhibit especially large percentages. This also applies to the Irish case, which indicates that it is the level of professional ambulant care in a country, rather than the legal obligation of children to care for their parents, that plays the major role. Overall, these results exhibit fewer differences between countries compared to the pattern observed for help. However, there is some indication of crowding-out.

Further investigations (not presented in a figure) show that care is much more time-consuming than help. Adult children who support their elderly parents in dressing, bathing or showering, eating, getting in or out of bed, using the toilet etc. spend much more time on these tasks than those daughters and sons who 'only'

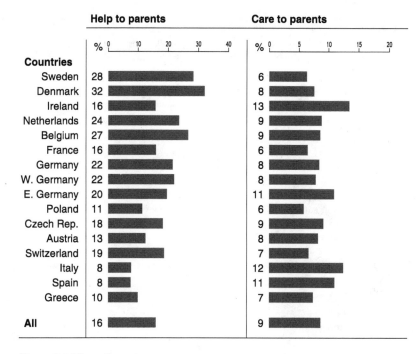

Figure 8.3 Time: Countries

Source: SHARE (n: 10,041/10,041). No coresidence.

provide practical household support or help with paperwork. More adult children help their parents for a shorter period of time. However, fewer carers spend many more hours.

Carers with a better education and higher household income spend less time on these tasks, indicating the relevance of resources (opportunities) to draw on additional outside sources, such as paid professional support. Daughters are not only more likely to provide care in the first place, but also give much more time when doing so. Migrants are less able to care for their parents (see above). However, when they do become carers they spend considerably more time than the native population. Besides cultural differences, migrants in general have fewer discretionary resources to draw on external support.

The occurrence of help follows a north-south gradient, whereas the occurrence of care, and the intensity of support in particular, reflect the opposite pattern, with carers spending many more hours in Eastern and Southern Europe, and Czech and Italian carers and helpers being much more involved than their Swedish and Danish counterparts. This is a further indication of a specific mixture of crowding-in (referring to less intense and less time-consuming help) and crowding-out (with regard to more demanding and extensive care).

Explanation

How can one explain differences in time transfers between adult family generations? Figure 8.4 summarises the net results of Table A8.2 (see Appendix), where
'+' signifies higher probabilities of help and care and '−' indicates fewer adult
children spending time on support for their parents. The analyses largely employ
the same independent variables as the contact models (Chapter 4), which facilitates
the comparison between time spent together in general and actual time transfers.

Opportunity structures are described in terms of education, income, bequests,
health and distance. The higher educational classes are in a better position to

		Help	Care
Opportunity Structures	Education: Lower (ref.)		
	Medium	+	+ +
	Higher	+ +	+ + +
	Income	+ +	
	Future inheritance	+ + +	+ +
	Health	−	
	Distance	− −	− −
Need Structures	Money transfer	+ + +	+ + +
	Age parent	+ +	+ + +
	Health parent	+	+ + +
Family Structures	Daughter-mother (ref.)		
	Daughter-father		− − −
	Son-mother	− −	− − −
	Son-father	− − −	− − −
	Married (ref.)		
	Partner		
	Widowed		
	Divorced		
	Single		
	Partner parent	−	− −
	Number of children	− −	
	Grandchild	−	
	Number of siblings	− −	
Cultural-contextual Structures	Migrant	− −	
	Social expenditure	+ +	− −
	Family expenditure	+ + +	
	Wealth per capita		
	Poverty rate	− − −	

Figure 8.4 Explaining time

Source: SHARE, Table A8.2, see Appendix (net). '+': more, '−': less help/care to parents. No
coresidence.

cover help costs and to offer assistance with bureaucratic affairs, such as filling out forms and settling financial or legal matters. Since better-educated children spend considerably less time on care (see above), one can also presume that the higher classes are, in general, more inclined to organise external support and thus share the care burden for their elderly parents with professional services (the increased education effect on care in Table A8.2, in the Appendix, is caused by health and distance). The higher classes are in a better position to occasionally offer 'a bit' of care across greater distances, whereas lower-class children more often find themselves in an 'all-or-nothing' situation.

Income also seems to play a role, at least with regard to help. This is again an indication that help (between households) with home repairs, gardening, transportation, shopping as well as spending time on providing support in financial matters often involves some monetary costs, which are easier to bear for those who are in a better financial situation.

The prospects of a future inheritance indicate opportunities for parents to encourage their adult children to provide personal support. If the offspring anticipate future financial gains, they are much more likely to help and care for their parents. The health of the respondents plays a role as well, at least when it comes to help (the difference between the gross and the net effect with regard to care is due to the age and health of parents). Adult children with poor health are less able to help a parent.

Geographical distance is extremely important for giving time. Of course, personal help and care depend on the opportunity to meet the other person without great effort. The closer generations live to each other, the more personal support is provided. This also shows that spatial distance has to be taken into account in assessing the influences of the other potential factors.

Need structures of both parents and children are also essential. Giving help and care often involves financial returns. The results indicate reciprocity of upward time support and downward financial transfers along the generational line. It is not only the expectation of a future inheritance but also current monetary transfers that may encourage adult children to spend time supporting their elderly parents.

The older the parents, the more likely the receipt of help, and especially of care. It goes without saying that the needs of parents are a crucial prerequisite of personal support, and age is a suitable indicator for assessing those needs. Moreover, the poor health of a parent increases the likelihood of receiving help from an adult child. The effect of parental health on care is even considerably more pronounced, indicating that adult children caring for their parents is indeed rooted in corresponding needs arising from deteriorating health.

Family structures involve gender combinations as a key component. Daughters are much more likely than sons to help, and especially to care. As long as women in particular are made responsible for household and caring tasks, intergenerational time support for elderly parents will remain a matter especially for daughters. Compared with fathers, daughters in particular take over responsibilities of mothers, which is also a reflection of the lifelong closer relationships between mothers and daughters.

The contact analysis in Chapter 4 shows that adult children who are singles have more contact with their parents. The situation is similar in the gross models with regard to help and care (see Appendix, Table A8.2). However, the multivariate analyses show no significant effects (owing to the number of children and gender, respectively). In contrast, when the parent has a partner, time support from children is less necessary and therefore less likely. Particularly with regard to care, it is first partners and second children that are responsible for personal support.

As expected, the presence of children, grandchildren and siblings plays a role as well. The more children the respondents have, the less likely it is that they help their parents, indicating less remaining time and attention on the part of the middle generation. The same applies when the adult children have a grandchild. The number of siblings also decreases the likelihood that an adult child provides help to parents. From the elderly parents' perspective, the more children they have, the less likely it is that each individual child is available to help. The multivariate analysis does not yield corresponding significant effects for care. This may be a result of the lower number of cases, but also of the fact that it is easier for an adult child to withhold less essential help than absolutely necessary care.

The *cultural-contextual structures* considered here reveal considerably smaller migration effects when taking spatial distance into account. Regarding care, the difference is no longer significant. With respect of help, migrants still show a lower probability of support. This is an indication of at least some (cultural) differences between migrant children and their elderly parents, including some intergenerational 'drifting apart' due to residences in different countries as well as the new experiences of the migrating generation.

Most importantly, welfare state conditions show stark effects on private intergenerational help. Again, the crowding-in hypothesis is confirmed: the higher the social and family expenditure, the more adult children help their parents. Strong welfare states obviously do not crowd out family solidarity in principle. Higher public expenses are associated with more functional solidarity in terms of adult children's help to parents. However, with regard to care, the results for social expenditure show a totally different pattern. Here, more public spending is associated with less intergenerational support. Although the coefficients for family expenditure are not statistically significant, they point in the same direction (ordinary logistic regressions result in significant effects, too). In any case, the findings for social expenditure indicate that adult children provide less care in contexts in which it is more common for professionals to take over those tasks.

These results also provide empirical evidence of the interpretation that strong welfare states tend to relieve families of strenuous and demanding care tasks and, in so doing, open up possibilities and free resources for personal help. Sometimes, 'help with paperwork, such as filling out forms' and 'settling financial or legal matters' (see the survey questions cited earlier in this chapter) may include help with dealing with public authorities and other relevant agencies that take over the care burden. At any rate, there is less strain on adult children in countries that offer the respective services.

Further analyses indicate that social and family expenditure have a particularly pronounced effect on adult children with a lower educational degree. A stronger welfare state increases help and decreases care among the lower classes in particular. This is an indication that public policies have the greatest influence on intergenerational time transfers among population groups with relatively few resources.

General wealth does not seem to have a significant effect on time support provided by adult children to elderly parents, and this also holds for poverty with regard to the provision of care (the decrease from the gross to the net model is mainly due to distance and grandchildren). However, greater poverty does reduce help. This result again evidences the cost argument, considering that help with home repairs, gardening, transportation, shopping and financial matters is often associated with expense, and thus requires sufficient monetary means.

Summary

Who helps, who cares? Above all, it is the family. Friends, neighbours, colleagues and acquaintances are seldom amongst those who give valuable support in the form of time. Most of those who help and care from household to household are adult children and parents. The respondents provide household help and assistance with formalities to their children and parents, care for their parents and receive support from their offspring. Family generations do not leave one another to fend for themselves when they are in need of help and care.

However, there are striking differences among individuals, families and countries. Education and money play a relevant role. Giving help is often associated with financial costs. Thus, population groups who are better off have greater means for helping with home repairs, gardening, transportation, shopping and for providing support with financial matters. Conversely, parents who support their adult children financially – or hold out the prospect thereof – are much more likely to be helped and cared for. The exchange of time for money means that wealthy parents who have more resources have better chances of receiving personal time support from their offspring, and their adult children are more strongly motivated to provide help and care if they can expect something in return. In this way, the need (for time) and opportunities (of money) of one generation are met by the need (for money) and opportunities (of time) of the other generation. The findings indicate both short-term and long-term connections between time and money. Adult children who currently receive financial transfers from their parents provide considerably more help and care, and this also applies in the case of an expected future inheritance.

Of course, geographical distance is a crucial factor for personal practical support. Moreover, poor health decreases the provision of help and greatly increases the likelihood of receiving support, in particular of care. Gender is of major importance as well; women remain the major helpers and carers. The existence of other family members such as parents' partners, (grand)children and siblings reduces the help from adult children to parents.

Theoretical reasoning and empirical evidence have underscored the importance of differentiating between help and care. Studies that do not distinguish between these different kinds of support forgo valuable theoretical and empirical insights. It makes a huge difference whether a person provides practical *help* – for instance, with home repairs, gardening, transportation, shopping, household chores and help with paperwork, such as filling out forms and settling financial or legal matters – or personal *care*, involving support with dressing, bathing or showering, eating, getting in or out of bed and using the toilet.

This differentiation is especially fruitful when it comes to international comparisons. A crucial result is that help and care follow opposite patterns across countries. Help is provided much more often in strong welfare states, where intergenerational care is considerably less pronounced. Personal family care is rather a feature of a weak welfare state, where help is quite rare.

These empirical results give a strong indication of the significance of 'crowding-out' and 'crowding-in'. Crowding-out can be seen when it comes to personal care. Crowding-in is observed with regard to help. Therefore, general fears of a termination of private support in the wake of the welfare state 'taking over' are unfounded. When family members are relieved of particularly strenuous tasks such as caring for frail elderly 24 hours a day, seven days a week, they are more likely to help with household tasks and formalities. Nowhere do adult children leave their parents on their own. However, when children live in a country with more public solidarity, more offspring are inclined to provide private support, albeit to a lesser degree. In strong welfare states, more children give less time. In weak welfare states, fewer children give more time.

The findings point to a specialisation of family and state in terms of the tasks that they are especially suited to perform. In this context, family members, including adult generations, have the choice to take over less strenuous kinds of support such as temporary household help and bureaucratic tasks. This help is more voluntary, less burdensome in both emotional and physical terms, and less intense. Helping elderly parents with household tasks and formalities still gives adult children the chance to get on with their own lives without being caught up in the permanent personal care of frail parents. At the same time, elderly parents receive professional support, and close family members can provide emotional attention and help, including support for a suitable mix of personal help and professional care.

9 Inheritance

To him that hath

Introduction

One of the most dramatic events in life is the death of one's parents. When a mother or father dies, what in most cases has been a lifelong relationship, comes to an end. Parents are not only the most significant others during childhood and adolescence, but also the relationship does not end upon leaving the parental home. The previous chapters have shown generally low distances between residences, frequent contact over a whole lifetime and a wide range of support, be it via space, money or time. The death of one's parents thus represents a tremendous loss, which is reflected accordingly in a long mourning period (Archer 1999; Valentine 2008; Parkes and Prigerson 2010).

For some, the loss also comes with significant financial gain. This is the case if possessions are passed on from one generation to another. Bequests create a bond between the living and deceased generations of a family. Memories are evoked, family traditions continued, and an inheritance may involve responsibilities and commitments. Oftentimes it is not a single event but a prolonged process. Before the inheritance, the parents' possessions can constitute power relations within the family or motivate reciprocity, for instance, in the form of contact, help and care, which is then 'reimbursed' post mortem (Chapters 4, 5 and 8). After receiving the inheritance, it may take some time until the heir actually perceives him- or herself as the owner of the bequest.

Transfers as a result of death thus also have a special emotional significance: who gets more, who gets what, who is the keeper of the 'family memory' (Halbwachs 1925) – for instance, by receiving or appropriating relevant objects, such as the family Bible, family jewellery, diaries and documents. Bequests can involve interpretations regarding affection and the quality of the relationship with the deceased, not least in a situation when the death of the parents requires readjusting the family fabric. Here, even objects with little economic value may be vested with major emotional significance. After all, passing belongings on to the next generation is, in a way, the last 'act of communication' between the deceased and living family members (Ariès 1977; Kosmann 1998; Lettke 2004; see Szydlik 2000: 146f.).

However, bequests are not only of great relevance to individuals and families, but also have economic implications. Whether a (family) business is handed over successfully or not can have far-reaching consequences for the future of the enterprise and the jobs involved. It may also affect economic competition, including prices for goods and services if, for instance, the transfer fails, a suitable successor is not available, or a local business is taken over by a larger enterprise. Moreover, bequests can have an impact on the property market, especially since a large share of bequeathed wealth is residential property (Szydlik and Schupp 2004: 619). If, in a wave of inheritances, large numbers of houses and apartments become available for sale, this can put considerable pressure on (local) property prices.

Another issue is financial resources in old age. This is particularly true when social security benefits are subject to cutbacks so that some form of compensation would be welcome. The resulting situation might be described as a 'pension-inheritance paradox' (Szydlik and Schupp 2004): on the one hand, reductions in welfare state transfers lead to smaller pensions; on the other, the image of a so-called inheritance wave suggests that there is a significant increase in economic gain from bequests. In this case, lower public transfers would go hand in hand with greater private transfers, which in an ideal scenario could offset cuts in retirement benefits in the wake of demographic change.

Yet, although most people are forced to cope with the loss of their parents at some point in time, by far not all of them benefit economically. The aim of this chapter is thus to investigate who benefits most from inheritances, who hardly benefits at all, and what this implies for individuals, families and societies. Who has greater or smaller chances of receiving a bequest? What are the relevant causes and inheritance patterns? In what way do population groups and countries differ in this respect? The analyses refer to both past and expected inheritances in order to also find out whether the previous patterns are likely to hold in the future (see Szydlik 2011b).

Research and hypotheses

What is inheritance?

Inheritances are mortis causa transfers, i.e., the gain is based on another person's death. The possessions of a deceased person are transferred to a living person. In some cases, these transfers are the result of an explicit will of the testator. Often these transfers are governed entirely by legal rules, such as inheritance law with regard to surviving partners and children in the event that no individual will has been made. In other cases there is a combination of the two, for example, when an heir 'just' receives her or his legal share, and the other part of the bequeather's wealth is distributed according to his or her will.

As in the analysis of monetary transfers between living generations above, the following investigation of inheritance also applies a threshold of financial value. Personal items such as letters, diaries or photo albums may be of immense emotional relevance. However, many of these items are not very likely to involve noteworthy financial value, and were we to consider all kinds of objects, including used clothes, books, household goods etc., many more adult children with deceased parents would be counted as heirs. It makes sense to neglect those items when economically relevant transfers are the issue, especially when conducting empirical analyses on questions such as who receives a notable inheritance and why.

The Survey of Health, Ageing and Retirement in Europe concentrates on inheritances that exceed a certain amount and, in this respect, resembles more the German Socio-economic Panel than the Ageing Survey. This results in lower inheritance rates as opposed to a survey that also includes small bequests. In the study presented here, only transfers of some financial significance will be considered. However, in doing so, we need to bear in mind that the chosen threshold may represent different economic value in different countries.

A second issue refers to the time frame. Asking about inheritances received within a specific period of time – during the last ten or twenty years, for example – would result in neglecting previous bequests. This procedure would only paint a fragmentary picture. Therefore, it makes sense to include notable inheritances that were received at any point in time.

Thirdly, it is of great value not to limit the analyses only to past inheritances. In order to get the whole picture it would be preferable to address future bequests as well. Again, we need suitable data to conduct these thorough analyses, which are fortunately provided by the survey at hand (see below).

Research

In spite of their great relevance, inheritances were a long-neglected area of research. This may have been due to a lack of suitable data (see, for instance, Keister and Moller 2000: 75f.). Questions related to bequests were almost never asked in major representative surveys, also because this involves treading into sensitive territory in two areas (inquiring about wealth and the death of close relatives), and thus the fear of high non-response rates. Although still unsatisfactory, the situation has improved somewhat in the meantime.

There are two data sets especially worth mentioning that provide representative inheritance information: the German Ageing Survey and the German Socio-Economic Panel. In 1996, the Ageing Survey asked 40–85-year-old Germans in the Federal Republic of Germany about all past and future inheritances; for the first time, this included inheritances of East Germans as well (Szydlik 2000, 2004). In 1988, the Socio-economic Panel (SOEP) collected information about inheritances in West Germany for the period from 1961 to the time of the survey, enquiring about residential property, stocks and shares, business ownership and other assets (Lauterbach and Lüscher 1996; see also Schlomann 1992). In 2001, the SOEP focus issue was 'social protection'. In this context, more comprehensive inheritance data was gathered, including information for a longer period of time as well as on East Germans and the immigrant population (Szydlik and Schupp 2004; Schupp and Szydlik 2004b).

This previous research for Germany consistently finds that inheritances stem largely from parents, and that it is the higher educational classes in particular that benefit from bequests. West Germans are also much more likely to be amongst the heirs, whereas East Germans face considerably lower chances of receiving an inheritance.

Although there are a few studies for some countries, the major problem is that these investigations lack comparability and in the end do not allow us to draw solid conclusions on similarities or discrepancies between inheritance in different countries. The differences in survey designs are indeed so substantial that even comparing the findings of inheritance studies within the same country is often hardly possible. The studies differ not only in terms of the time of the survey and the population groups included but also, above all, with regard to the questions asked. Some studies enquire about all inheritances, including small ones. Others place the emphasis on large transfers. One study probes the personal inheritances of the respondents, whereas others include those of spouses, partners and other household members. Some studies are concerned with inheritance during a certain period of time, others with transfers received at any point in time. Additional information collected also varies considerably, for instance, regarding the testators, kinds and values of inheritances as well as expected inheritances in the future (for more information on previous inheritance research, see also Szydlik 2000, 2004, 2011b; for a scheme of bequest motives, see Szydlik 2011a).

Hypotheses

The ONFC model (Figure 2.2) also offers arguments and hypotheses with regard to inheritances. As in the other chapters of this book, education is treated as the first indicator of *opportunity structures*. The respondents' educational background is viewed in a life course perspective. Lifelong solidarity between parents and their children from cradle to grave is a fundamental principle in intergenerational relations (Table 2.1). During childhood and beyond, the greater resources available to higher-class parents have an impact on their children's path of educational attainment, and this support from parents does not stop once their children have also reached a higher level of education. It can therefore be assumed that adult children who have benefited from parental resources in childhood, youth and early adulthood are also more likely to receive a higher inheritance after their parents have passed away.

This applies in a similar fashion to the respondents' income situation. On the one hand, having fewer financial resources can entail a greater need for an inheritance. On the other hand, lifelong parental solidarity is likely to contribute to a more favourable income situation for their adult children, which may even be further enhanced by bequests. From this perspective, those who have already received a bequest may well also have a better chance of receiving another one.

A likely factor to affect both past and future inheritances is whether the parents are still alive or have already passed away. On the basis of the assumption that most inheritance comes from parents, a person is more likely to have received a bequest if that person's parents have passed away. Conversely, expecting an inheritance in the future should be most likely if both parents are still alive.

Need structures apply to both testators and heirs. There is a potential contradiction between the needs of parents as prospective testators and children as future heirs. It is in the interest of the latter to gain possession of the estate as soon as possible, which implies receiving the legacy in the form of a gift instead of a bequest. However, from the point of view of prospective testators, it makes sense to not part with their possessions too early. For instance, parents may not want to end up living in what would then be their children's house after having spent much of their lifetime building or paying for it. Passing one's property on to one's children may also modify power relations, and parents may not be totally sure that their children will still provide attention and care once they have already received it all ('King Lear effect'). If parents prefer to bequeath their property rather than to transfer it earlier inter vivos, well-off adult children might acquire their own home early on, expecting a future inheritance later. This pattern would also correspond with the general preference of both adult children and parents to live in separate homes if possible (Chapter 6).

Age may play a role, too. The elderly are likely to need more financial resources owing to deteriorating health and increasing health costs in old age. However, when considering age, one might also find a cohort effect in that especially younger cohorts are increasingly likely to benefit from their parents' better economic situation after World War II.

Chapter 8 has shown that adult children who expect a future inheritance are more likely to help or care for a parent. This finding points to reciprocal bequests inasmuch as adult children's financial needs can correspond with the needs of elderly parents for time transfers, which might then be 'remunerated' post mortem (Kotlikoff and Spivak 1981; Bernheim et al. 1985; see Künemund and Motel 2000; Szydlik 2011a).

What is the influence of *family structures*? Regarding gender, sons were traditionally favoured over daughters when family property was passed on (see Rosenbaum 1982; Kosmann 1998). Yet gender roles, norms, laws and economic structures have changed, which makes it quite unlikely that sons are still significantly preferred over daughters when it comes to bequests. Succession law in modern society makes it virtually impossible to disinherit a particular child, let alone daughters in general. The decline in the number of farms and craft businesses to be passed on may also have an impact. Moreover, differential treatment of children in the event of an inheritance might also be interpreted as indicating different levels of parental affection, so that parents generally can be expected to refrain from favouring one child over the other when passing on their estate (Bernheim and Severinov 2003: 735). Although the empirical analyses may unearth some traditional remnants of gender inequality in bequests, one may assume that they no longer play a major role, especially compared to other factors such as social background or country.

Chapter 7 has shown that adult children who have a partner are less likely to receive money from their parents, indicating (the perception of) less financial need. In this vein, one could expect a similar situation with regard to mortis causa transfers. Furthermore, bequests to an adult child are also likely to benefit the child's partner. Thus, it will be interesting to see whether divorced or single children are more likely to be considered, be it because of financial need or to ensure that the whole estate will stay within the family of origin.

On the one hand, testators might favour adult children who have children of their own (grandchildren in the view of the testator) and thus continue the family line. On the other hand, grandchildren also represent alternative options when dividing the estate. This would make children and grandchildren competitors for an inheritance. From the testator's point of view, the number of children could be a significant factor, too. Higher expenses of large families can result in less wealth that can be bequeathed. Moreover, the remaining estate must be divided among a larger numbers of heirs. Thus, from the viewpoint of the prospective heirs, siblings may be rivals for the parental estate.

With regard to *cultural-contextual structures*, we can expect differences between migrants and natives. Migration is frequently triggered by a lack of opportunities and resources in one's native country. These are conditions that make it quite unlikely that there will be much wealth to bequeath from one family generation to the next.

In general, a strong welfare state can be associated with more inheritances. More financial resources in a country can contribute to both more public spending and more private bequests. Another possible reason for larger inheritances is that more public spending leaves more means in the hands of the elderly, which can later be bequeathed.

One can assume greater economic prosperity in a country to entail more bequests. Conversely, more poverty is likely to be associated with fewer inheritances. People who own more can also pass on more to the next generation. From this perspective, political and economic regimes are likely to play an important role. Economies that offer vast opportunities for building wealth are also likely to be ahead in terms of inheritances. Assessing this requires taking long time spans into consideration, particularly the parents' and grandparents' chances of accumulating private wealth.

Therefore, the empirical analyses are also likely to show notable discrepancies reflecting long-term consequences of planned versus market economies. The former socialist countries only allowed limited opportunities for accumulating private property and wealth, including homes, businesses, stocks and shares, so that there has been much less to bequeath. For Poland and the Czech Republic, we can therefore expect much lower inheritance rates. In the same vein, it should be promising to differentiate between West and East Germans when analysing inheritances. One can assume long-lasting effects of the specific conditions in the German Democratic Republic and the 'former' Federal Republic of Germany, including different opportunities for property acquisition owing to political regulations and economic contexts.

Explaining inheritance

Questions

The Survey of Health, Ageing and Retirement in Europe gathers information on (up to five) past transfers of wealth, including inheritances, on the basis of the following main question:

Not counting any large gift we have already talked about, have you or your [husband/wife/partner] ever received a gift or inherited money, goods, or property worth more than 5,000 euro (in local currency)?

The next questions refer to the point in time, the giver and the value of the various transfers:

In which year did you or your [husband/wife/partner] receive it?

From whom did you or your [husband/wife/partner] receive this gift or inheritance?

What was the value of this gift or inheritance at the time you or your [husband/wife/partner] received it?

When focusing on inheritances, the analyses only take wealth transfers from parents into account, concentrating on respondents with deceased parents. This does not totally rule out that the respondents may have received previous gifts inter vivos from their since deceased parents. However, this can be expected to apply to only a few cases since (a) gifts are much rarer than inheritances (and thus more seldom reported in response to the corresponding question), (b) gifts are much smaller (and are thus more likely to not exceed the threshold of 5,000 euros), and (c) it is very likely that parents who gave a substantial gift inter vivos to an adult child will have additionally bequeathed even greater wealth later on. From this it follows that the information on received inheritances documented below provides an accurate picture even if these interviewees did also receive a large gift from their parents at an earlier point in time.

The main question on future inheritances reads as follows:

Thinking about the next ten years, what are the chances that you will receive any inheritance, including property and other valuables?

The respondents are asked to assess the likelihood ranging from 0 to 100 per cent. This study assumes a prospective inheritance when the respondent states an at least 50 per cent chance of receiving one. Of course, these responses are predictions that must be treated with caution. There are, however, a number of arguments in favour of this question. First, the prediction does not generally extrapolate past events into the future, as many general prognoses more or less implicitly tend to do. Instead, the survey participants are asked directly. Second, the question does not require the respondents to do much 'guesswork'. Ultimately, an assessment of inheritances to come involves no more than knowing whether one's parents are still alive, whether they have any relevant assets, and whether these assets can be expected to represent some financial value after being divided up among the respective number of siblings. Third, the fact that in the findings presented below, prospective inheritances are pretty much in line with patterns of past inheritances indicates that the respondents' answers are mostly realistic.

Description

Where do the transfers stem from, and when do they take place? Is it actually an intergenerational issue at all? In light of the pension-inheritance paradox, one might also raise the question of whether these gains are a potentially viable source of financial security in old age considering the time of occurrence. Figure 9.1 answers the latter two questions in the affirmative.

Most transfers follow the generational line, and most of them, by far, originate from parents (since multiple answers are possible, the total adds up to more than 100%). This suggests that the financial gain is embedded in fundamental family processes and influences intergenerational relationships, be it implicitly or explicitly, long before the actual act of inheriting. Second come parents-in-law, which points to the significance of marriage homogamy. Since higher social classes frequently choose partners of similar social background, they are often in line for several inheritances: directly from their own parents and indirectly from their in-laws. Although transfers from grandparents are relatively rare, the findings for parents and parents-in-law clearly underscore the significance of the generational line. Therefore, studying inheritances for the most part means studying intergenerational family relations.

In this light, the findings for age groups come as no surprise. Since inheritances stem mainly from parents, the transfers occur mostly in the second half of life. As expected, parents make sure not to part with their possessions too early. This is also supported by my calculations for Germany based on the Socio-economic Panel. They show that gifts are not only received much less frequently than inheritances, but also at a much earlier point in time. Moreover, gifts tend to be of smaller value (see also Schupp and Szydlik 2004a). The age rates provide preliminary evidence regarding the pension-inheritance paradox. Bequests from parents could indeed play a role in providing security in old age – at least their children have little opportunity to consume the parental estate at an earlier point in time. However, for a sound assessment of the paradox, we must take a closer look at the opportunity and need structures of the heirs.

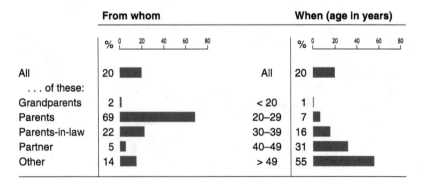

Figure 9.1 Inheritance: Overview

Source: SHARE (n: 38,635/38,635).

Owing to the wording of the questionnaire, Figure 9.1 refers to all respondents and includes inheritances and gifts. However, from Figure 9.2 onwards, the focus shifts to bequests from parents. Thus, the following analyses for previous inheritances refer to respondents with at least one deceased parent, while only a wealth transfer from a parent is counted as a previous inheritance. Conversely, with regard to future inheritances, only interviewees with at least one living parent are included.

As Figure 9.2 shows, 15 per cent of the respondents with at least one deceased parent received a transfer of more than 5,000 euros from that parent. This testifies to the fact that rather small proportions of the population are beneficiaries of noteworthy inheritances. It is notably not the classes with lower levels of education whose comparatively difficult situation is counterbalanced by transfers of wealth. Some people with lower education benefit from inheritances. However, the rate is much higher among classes with medium to higher education. The findings thus support the existence and impact of lifelong intergenerational solidarity: higher-class parents are much more successful in ensuring that their children attain higher-level education as well, while the same parents also have more assets to pass on to their adult children decades later. Furthermore, this situation will not be reversed in the future – on the contrary, the better educated are also the ones that can expect to benefit most from future bequests.

The highest income group reports the most inheritances. In cases where respondents have received a bequest in the past, one cannot entirely rule out that

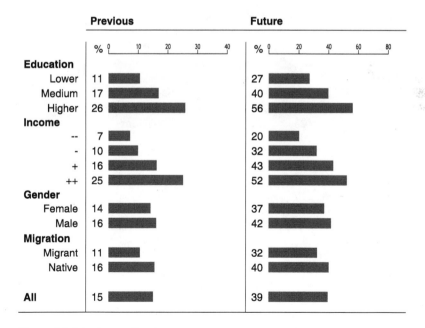

Figure 9.2 Inheritance: People

Source: SHARE (n: 36,105/9,824).

the household's current financial situation could also be the outcome of that previous transfer of assets. However, the same pattern exists with regard to expected inheritances: those experiencing difficulties in making ends meet are also less likely to expect financial gains from future bequests. The discrepancies between the income groups are very pronounced.

Gender seems to have much less impact in this respect. The figure suggests that women are at a slight disadvantage in terms of past and future inheritances. It will be investigated whether this holds true in the context of the multivariate analyses.

The differences between migrants and natives are also not as great as those related to education and income. However, they are still considerable and point in the expected direction: in contrast to the native population, migrants are and will continue to be less likely to receive an inheritance. The findings thus indicate that, compared to natives, migrants are less likely to have had or have parents with notable monetary resources.

Figure 9.3 shows the share of respondents having received an inheritance or expecting to do so for 14 European countries while it also distinguishes between West and East Germany. The figure gives evidence of very pronounced differences between the countries and underscores the importance of comparative international analyses of inheritances. The incidence of past inheritances ranges from 6 to 32 per cent,

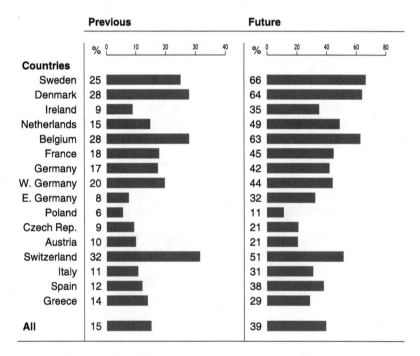

Figure 9.3 Inheritance: Countries

Source: SHARE (n: 36,105/9,824).

whereas the rates span from 11 to 66 per cent for ones to come. With regard to past inheritances, Switzerland, Denmark, Belgium and Sweden are the leaders. West Germany, France and the Netherlands represent the upper middle range. The lower middle range stretches from Greece, through Spain and Italy, to Austria. At the lower end are the Czech Republic, Ireland, East Germany and Poland.

On the whole, the results for expected future legacies confirm the country ranking by past inheritances. Hence, there is no future compensation in sight to offset poorer chances of inheriting in the past. An interesting observation is that in Ireland and East Germany, somewhat counter to the trend, around a third of the respondents expect future inheritances. This relatively higher share than in the past could suggest a partial catching-up process.

Further investigations (not shown in a figure) indicate that most bequests do not exceed a certain sum. Two-fifths amount to less than 20,000 euros, two-thirds are lower than 50,000 euros, and more than four-fifths of the transfers are below the threshold of 100,000 euros. Of course, these sums are considerable, and inheriting any sum is likely to be considered a welcome financial gain. Nevertheless, very high sums are very rare.

The size of inheritances is unequally distributed amongst population groups and countries. The lower educational classes not only inherit less often, but also receive smaller sums if they do. Over half of the bequests for the least educated are below 20,000 euros, whereas this applies to only 30 per cent of the academics. There is no sign of gender inequality in this respect. The investigations show impressive country disparities; yet owing to the relatively low number of inheritance cases in several countries, these results have to be treated with caution. The highest sums and the lowest share of relatively small inheritances can be found in Switzerland. By contrast, an especially large proportion of the bequests in Eastern and partly Southern Europe tend to be rather small. This is in line with the findings on inheritance chances presented above.

Explanation

What factors account for better or poorer chances of receiving an inheritance? Figure 9.4 displays the summarised net results of the multilevel multivariate analyses shown in Table A9.2 ('+' stands for higher inheritance chances, '−' indicates fewer respondents having received or expecting a bequest).

The analyses confirm the extraordinary relevance of *opportunity structures*. First of all, testators have to own something that they can bequeath. From the point of view of the adult child as the prospective heir, having resourceful parents obviously increases the chances of an inheritance. The findings again confirm lifelong intergenerational solidarity, according to which higher-class parents foster the educational success and thus the income opportunities of their children while – apart from providing support in many other ways – they are also able to pass on legacies of some value in the end. Thus, already privileged children obtain further advantages through bequests. Conversely, those at a disadvantage because of lower education can rarely expect this kind of financial gain.

		Previous	Future
Opportunity Structures	Education: Lower (ref.)		
	Medium	+ +	+ +
	Higher	+ + +	+ + +
	Income	+ +	+ +
	Previous inheritance	/	+ +
	Mother alive	– – –	– –
	Father alive	– – –	–
	Parents deceased (ref.)		– – –
	Parents alive (ref.)	/	
Need Structures	Property	/	+
	Age	– – –	– – –
	Time transfer	/	+ +
Family Structures	Woman		
	Married (ref.)		
	Partner	–	
	Widowed		–
	Divorced	+	
	Single	+ +	
	Child		
	No sibling (ref.)		
	1 sibling		
	2 siblings	–	
	3+ siblings	– –	–
Cultural-contextual Structures	Migrant	– – –	– –
	Social expenditure	+	+ +
	Family expenditure	+	+
	Wealth per capita	+ +	+ + +
	Poverty rate	– –	– –

Figure 9.4 Explaining inheritance

Source: SHARE, Table A9.2, see Appendix (net). '+': more, '–': less inheritance.

Also, inheritances mostly benefit those who already belong to the highest income groups. Low household income rarely comes with high chances of inheriting, so bequests generally cannot be counted upon to meet this greater financial need. The empirical results also confirm that the favourable position of the higher classes regarding past inheritances extends into the future. The fact that previous heirs are even more likely to expect future inheritances completes the picture.

If the mother or father is still alive, the likelihood of having received an inheritance in the past is much lower compared to persons whose parents are already deceased. In fact, inheritances originate primarily from parents. Since past transfers from parents are considered only for respondents with at least one deceased parent, the variable 'parents alive' is not included in this case. However, this group constitutes the reference group for inheritances expected in the future: the other constellations involve considerably lower chances of inheriting. As expected, this holds particularly for respondents whose mother and father are both deceased. Parents remain the main source of inheritances also in the future.

The results with regard to education, income and a previous inheritance already indicate that the *need structures* of adult children play a minor role when it comes to bequests. This also applies to property. For someone who does not own property, an inheritance would be especially handy. However, in this respect, too, the greater need is less likely to be met (since property can also be the result of a past inheritance, it is not considered in this context). This finding further indicates that parents who own property are rather inclined to bequeath their estate instead of transferring it to their offspring during their lifetime in the form of a gift, which testifies to the aforementioned 'King Lear effect'.

One can assume that the elderly are in greater financial need owing to deteriorating health and the corresponding costs that this involves. However, the fact is that older respondents report fewer inheritances. The findings thus rather point to a cohort effect. Amongst the SHARE respondents, the older cohorts more often had parents who had lost their possessions through war and hyperinflation. The younger cohorts, by contrast, are more likely to have parents who experienced considerably better chances to accumulate wealth after World War II.

The provision of help or care from respondents to their parents is an indicator of parental needs, whereas the monetary needs of the adult child may play a role as well. The available data does not allow us to investigate whether support of this kind has actually been remunerated post mortem. Yet, those providing time transfers to parents are more likely to expect future inheritances. This result suggests (the expectation of) intergenerational reciprocity, in that adult children give time today and parents provide monetary 'rewards' tomorrow.

The present study includes analyses of the relevance of *family structures* with regard to gender, partnership, parenthood and siblings. The findings indicate that parents hardly distinguish between daughters and sons anymore in passing on their estate. The traditional favouritism of male heirs is no longer significant. This underscores the relevance of changes in gender roles, norms, inheritance laws and economic structures.

In contrast to married children, living with a partner without being married seems to result in a somewhat lower chance of having received a larger inheritance in the past. This is an indication that parents (previously) favoured married children, whereas such an effect cannot be observed regarding future bequests. Widowed children are less likely to expect an inheritance; at least, widowhood precludes inheritances from parents-in-law. Also, similar to the findings for current transfers (Chapter 7), divorced and especially single children more often report a previous inheritance, be it due to their (perceived) more fragile financial situation, or because parents are inclined to favour children who are less likely to share the inheritance with someone outside the family of origin. Other possible factors might be that a huge inheritance contributes to staying or becoming single as well as to singles having closer bonds with their parents (e.g., more contact and coresidence, as shown in Chapters 4 and 6). However, there is no corresponding effect with regard to expected bequests.

The existence of children (or grandchildren from the viewpoint of the testator), in principle, can lead to being 'rewarded' for the continuation of the family line, but it can also result in skipping the middle generation. Here, the empirical analyses do not come to a definite conclusion. Either none of the divergent hypotheses is true, or the two options offset one another.

Siblings can be rivals for a parental estate, especially if there are three or more siblings. The costs of raising several children can result in fewer assets to be bequeathed, and those fewer assets amount to less for each individual child the greater the number of children among whom the estate must be divided.

Cultural-contextual structures are represented by migration, welfare states, wealth and poverty. Migrants clearly have fewer chances of receiving an inheritance compared to the native population. Migration frequently occurs for economic reasons, and the findings indicate that parents of migrants have fewer resources. Substantial inheritance-related disadvantages can be observed not only in the past but also extend into the future.

As expected, a stronger welfare state is associated with more inheritances, both in the past and in the future. The more social and family expenditure in a country, the more bequests. On the one hand, more resources in general can lead to both more public expenditure and more private bequests. On the other hand, social and family expenditure relieve the elderly from having to spend money for offspring in financial need and for their own health costs, while higher pensions put them in a better position to cover their own expenses without having to spend their savings. All in all, a strong welfare state leaves more money in the hands of the elderly, resulting in more bequests.

Countries with low wealth per capita are on the losing side in terms of inheritance. Where there is more wealth, there is more to bequeath and inherit. This means that historical circumstances, national political decisions and economic success or failure have a substantial impact on the financial gains to be obtained through intergenerational family solidarity. Countries offering greater opportunities for accumulating wealth also offer better chances of inheriting some. From this it follows that inheritance practices are most likely to influence intergenerational family relations in wealthy countries.

In contrast, a huge poverty rate is associated with considerably fewer bequests. If large segments of the population are poor, inheritances are generally less likely. Wealth and poverty play a tremendous part in mortis causa transfers, both in the past and in the future.

Summary

In many countries, an immense fortune has been accumulated that has not been wiped out either by an act of war or inflation. This fortune is now being transferred from one generation to the next. However, only a fraction of the population actually benefits from such a legacy. It is a particular group of people that receives most of the possessions. Who are these heirs, and who has rather slim chances of receiving a substantial bequest?

First of all, inheritance is an important form of intergenerational solidarity. Most legacies stem from parents. Heirs often have at least one deceased parent, and those who are most likely to expect a bequest in the future are those whose mother and father are still alive. This implies that the financial gain goes hand in hand with deep personal loss and is embedded in fundamental family processes. Research concerned with bequests must therefore consider intergenerational family relations. Inheritance research is intergenerational research.

The empirical analyses document the immense importance of resources for mortis causa transfers. Parents of the higher social classes have far greater means at their disposal for exercising lifelong intergenerational solidarity than their lower-class counterparts. Even after their death, their children are much more likely to receive considerable financial assets. The greater monetary needs of the lower classes, on the other hand, are barely met. Although some adult children from the lower and middle classes also inherit legacies of some value, which may even represent a proportionally larger gain in relation to their previous 'wealth', this occurs much less frequently. One in ten respondents with a lower education received an inheritance of more than 5,000 euros. This applies to one in four of the academics. Moreover, the better educated not only receive more bequests but also higher sums.

The prevalence of the 'Matthew principle' – 'To him that hath shall be given, and he shall have abundance' (Matt. 13: 12) – is validated by a number of other findings. Those with a particularly high income are much more likely to be heirs. Those who already have inherited in the past are much more likely to expect a further legacy, and this also applies to owners of property. While there are no significant gender differences, the native population has much better chances of inheriting compared to migrants.

The Matthew principle also solves the pension-inheritance paradox: those population groups that might need a substantial bequest the most are the ones that are least likely to receive it. Increasing inheritances do not offset a retreat of the welfare state. Instead, stronger welfare states give and leave more monetary means in the hands of the elderly, ultimately leading to more bequests. This matches the finding that higher social and family expenditure in a country are associated with considerably more inheritances. From this perspective, lower pensions and higher costs of living owing to public cutbacks may diminish the estates to be passed on. A retreat of the welfare state could thus lead to fewer bequests.

Wealth per capita and poverty in a country have also proven to be immensely important factors in explaining inheritances. In countries where people own more assets and the previous generation has experienced more favourable conditions for accumulating wealth, there are many more legacies available for descendants. In fact, Switzerland, Denmark, Belgium and Sweden display the highest inheritance rates. West Germany, France and the Netherlands are in the upper middle range, whereas Greece, Spain, Italy and Austria represent the lower middle range. The fewest estates are passed on in the Czech Republic, Ireland, East Germany and Poland. These findings also indicate that it makes sense to consider differences in bequests between West and East Germany. The distinct political and economic conditions in the 'former' Federal Republic of Germany and the German Democratic Republic cast a long shadow.

What future developments can be expected on the basis of the empirical results? The better-educated and more affluent population groups anticipate considerably more future inheritances. At the same time, property is most frequently expected to be passed on from one generation to the next in countries that have the most heirs in the first place. Particularly high bequest rates in the past are associated with particularly high bequest rates in the future. The empirical findings thus indicate increasing inequality in inheritances both within and between countries.

10 Conclusions

Sharing lives

Family generations indeed share their lives. (Adult) children and their parents not only have the longest possible joint time in the history of mankind, they also make intense use of it. Intergenerational relations span from infancy all the way to old age. They are generally stable, long-lasting and intense. Without exaggeration, we can conclude that there is indeed 'lifelong solidarity'. Even the relationship between adult children and parents who no longer live in the same household is marked by strong bonds, ranging from frequent contact to impressive functional solidarity, including financial support, help with household chores and even long-term care for frail elderly relatives. The adage, 'Out of sight, out of mind', definitely does not apply to children and parents. This also shows that when looking at human bonding (Rossi and Rossi 1990), one has to consider intergenerational family relations.

In the introduction to this book, three possible scenarios characterising family relationships were distinguished: autonomy conflict and solidarity. The empirical investigations come to a clear result: the most dominant pattern is solidarity. Thus, this study contradicts common myths. It is simply not true that generations live in permanent conflict, let alone in a 'battle' or even a 'war'. The same applies to the notion of individualisation or autonomy in the sense of isolated individuals with no nameable connection to others. General break-ups are as disconnected from reality as are fierce conflicts. Instead, only 5 per cent of the respondents report frequent generational conflict, whereas more than four out of five adult generations are in at least weekly contact. Given notions of conflict, isolation and crisis of the family, these are indeed surprising and impressive results.

Frequent contact and few conflicts are only one part of the typical intergenerational relationship. The other part is functional solidarity, that is, the giving and receiving of space, money and time. This support is manifold. It includes the provision of living space, for example, when young adult children do not yet have the means to stand on their own feet. It includes help with household chores, gardening and repair work, shopping for groceries, filling out forms and assistance with other bureaucratic tasks all the way to immensely intense permanent care for frail elderly parents. It includes financial assistance in the form of regular payments, or special monetary support in times of emergency, right up to smaller or larger bequests. The empirical results prove the relevance of the so-called 'cascade model', according to which monetary transfers tend to flow from parents to their offspring rather than the other way around. While this is the case for money, the reverse is true for time. Time is more likely to run up the generational line, that is, from adult children to parents.

Yet despite this immense cohesion and solidarity, one should avoid the temptation to idealise intergenerational relations. To only emphasise frequent contact, rare conflict and pronounced support between the generations is to paint an incomplete picture. Noteworthy conflicts are relatively rare, but should not be neglected either, and they can often lead to generations drifting apart. Intense controversies are more of a risk to than an opportunity for intergenerational solidarity. They are destructive rather than constructive, and there is a danger of terminating the relationship (Szydlik 2008a).

Also, intergenerational solidarity is not in principle and in general an indication of a 'good' family. Indeed, we would be mistaken to think of 'solidarity' as being necessarily 'good'. Sharing lives means sharing bad times, too. Frequent contact includes sharing sorrow and pain, and not all contact is desired at all times. Staying in touch may be owing to a feeling of obligation. Some generations would like to have more contact, others would prefer less. Intergenerational relations may even be too close and symbiotic, such as when parents cling to their children or adult children have difficulty living their own lives. Moreover, coresidence of adult generations is often not the preferred form of living, but stems rather from necessity. Giving money or time may lead to postponing or giving up one's own wishes, and receiving support may come with undesired feelings of dependence and the obligation to give something in return. Personal care in old age is often accompanied by stresses and strains for both parties. In other words, there can be too much solidarity, and intergenerational cohesion may be 'good' or 'bad', sometimes even at the same time.

Furthermore, it is important to bear in mind that empirical social research deals with social regularities and not natural laws that apply to every single case. General patterns do not reflect the situation of every individual, and one's own personal situation may sometimes correspond to the general pattern, and sometimes not. Thus, when intergenerational relations are assessed as close and supportive, it should also be taken into account that there are those who do not fall into the general scheme. Some members of family generations do not help one another at all. There are adult children and parents who very rarely meet or talk, others have totally lost contact, and some who have deliberately ended the relationship.

Education, income, gender, migration, country

Although, in general, intergenerational solidarity is lifelong and intense, the empirical investigations also show striking discrepancies between population groups and countries.

Lower and higher education

Academics report greater geographical distances both from their parents and adult children, and feel fewer family obligations both towards children and the elderly. Furthermore, the empirical analyses find more intergenerational conflict between better-educated parents and their adult children. These results speak of less intergenerational cohesion among the higher educational classes. However, the picture is reversed when considering time and, most notably, money. The better educated more often provide support with household tasks and help with paperwork, such as filling out forms and settling financial or legal matters. This is an indication that educational resources enhance the ability to give time. Moreover, differences between educational classes are particularly pronounced in the case of current financial transfers and inheritances. The better educated give much more money to their adult children, and also have a much higher chance of receiving a notable inheritance from their parents.

Rich and poor

In many ways similar patterns to educational classes emerge when one observes income groups, with a notable exception: considerably less conflict with adult children occurs when the household is easily able to make ends meet. A favourable economic situation obviously reduces reasons for quarrels and fights. Well-off adult family generations are also forced to share the same four walls less often. The lower income groups are more likely to provide space, whereas the affluent give money. Financial transfers from parents to adult children are much more common when parents belong to the best-off income group. Here we find extraordinary differences from parents who have great difficulty in making ends meet (9 vs. 33 per cent). A great discrepancy is also found when observing inheritances. In the lowest income group, only 7 per cent have received a bequest. In the highest group, it is 25 per cent. A fifth of those with few resources see a chance of a future inheritance. In contrast, this applies to every second affluent person.

Women and men

Women hold families together. The expression 'kinkeeper' is certainly justified. In comparison to men, women maintain closer contact with children and parents across households. Adult daughters leave the parental home earlier, yet stay in touch with their parents more often than sons. By far, daughters and mothers have the closest relationship. The kinkeeper situation becomes especially obvious when one looks at support in the form of time. Help is more often provided by women, and this applies particularly to personal care. When parents are cared for by an adult child, it is mostly a daughter who shoulders the task. At the same time, the empirical investigations document slightly more frequent conflict between daughters and parents. However, the analyses find no gender differences with regard to larger monetary transfers, including inheritances. When it comes to considerable transmissions of financial means from one generation to the next, parents nowadays generally do not distinguish between daughters and sons.

Migrants and natives

It comes as no surprise that moving to a different country increases the geographical distance between migrants and their parents and thus reduces the frequency of contact with and help and care for older parents. However, when considering geographical distance, intergenerational contact of migrants is even more frequent, which supports the 'safe haven' hypothesis. Regarding the frequency of parents' contact with their adult children, migrants seem to differ considerably less from the native population. Nevertheless, there is more conflict. Possible reasons are strains due to migration and the situation in the host country as well as a 'drifting apart' of migrant parents and their offspring owing to the different cultural contexts ('drift' hypothesis). Moreover, since migration is often triggered by economic circumstances, it is safe to assume that migrants are less likely to have rich parents, which in turn means that migrants represent a population group with substantially lower chances of receiving a notable inheritance.

Region and country

The country in which one lives is of great importance for intergenerational relations. From a global perspective, one might assume that European countries are quite similar. However, this is far from true. Every country is unique, and it is important to have a close look at country-specific differences. Nevertheless, the patterns we do find are also associated with the wider regions of Northern, Western, Eastern and Southern Europe. In the north, (near) coresidence with adult children is relatively rare. At the same time, Sweden and Denmark show particularly low levels of conflict as well as high rates of help and inheritance. A generally different pattern can be found in the south, where there are particularly high rates of contact, coresidence and care. However, help is less frequent and so are inheritances. Eastern European countries are marked by low rates of conflict, frequent instances of shared living space and rare bequests. The latter also applies to East Germany, reflecting the long-term effects of differing political and economic regimes.

Opportunity, need, family, society

One of the main arguments of this book is that the relationships between adult children and parents are influenced by individual, familial and societal factors. From this it follows that three levels of analysis need to be addressed: micro (individual opportunities and needs), meso (family) and macro (society). This multilevel approach is at the core of the ONFC model and supported by the empirical results.

Opportunity

Intergenerational relations are closely linked with resources. Education and income have already been mentioned as highly significant means of providing support. Possession of greater financial resources gives ample opportunity to assist other generations. This is also true for property. Moreover, expected monetary returns seem to encourage solidarity. For example, an expected future inheritance is clearly associated with more frequent contact and the willingness to provide help and care. This is an indication that the financial means of one generation are an opportunity to motivate attention and support from the other generation. Another crucial factor is geographical distance. The closer the generations live to one another, the more contact, help and care is possible. By contrast, the farther they live apart, the less opportunity there is for personal contact and support. Having more space enhances the opportunity for generations to live in the same household. Parents with larger homes are more likely to still have adult children living with them.

Need

Much intergenerational solidarity is due to necessity. Family members do not leave one another to fend for themselves when problems strike. Parents support their offspring when they are in need, and adult children care for their parents, for example, when they become frail – and doing so often comes with considerable sacrifices in either case. One particularly crucial need factor is health. When their parents' health is poor, adult children are more likely to help, and the poor health of parents is the most important factor responsible for adult children providing care. Poor health is also associated with more conflict, which is further evidence supporting the strain hypothesis. Another need factor is the employment situation. When adult children are in education, parents are much more likely to provide living space or give money. Age plays a relevant role, too. Parents particularly support their young adult children by giving space and money, whereas children are more likely to provide help and care to older parents.

Family

There are a number of family aspects that influence intergenerational relations. Gender combinations have already been mentioned. Another crucial factor is partnership. Married parents have the most frequent contact with their adult children, whereas divorced and single parents show particularly low contact rates with their offspring. Parents who have a partner also give money more frequently, whereas adult children with a partner are less likely to receive financial transfers. Moreover, it is especially rare that these children still live with their parents. The number of offspring plays a role, too. Having more children leads to partitioning resources. The more children, the less contact and coresidence with each child, the less money given to each child, and the less help provided to parents.

Having a grandchild also diminishes coresidence, money and help, while increasing the likelihood of near coresidence. The number of siblings lessens contact with and help to parents, again showing that having more offspring reduces the support received from each child.

Society

Migration – and thus cultural differences – is one crucial factor for intergenerational cohesion. Welfare states and social stratification have also been shown to be of utmost importance for the relationships between adult children and parents. A strong welfare state and more family expenditure in particular are associated with fewer generational conflicts, fewer adult children still having to live with their parents, more frequent help to parents, more current monetary transfers to adult children, and more bequests. By contrast, relatively small public expenditure for families is accompanied by more conflict and coresidence as well as less money, help and inheritances. Wealthy countries show more intergenerational contact and conflict, less (near) coresidence, more large inter vivos transfers of money and more bequests. Living in a country with a high poverty rate also goes hand in hand with more contact and conflict, but at the same time with more (near) coresidence, less help and fewer large monetary transmissions including bequests.

Connections

A core feature of intergenerational relations is 'connections' (Szydlik 2012b). Family generations connect (a) individuals, (b) people with time, (c) forms and factors of solidarity, (d) research agendas and (e) individuals and families with society.

First of all, intergenerational relations connect individuals. The analyses in this book provide ample evidence of the lifelong bonds between parents and children. Intergenerational relations connect the young with the old. Family life offers opportunities for mutual recognition and understanding, but also for conflict.

Family generations connect individuals with (historical) time, linking present, past and future. Listening to one's parents' or grandparents' life stories means reflecting on former times. Interacting with children gives parents the opportunity to look at new times, new technologies, new ways of thinking and seeing things through their children's eyes.

Various forms of solidarity are connected with one another, for example, when it comes to reciprocity between money and time. Solidarity factors are linked in many ways, too, which has been shown via the ONFC model and the empirical analyses based thereon. There are links among micro, meso and macro levels, that is, individual, family and society.

When investigating intergenerational relations, it is crucial to combine theoretical reasoning with empirical investigations, and vice versa. Research on generations also connects various sociological subdisciplines such as economic, family, gender, health, life course, migration and political sociology as well as social stratification research. Furthermore, generation research connects scientific disciplines. For example, Künemund and Szydlik (2009) compiled generation research in sociology, biology, Egyptology, history, pedagogy, ethnology, psychology, literary studies, media studies, economics, law and political science.

Family solidarity is a basis for social cohesion and thus connects individuals and families with society. There exist connections between family and social generations, be it in political, cultural or economic terms. Intergenerational family relations link societal domains and political fields, such as education, family, finance, labour, law etc. There is also a link between family generations and demographic change. Fertility is a key aspect of demography, and longevity has a great influence on intergenerational relations. Moreover, there is a strong private-public welfare link, including connections between private and public intergenerational solidarity. Last but not least, there are important connections between intergenerational family solidarity and social inequality.

Generation and state

Welfare states have enormous consequences for intergenerational relations. There are striking differences among social-democratic, conservative, familistic and post-socialist countries, and also between individual states within the same group of nations. The country in which they live makes a huge difference to individuals and families.

What is the nature of the connection between generation and state? The empirical results support both 'crowding-out' and 'crowding-in'. The welfare state reduces and enhances family solidarity at the same time. Living in a weak welfare state means that family members are more obliged to support one another. Here, women in particular are expected to assume care responsibilities for their dependent parents. In contrast, in a strong welfare state, families are more likely to have the option of leaving the burden of intense personal care to professionals. However, the results show that this crowding-out in the area of intense care would be misinterpreted if taken as a general retreat of family members from solidarity per se. On the contrary, family solidarity is still strong in strong welfare states. Here, help below the threshold of intense personal care is even more frequent, indicating crowding-in.

Taking both results into consideration suggests a welfare mix of family and state, a 'refined specialisation' of private and public support. A stronger welfare state offers adult children and parents greater choice. In this case, family members and public services can concentrate on the tasks that they are especially suited to perform. This division of labour leaves it to professionals to take care of regular, plannable and intensive work, whereas family members can focus on sporadic, short-term and less arduous tasks (Brandt et al. 2009; Igel et al. 2009). For example, adult children would assume tasks such as practical household help, organising care provision amongst family members and professionals, helping with paperwork and bureaucratic matters and in general providing attention to and emotional support for their parents. Such a 'refined specialisation' could be to the benefit of frail elderly, and would also benefit adult children because intense care often places an extreme burden on the caregivers, even to the point of over-burdening them (e.g., Colombo et al. 2011: 85ff.). Furthermore, reconciling work and family is not only a problem for parents of small children, but also for adult children with frail parents. In any case, according to Figure 3.4, a combination of private and public responsibility would reflect the opinion of the overwhelming majority of the respondents.

However, offering a refined mix of public and private welfare is rendered even more difficult by a number of major challenges. One such challenge is demo-graphic change. Longer lives belong to the best news of our time. Family gen-erations obviously make use of those gained years. Nevertheless, demographic change also involves many more people being in need of intense support and care. Another challenge is the increased flexibility demands in working life ('flexibili-sation'; Szydlik 2008b). Flexible time demands put a daily strain on the employed and their relatives: families need stability and reliability, whereas employers demand flexibility. At the same time, increased work-induced demands for geo-graphical mobility make it increasingly difficult for adult family generations to support one another (BMFSFJ 2006: 142). This is all the more important since the analyses show that spatial proximity is one of the most significant conditions for intergenerational contact, help and care. Developments in family structures rep-resent a further challenge. Less stable partnerships and fewer siblings who could share care work decrease support resources, and put more strain on those who are still available (Szydlik 2012b: 101f.). All in all, the greater need for solidarity comes up against fewer opportunities to provide it.

Against this background, the retreat of the welfare state poses a serious addi-tional problem. The availability of fewer public services puts much more pres-sure on family members – and especially women – to provide intensive support (Schmid 2014; Haberkern et al. 2015). The analyses in this book have further shown that private financial transfers are extremely dependent on resources. Part of the money that is publicly transferred from young to old (i.e., from the employed population to pensioners) is privately returned by the old to the young (Kohli 1999). Diminished means thus equate to less monetary support for fam-ily generations in need. The connection between public and private transfers is of particular significance to the lower classes. Smaller pensions for less affluent groups would not only reduce the quality of life of those pensioners, but would also result in less private support for their offspring. Instead, adult children might be urged to give money to their parents in need – if they can afford to do so. This interplay of public and private intergenerational solidarity could ultimately also reduce the acceptance of the public 'intergenerational contract'.

Strong family cohesion might inspire the political protagonists of a 'lean' wel-fare state to champion the reduction of public spending, since an argument might be made that, in this case, the family would take over. However, the connection of family and welfare state is less one of competition than of complementarity. Precisely because relatives support one another in difficult situations, they should not be left on their own. Instead, a refined specialisation of family and state is more likely to avoid excessive strains and an overburdening of caring relatives, and thus consequential costs for individuals, families and societies.

Generation and inequality

There is a precarious relation between intergenerational solidarity and social inequality. Family cohesion is closely connected with social stratification. The relationship goes in both directions. On the one hand, education and income as well as societal wealth and poverty greatly influence how parents and children share their lives: social inequality affects intergenerational solidarity. On the other hand, parents' lifelong support for their children has immense consequences for social stratification. Intergenerational solidarity is one of the main driving forces for the preservation and even widening of social disparities.

Parents care deeply for their offspring. Lifelong solidarity lasts from cradle to grave, and even beyond. This family cohesion 'transfers' social inequality from one generation to the next (Swartz 2009: 207). The mechanisms are elaborated in Chapter 2. At each stage of their children's life course, parents support their offspring as well as they can, but affluent parents can do more. In fact, one can observe an accumulation of social inequality over the life course (Szydlik 2012a). Better-educated and rich parents have abundant resources that they use for the benefit of their offspring. Children are born into higher- or lower-class families, which has tremendous consequences for their whole lives, including education, school, vocation, job, career, income, prestige, job security, (un)employment, partnership and the social background of their partner, poverty or wealth, housing, travel, quality of life, self-esteem, health, pension, morbidity and mortality.

The connections between intergenerational solidarity and social inequality also apply to functional solidarity (the giving and receiving of space, money and time) between generations in adulthood. Providing living space can be seen as part of an investment of resourceful parents in a better education for their adult children, including university studies. At the same time, high poverty and youth unemployment greatly increase the proportion of young adults still living in their parents' home. In both cases, those adult children who can rely on their parents to provide space have an advantage. Nevertheless, the empirical findings also suggest that permanent coresidence of adult family generations is more a result of economic pressure and less a matter of choice. The fact that higher income is associated with less intergenerational coresidence attests to this. Although adult children and parents do prefer to share their lives, they would rather do so at a (preferably short) distance. The affluent have the ability to put that preference into practice.

The other forms of functional solidarity – money and time – display a positive correlation between resources and solidarity. Having more money increases the frequency of help, not least because helping others often requires a certain amount of financial resources, too. This applies to monetary transfers from parents to adult children by the very nature of the transaction. Since current financial support goes particularly to adult children in education, this may even lead to less inequality between young adults in employment and those still in education.

However, in the long run, these transfers can be seen as investments in higher education, leading to more subsequent inequality between children of poor and of affluent parents. Wealthy parents are in a much better position to support their children with money, and these children are much more likely to receive something.

This also applies to the transfer of wealth from one generation to the next. An argument could be made that, on the whole, bequests do not greatly affect social inequality, since inheritances stem mostly from parents and thus stay within families: rich families stay rich, poor families stay poor. One might also point to relatively high gains of the less affluent in relation to their previous 'wealth'. Nevertheless, the empirical results show that it is affluent adult children in particular who benefit from notable bequests. From a life course perspective, wealthy parents pass on their assets to affluent children in the second half of their lives, while these children have already profited substantially from the previous support of their parents. Those who have, give – and those whose parents have, receive. Adult children with no or few resources are in particular financial need. However, poor children rarely have wealthy parents. The findings confirm the Matthew principle: 'To him that hath shall be given, and he shall have abundance'.

Last but not least, it is important to emphasise that the connections between generation and inequality are orchestrated by political decisions. Three brief examples from a life course perspective serve to underline this. First, in the early stages of life, the division of pupils into basic and advanced schools by state-regulated educational systems plays a major role in lifelong inequality. Dividing up children at an early stage favours the offspring of affluent parents by facilitating their path toward a better education, and thus more favourable social positions throughout life. Second, in later years, the extent of public support for families in need is crucial. Living in a weak welfare state puts greater strain on less affluent families, in particular, to care for their relatives, thus leading to less choice in accommodating different needs and preferences. Third, a pension, health and tax system with only weak redistributive elements ultimately contributes to ever increasing social disparities that are perpetuated from one generation to the next. It is thus a task of society as a whole to closely address the unwelcome 'side effects' of otherwise welcome intergenerational solidarity.

Appendix: Data

Survey, sample, statistics

This Appendix provides information on the survey, sample and statistical procedures. Furthermore, it documents the number of cases (Table A1), operationalisations of the dependent and independent variables (Tables A2 and A3) as well as the results of multivariate analyses (Tables A4.1 to A9.2).

Survey

The empirical analyses are based on the 'Survey of Health, Ageing and Retirement in Europe' (SHARE), a representative survey of the population aged 50 years and older that offers detailed information on respondents and their family members, including parents and (adult) children. This book uses the release of SHARE data that was distributed to researchers in 2014, which offers the best available data quality for the first two SHARE waves, whereas investigations based on previous releases need to be treated with more caution.

Researchers using SHARE data are asked to issue the following declaration:

This paper uses data from SHARE Waves 1 and 2 release 2.6.0, as of November 29th 2013 (DOI: 10.6103/SHARE.w1.260 and 10.6103/ SHARE.w2.260). The SHARE data collection has been primarily funded by the European Commission through the 5th Framework Programme (project QLK6-CT-2001-00360 in the thematic programme Quality of Life), through the 6th Framework Programme (projects SHARE-I3, RII-CT-2006-062193, COMPARE, CIT5-CT-2005-028857, and SHARELIFE, CIT4-CT-2006-028812) and through the 7th Framework Programme (SHARE-PREP, N° 211909, SHARE-LEAP, N° 227822 and SHARE M4, N° 261982). Additional funding from the U.S. National Institute on Aging (U01 AG09740-13S2, P01 AG005842, P01 AG08291, P30 AG12815, R21 AG025169, Y1-AG-4553-01, IAG BSR06-11 and OGHA 04-064) and the German Ministry of Education and Research as well as from various national sources is gratefully acknowledged (see www.share-project.org for a full list of funding institutions).

Sample

The first two waves of the SHARE survey, on which the empirical investigations of this book are based, were collected in 2004/05 and 2006/07. The third wave (2008/09), focusing on people's life histories, does not contain sufficient information on intergenerational solidarity so it was not possible to use this data for the book at hand. The fourth wave (2010/12) did replicate a number of relevant generational questions of the first two waves. However, crucial information is missing. On the one hand, the fourth wave only partly tells which adult child received/gave time or money from/to parents. In fact, this information is limited to the respondents' social network, which considerably restricts the possibility of conducting thorough analyses on intergenerational time support and financial transfers. On the other hand, the fourth wave provides no information on (intergenerational) conflict, making it impossible to use this data to conduct the corresponding analyses documented in Chapters 2, 3 and 5.

All analyses refer to first-time respondents. This decision has three important advantages:

1   The underlying time frame is crucial to a number of key questions of this study. For example, in the first interview, each respondent is asked whether he or she received/provided help or care in the *last twelve months*. In the following interview, the respondents are asked whether this applied to the time *since the last interview*. The same time frame was used when asking about giving and receiving financial transfers. As the time period between the interviews varies from 11 to 40 months, the question is hardly comparable across respondents, since a different time frame for various respondents greatly affects the respective reply. The longer the time frame, the greater the likelihood of the occurrence of help, care or financial transfers. This problem is avoided by concentrating on first-time respondents.
2   Since all questions were answered by the respondents for the very first time, this avoids a possible survey effect from asking the same question repeatedly and treating first- and second-time responses in the same way.
3   Concentrating on the first interview of both waves offers information on more observations than by only focusing on the second wave.

The following 14 European countries are included in the analyses (ordered from north to south): Sweden, Denmark, Ireland, the Netherlands, Belgium, France, Germany, Poland, Czech Republic, Austria, Switzerland, Italy, Spain and Greece. A further distinction is made between West Germany and East Germany in order to observe long-term influences of the different political and economic regimes in the 'former' Federal Republic of Germany and the German Democratic Republic. Thus, the model statistics count East and West Germany as separate observations, which technically amounts to a total of 15 'countries'.

The Survey of Health, Ageing and Retirement in Europe, although in general referring to respondents aged 50+, also interviews younger partners of the main respondents. In order to avoid possible age-related effects, all empirical analyses refer to respondents who are at least 50 years of age. Furthermore, people living in institutions such as nursing homes are excluded, and this also applies to those who, according to the interviewers, were on the whole not able to understand the survey questions. All in all, the investigations include over 39,000 respondents, 12,500 child-parent and over 82,000 parent-child dyads (see Table A1).

The results documented in the figures are weighted, except for Ireland, for which SHARE provides no weighting factor.

Statistical procedures

The theoretical considerations as well as the structure of the data suggest distinguishing up to four levels: dyads, individuals, households and countries. To do justice to the influences and differences at all levels, multilevel models are applied (Hox 1995; Guo and Zhao 2000; Snijders and Bosker 2012). Even though, from a statistical standpoint, only relatively 'few' countries are considered, multilevel analyses have a number of advantages. They make it possible to take into account the hierarchical structure of the data and the theoretical model. They also take into consideration that the hierarchical data structure generally makes it impossible to ensure the independence of observations (multiple individuals in the same household, individuals and households in the same country), so that we cannot assume unbiased and efficient coefficient estimates when performing ordinary ordered probit models or logistic regressions.

The model statistics for the multilevel models include (a) the variances for the various levels, (b) the intraclass correlation and (c) the number of cases. The variances refer to the full model including the first macro indicator (social expenditure). The total variance of the dependent variable is partitioned into the variances for the various levels, where the lowest level is set to $\pi^2/3$ (=3.29) as the standard logistic distribution (Snijders and Bosker 2012). The intraclass correlation (ICC) is calculated for the empty model. It refers to the 'highest' (=country) level. The letter 'n' stands for the number of cases.

Because of the number of cases (countries) at the 'highest' level of the multilevel models, the macro variables are included in the multivariate models one at a time. The listed net coefficients of the other independent variables always refer to the model with the first documented macro variable (social expenditure). Stata software (GLLAMM) was used to estimate the multilevel models.

Tables A4.1–A9.2 list the results of the ordered probit models and (multinomial) logistic regressions. In the case of the ordered probit models, a negative coefficient indicates a statistically negative association of the corresponding independent and dependent variables, whereas a positive parameter denotes a statistically positive relation. The documented coefficients of the (multinomial) logistic regression analyses are odds ratios. Coefficients greater than 1 indicate a greater likelihood with regard to the dependent variable (e.g., of receiving an inheritance) compared to the reference group, whereas those less than 1 indicate fewer chances (of doing so).

When interpreting the results in terms of their relative relevance, one needs to consider the scale of the independent variable. For example, a coefficient for a variable with only two values (e.g., gender) is likely to be higher than a coefficient for a variable with ten values. This fact is also taken into account when transferring the net parameters into (more or fewer) '+' and '−' in the overview figures of this book. In this case, only significant coefficients (5% level) are considered. The following limits are applied to positive and negative relations, respectively: contact (0.4/0.8, −0.4/−0.8), conflict (0.1/0.2, −0.1/−0.2), space, money, time, inheritance (1.5/2, 0.67/0.5). For metric variables, half of the range is used as a basis.

In the 'gross' models, the influence of independent variables is estimated without considering control variables, as opposed to the 'net' models in which the coefficients are determined including the other independent variables (except for the macro variables in the case of the country models).

In the country models (Tables A4.1, A5.1, A6.1, A7.1, A8.1, A9.1), West Germany serves as the reference group. West Germany not only offers a fairly large number of observations, but is also a medium case, which leads to a conservative estimate without running the risk of exaggerating the country differences.

The units of analysis are either individuals or dyads; 'dyad' means that intergenerational relationships are considered. For instance, the relationship of a mother with her first daughter is considered as one unit of analysis (one dyad), whereas the mother's relationship with her second daughter is another dyad.

Information on the operationalisation of the dependent and independent variables is provided in Tables A2 and A3. If not specified otherwise, the independent variables refer to the respondent. For example, the variable 'education' refers to the education of the respondent. The abbreviation '(ref.)' stands for 'reference group'.

Cases, variables, analyses

Table A1 Cases

	Respondents			Dyads	
	Wave 1	*Wave 2*	*Waves 1+2*	*Resp. – parent*	*Resp. – child**
Education: Lower	13,242	6,464	19,706	4,378	44,166
Medium	7,502	4,984	12,486	4,924	24,186
Higher	4,645	2,515	7,160	3,226	14,011
Income: − −	2,591	1,832	4,423	1,290	10,074
−	6,533	4,520	11,053	3,232	23,577
+	8,991	4,479	13,470	4,357	27,565
+ +	7,274	3,132	10,406	3,649	21,147

Female	13,704	7,510	21,214	6,718	45,225
Male	11,685	6,453	18,138	5,810	37,138
Migrant	2,010	913	2,923	994	6,248
Native	23,379	13,050	36,429	11,534	76,115
Sweden	2,838	643	3,481	1,207	7,811
Denmark	1,517	1,257	2,774	960	5,917
Ireland		1,033	1,033	200	2,946
Netherlands	2,693	755	3,448	1,118	7,721
Belgium	3,506	285	3,791	1,295	7,823
France	2,790	825	3,615	1,503	7,621
Germany	2,745	895	3,640	1,156	6,612
West Germany	2,226	720	2,946	942	5,273
East Germany	519	175	694	214	1,339
Poland		2,294	2,294	540	5,693
Czech Republic		2,598	2,598	693	4,977
Austria	1,476	54	1,530	357	2,916
Switzerland	856	713	1,569	604	3,058
Italy	2,326	1,113	3,439	982	6,816
Spain	2,047	661	2,708	699	6,169
Greece	2,595	837	3,432	1,214	6,283
All	25,389	13,963	39,352	12,528	82,363

Source: SHARE. First-time respondents, unweighted. Resp.: respondent. *: child at least 18 years old.

Table A2 Dependent variables [Chapter in this book]

Contact [4]	0: Less often. 1: About once a week. 2: Several times a week. 3: Daily. Time: Last twelve months. Level: Dyads
Conflict [5]	0: Never. 1: Rarely. 2: Sometimes. 3: Often. Time: Current. Level: Individuals
Space [6]	0: Parent and adult child live in different houses. 1: Parent and adult child live in the same household (coresidence). 2: Parent and adult child live in the same house but in different households (near coresidence). Time: Current. Level: Dyads
Money [7]	1: Financial transfer to adult child of at least 250 €. 0: No transfer of at least 250 € to adult child. / 1: Financial transfer to adult child of at least 2,000 €. 0: No transfer of at least 250 € to adult child. Time: Last twelve months. Level: Dyads
Time [8]	Help: 1: Household help or help with paperwork to parent, no care. 0: No help or care to parent. / Care: 1: Personal care to parent averaging at least one hour per week. 0: No personal care to parent. Time: Last twelve months. Level: Dyads
Inheritance [9]	Previous: 1: Inheritance from deceased parent worth more than 5,000 €. 0: No inheritance of more than 5,000 € from deceased parent. Time: Ever. / Future: 1: At least 50% chance of receiving an inheritance. 0: Less than 50% chance of receiving an inheritance. Time: Next ten years. Level: Individuals

Table A3 Independent variables [Chapter(s) in this book]

Age	In years [4, 5, 6, 7, 8, 9]
Child	Respondent has at least one child [9]
Contact	Day: Daily contact. Week: Several times a week. Month: 'About once a week' or 'About every two weeks' or 'About once a month'. Year: 'Less than once a month' or 'Never' [5, 7]
Distance	1: Same house/2: < 1 km/3: 1–5 km/4: 5–25 km/5: 25–100 km/6: 100–500 km/7: > 500 km/8: > 500 km, other country [4, 8]
Education	Highest level of formal education completed according to the International Standard Classification of Education (ISCED) 1997 (see OECD 1999). Lower: Lower secondary education/Medium: Upper or post-secondary education/Higher: Tertiary education (academics) [4, 5, 6, 7, 8, 9]
Employment status	Education: In vocational training/retraining/education/Full-time employed or self-employed/Part-time employed (< 30 hours per week)/Unemployed/Not in workforce: Parental leave or looking after home/family or (early) retirement or permanently sick/ disabled or other [6, 7]
Family status	Married: Married and living with a spouse or in a registered partnership/Partner: Never married, but living with a partner/ Widowed/Divorced: Divorced or living separated from the spouse/Single: Never married, no partner [4, 5, 6, 7, 9]
Future inheritance	Contact/conflict with parents: At least 50% chance of receiving an inheritance in the next ten years, including property and other valuables. Contact/conflict with children: Respondent or partner has at least 50% chance of leaving an inheritance, including property and other valuables [4, 5]. Help/care: At least 50% chance of receiving an inheritance in the next ten years, including property and other valuables [8]
Gender dyads	Daughter-mother, daughter-father, son-mother, son-father dyads (and vice versa) [4, 6, 7, 8]
Grandchild	Respondent has at least one living grandchild [4, 5, 7, 8]. Child of respondent has at least one living child [6]
Health	1: Health is less than good (worst two of five values). 0: Health is good/excellent (best three of five values) [4, 5, 6, 8]
Income	1: Thinking of household's total monthly income: Household is able to make ends meet (fairly) easily. 0: … with some/great difficulty [4, 5, 6, 7, 8, 9]
Migrant	1: The country of birth is not the country of residence or the respondent does not have the citizenship of the country of residence. 0: The country of birth is the country of residence and the respondent has the citizenship of the country of residence [4, 5, 6, 7, 8, 9]
Money in bank	Money of respondent and partner in the bank, transaction or saving accounts at the end of the year before the interview in 1,000 € (more than 100,000 € (approx. 2%) are set to 100). Range: 0 to 100 [7]

Money transfer	Financial transfer of at least 250 € within dyad in the last twelve months, either given or received [4]. Financial transfer of at least 250 € from respondent to parent/adult child in the last twelve months [5]. Financial transfer of at least 250 € from parent to respondent in the last twelve months [8]
Mother/ father alive	Mother alive: Mother is alive, father is deceased/Father alive: Father is alive, mother is deceased/Parents deceased: Mother and father are both deceased/Parents alive: Mother and father are both alive [9]
Number of children	Range: 0 to 10 (the few cases with more than ten children are set to 10) [4, 5, 6, 7, 8]
Number of rooms	Number of rooms for household members' personal use, including bedrooms, excluding kitchen, bathrooms, hallways and (sub)let rooms. Range: 0 to 8 (the few cases with more than eight rooms are set to 8) [6]
Number of siblings	Range: 0 to 10 (the few cases with more than ten siblings are set to 10) [4, 5, 8]. No sibling: Respondent has no sibling/1 sibling: Respondent has one sibling/2 siblings: Respondent has two siblings/3+ siblings: Respondent has at least three siblings [9]
Partner	Married and living with a spouse or in a registered partnership, or never married but living with a partner [7]
Partner child	Child has a partner who lives with her/him [4, 7]
Partner parent	Both parents of the respondent are alive, and both parents live in the same geographical distance to the respondent (=assumption that parents live together, due to a lack of direct information on parents' partnership in the survey) [4, 8]
Previous inheritance	Respondent or partner has ever received a gift or inherited money, goods or property worth more than 5,000 € [9]
Property	Property ownership (including own residence, secondary homes, holiday homes, other property, land or forestry; not including special time-sharing arrangements) [9]
Time transfer	Help or care from respondent to parent/adult child in the last twelve months [5]. Help or care to respondent from child in the last twelve months [7]. Help or care from respondent to parent in the last twelve months [9]
Woman	Respondent is female [5, 9]

Macro variables [Chapter(s) in this book] (see Figure 2.3)

Social expenditure	Total public expenditure (for old age, survivors, incapacity related, families, active labour market programmes, housing, other social policy areas) in per cent of GDP per country, 2005. Source: OECD 2012 [4, 5, 6, 7, 8, 9]
Family expenditure	Total public expenditure for families (family allowances, maternity and parental leave, other cash benefits, day care/home-help services, other benefits in kind) in per cent of GDP per country, 2005. Source: OECD 2012 [4, 5, 6, 7, 8, 9]
Wealth per capita	Per capita wealth per country adjusted for purchasing power parity in 10,000 €, in 2000. Source: Davies et al. 2007 [4, 5, 6, 7, 8, 9]
Poverty rate	Percentage of people below 60 per cent of the median net equivalent income in a country, mid 2000s. Source: OECD 2008 [4, 5, 6, 7, 8, 9]

A4 Contact

Table A4.1 Contact: Countries

	Contact with parents		Contact with children	
	Gross	*Net*	*Gross*	*Net*
Sweden	0.05	0.32***	0.10***	0.36***
Denmark	−0.06	0.15***	0.02	0.19***
Ireland	0.32***	0.72***	0.36***	0.81***
Netherlands	0.01	0.25***	0.12***	0.17***
Belgium	0.29***	0.31***	0.13***	0.14***
France	−0.04	0.37***	−0.03	0.23***
West Germany				
East Germany	0.24***	0.25***	−0.11***	−0.03
Poland	0.02	0.15**	0.08***	0.12***
Czech Republic	−0.07	−0.06	−0.02	−0.10***
Austria	0.25***	0.31***	0.06**	0.04
Switzerland	−0.18***	0.03	−0.13***	−0.08***
Italy	0.84***	0.91***	0.85***	0.91***
Spain	0.72***	0.91***	0.66***	0.77***
Greece	0.68***	0.91***	1.00***	1.10***
n	11,799	11,799	61,264	61,264

Source: SHARE. Ordered probit models, unweighted, no coresidence. Coefficients significant at the * 0.10-, ** 0.05-, *** 0.01-level.

Model statistics for Table A4.2

Variance (full model)		
dyads	$\pi^2/3$	$\pi^2/3$
individuals	7.04	0.00
households	2.29	1.38
countries	0.38	0.15
ICC (empty model)	0.03	0.03
n dyads	11,799	61,264
n individuals	9,553	29,712
n households	8,398	20,375
n countries	15	15

Table A4.2 Explaining contact

	Contact with parents		Contact with children	
	Gross	*Net*	*Gross*	*Net*
	Opportunity Structures			
Education: Lower (ref.)				
Medium	0.32***	0.33***	0.06***	0.03
Higher	0.18**	0.53***	−0.02	0.03
Income	0.30***	0.01	0.07***	0.02
Future inheritance	0.50***	0.52***	0.13***	0.11***
Health	−0.10	−0.08	−0.04***	−0.02
Distance	−1.13***	−1.22***	−0.46***	−0.47***
	Need Structures			
Money transfer	0.41***	0.82***	0.36***	0.34***
Age	0.02**	0.04***	−0.01***	−0.01***
Health parent	−0.23***	−0.26***	0.01	−0.02
	Family Structures			
Daughter-mother (ref.)				
Daughter-father	−0.63***	−0.65***	−0.05***	−0.05***
Son-mother	−1.27***	−1.51***	−0.40***	−0.48***
Son-father	−1.54***	−1.83***	−0.43***	−0.49***
Married (ref.)				
Partner	−0.45***	−0.25	−0.47***	−0.37***
Widowed	0.55***	0.23	−0.12***	−0.06**
Divorced	−0.07	−0.24*	−0.54***	−0.64***
Single	0.65***	0.52***	−0.40***	−0.59***
Partner parent/child	−0.88***	−0.24***	−0.10***	−0.15***
Number of children	−0.15***	−0.07**	−0.18***	−0.19***
Grandchild	−0.05	−0.14	−0.11***	−0.04
Number of siblings	−0.35***	−0.27***	0.01***	0.01***
	Cultural-contextual Structures			
Migrant	−1.64***	1.07***	−0.04	0.07**
Social expenditure	0.02*	−0.04***	−0.01	−0.01***
Family expenditure	−0.59***	−0.26***	−0.21***	−0.01***
Wealth per capita	0.03**	0.03***	0.11***	0.02***
Poverty rate	0.21***	0.19***	0.01	0.05***

Source: SHARE. Multilevel ordered probit models, unweighted, no coresidence. Coefficients significant at the * 0.10-, ** 0.05-, *** 0.01-level.

A5 Conflict

Table A5.1 Conflict: Countries

	Contact with parents		Contact with children	
	Gross	*Net*	*Gross*	*Net*
Sweden	−0.64***	−0.59***	−0.51***	−0.45***
Denmark	−0.47***	−0.47***	−0.43***	−0.44***
Ireland	−0.40***	−0.24*	−0.20***	−0.21***
Netherlands	−0.38***	−0.26***	−0.34***	−0.28***
Belgium	−0.17**	−0.12*	−0.21***	−0.17***
France	−0.17**	−0.10	−0.17***	−0.17***
West Germany				
East Germany	−0.04	−0.04	−0.08	−0.07
Poland	−0.71***	−0.69***	−0.52***	−0.52***
Czech Republic	−0.46***	−0.43***	−0.24***	−0.21***
Austria	0.22***	0.30***	0.14***	0.21***
Switzerland	0.13*	0.18**	0.04	0.09**
Italy	−0.01	0.06	0.15***	0.18***
Spain	−0.33***	−0.25***	−0.40***	−0.33***
Greece	−0.07	−0.01	0.07*	0.10**
n	5,468	5,468	19,637	19,637

Source: SHARE. Ordered probit models, unweighted. Coefficients significant at the * 0.10-, ** 0.05-, *** 0.01-level.

Model statistics for Table A5.2

Variance (full model)		
individuals	$\pi^2/3$	$\pi^2/3$
households	0.39	0.83
countries	0.20	0.07
ICC (empty model)	0.03	0.02
n individuals	5,468	19,637
n households	4,871	14,209
n countries	15	15

Table A5.2 Explaining conflict

	Conflict with parents		Conflict with children	
	Gross	Net	Gross	Net
	Opportunity Structures			
Education: Lower (ref.)				
Medium	0.07*	0.07	0.19***	0.07***
Higher	0.08*	0.07	0.29***	0.14***
Income	−0.08**	−0.04	−0.12***	−0.11***
Future inheritance	0.12***	0.10***	0.10***	0.06**
Contact: Day	0.16***	0.09**	0.27***	0.16***
Week (ref.)				
Month	−0.02	0.03	0.01	0.07**
Year	0.55***	0.61***	0.33***	0.38***
	Need Structures			
Money transfer	−0.03	−0.07	0.25***	0.12***
Age	−0.02***	−0.01***	−0.03***	−0.03***
Health	0.23***	0.26***	−0.05**	0.08***
Time transfer	0.10***	0.11***	0.04	0.03
	Family Structures			
Woman	0.07**	0.08**	0.02	0.02
Married (ref.)				
Partner	0.03	−0.01	0.05	−0.06
Widowed	0.06	0.01	−0.36***	−0.06*
Divorced	0.20***	0.11*	0.15***	0.06
Single	0.38***	0.22**	0.38***	0.24*
Number of children	−0.04***	−0.01	0.02***	0.06***
Grandchild	−0.17***	−0.12***	−0.46***	−0.23***
Number of siblings	−0.05***	−0.04***	0.01*	−0.01*
	Cultural-contextual Structures			
Migrant	−0.09	−0.09	0.18***	0.15***
Social expenditure	0.01	−0.03***	0.01***	0.02***
Family expenditure	−0.11***	−0.14***	−0.19***	−0.05***
Wealth per capita	−0.01	0.05***	0.06***	0.04***
Poverty rate	0.02***	0.03***	0.02***	0.02***

Source: SHARE. Multilevel ordered probit models, unweighted. Coefficients significant at the * 0.10-, ** 0.05-, *** 0.01-level.

A6 Space

Table A6.1 Space: Countries

	Coresidence		Near coresidence	
	Gross	*Net*	*Gross*	*Net*
Sweden	0.34***	0.30***	0.04***	0.04***
Denmark	0.33***	0.30***	0.06***	0.06***
Ireland	1.45***	1.02	0.03***	0.04***
Netherlands	0.82***	0.70***	0.05***	0.05***
Belgium	1.17***	1.81***	0.12***	0.12***
France	1.03	1.00	0.13***	0.12***
West Germany				
East Germany	0.53***	0.68***	0.84	0.78**
Poland	2.73***	10.72***	1.06	0.84**
Czech Republic	1.27***	3.06***	0.91	0.67***
Austria	0.84**	1.32***	1.22**	1.10
Switzerland	1.07	0.77***	0.37***	0.37***
Italy	3.66***	5.99***	1.13	0.88
Spain	2.94***	4.78***	0.43***	0.38***
Greece	4.02***	4.85***	1.77***	1.26***
n	74,372	74,372	74,372	74,372

Source: SHARE. Multinomial logistic regressions, unweighted, odds ratios. Parent (respondents)-adult child dyads. Coefficients significant at the * 0.10-, ** 0.05-, *** 0.01-level.

Model statistics for Table A6.2

Variance (full model)		
dyads	$\pi^2/3$	$\pi^2/3$
individuals	0.00	0.00
households	4.71	4.71
countries	0.95	0.95
ICC (empty model)	0.12	0.12
n dyads	74,372	74,372
n individuals	33,558	33,558
n households	23,419	23,419
n countries	15	15

Table A6.2 Explaining space

	Coresidence		Near coresidence	
	Gross	Net	Gross	Net
Opportunity Structures				
Education: Lower (ref.)				
Medium	1.67***	0.60***	1.22***	0.88**
Higher	2.11***	0.43***	0.79***	0.57***
Income	0.80***	0.74***	0.79***	1.04
Number of rooms	1.45***	1.31***	0.91***	0.90***
Need Structures				
Child: Education (ref.)				
Full-time	0.03***	0.32***	0.31***	0.57***
Part-time	0.03***	0.48***	0.23***	0.58***
Unemployed	0.16***	0.85*	0.56***	0.76*
Not in workforce	0.03***	0.84**	0.33***	0.80
Age child	0.80***	0.88***	0.93***	0.95***
Health	0.62***	1.38***	1.15***	1.18***
Family Structures				
Mother-daughter (ref.)				
Father-daughter	1.15***	0.84***	0.89*	0.94
Mother-son	1.95***	1.78***	1.48***	1.43***
Father-son	2.24***	1.53***	1.34***	1.36***
Child: Single (ref.)				
Divorced	0.03***	0.15***	0.28***	0.33***
Widowed	0.01***	0.11***	0.19***	0.25***
Partner	0.02***	0.02***	0.15***	0.16***
Married	0.01***	0.02***	0.14***	0.15***
Number of children	0.76***	0.82***	0.70***	0.76***
Grandchild	0.02***	0.66***	0.40***	1.41***
Cultural-contextual Structures				
Migrant	1.28***	1.34***	1.24**	1.35***
Social expenditure	0.91***	0.97***	0.92***	1.05***
Family expenditure	0.39***	0.35***	0.35***	0.50***
Wealth per capita	0.88***	0.83***	0.81***	0.88***
Poverty rate	1.18***	1.30***	1.14***	1.18***

Source: SHARE. Multilevel multinomial logistic regressions, unweighted, odds ratios. Parent (respondents)-adult child dyads. Coefficients significant at the * 0.10-, ** 0.05-, *** 0.01-level.

A7 Money

Table A7.1 Money: Countries

	At least 250 €		At least 2,000 €	
	Gross	*Net*	*Gross*	*Net*
Sweden	1.29***	1.48***	0.56***	0.64***
Denmark	1.15***	1.02	1.14	0.94
Ireland	0.55***	0.58***	0.88	0.85
Netherlands	0.77***	0.77***	0.69***	0.66***
Belgium	0.75***	0.93	0.73***	0.90
France	0.78***	1.08	0.81***	1.09
West Germany				
East Germany	1.21**	1.15	1.14	1.01
Poland	0.41***	0.95	0.09***	0.26***
Czech Republic	0.61***	1.11	0.13***	0.30***
Austria	0.85***	1.08	0.62***	0.80*
Switzerland	0.65***	0.62***	0.75**	0.68***
Italy	0.58***	1.15**	0.62***	1.37***
Spain	0.19***	0.38***	0.21***	0.46***
Greece	0.84***	1.40***	1.04	1.66***
n	59,623	59,623	53,231	53,231

Source: SHARE. Logistic regressions, unweighted, odds ratios. Parent (respondents)-adult child dyads, no coresidence. Coefficients significant at the * 0.10-, ** 0.05-, *** 0.01-level.

Model statistics for Table A7.2

Variance (full model)		
dyads	$\pi^2/3$	$\pi^2/3$
individuals	0.00	0.00
households	15.19	19.71
countries	0.34	0.73
ICC (empty model)	0.12	0.09
n dyads	59,623	53,231
n individuals	29,074	26,603
n households	19,926	18,336
n countries	15	15

Table A7.2 Explaining money

	At least 250 €		At least 2,000 €	
	Gross	*Net*	*Gross*	*Net*
	Opportunity Structures			
Education: Lower (ref.)				
Medium	2.59***	1.47***	2.73***	1.68***
Higher	5.67***	2.63***	6.95***	3.88***
Income	10.83***	4.90***	4.20***	3.87***
Money in bank	1.03***	1.02***	1.06***	1.04***
Contact: Day	1.01	1.08	1.20*	1.22
Week (ref.)				
Month	0.65***	0.73***	0.54***	0.70***
Year	0.30***	0.40***	0.22***	0.32***
	Need Structures			
Child: Education (ref.)				
Full-time	0.07***	0.17***	0.01***	0.05***
Part-time	0.11***	0.27***	0.01***	0.06***
Unemployed	0.23***	0.56***	0.02***	0.22***
Not in workforce	0.07***	0.25***	0.01***	0.05***
Age child	0.87***	0.91***	0.86***	0.92***
Time transfer	1.21**	1.87***	1.01	1.23
	Family Structures			
Mother-daughter (ref.)				
Father-daughter	1.29***	1.01	1.26**	1.09
Mother-son	0.75***	0.83***	0.85	0.99
Father-son	0.91	0.78***	0.87	0.90
Partner	4.02***	1.47***	4.83***	1.15
Partner child	0.33***	0.54***	0.38***	0.58***
Number of children	0.51***	0.54***	0.38***	0.54***
Grandchild	0.09***	0.75***	0.08***	0.44***
	Cultural-contextual Structures			
Migrant	0.86	1.10	0.80	0.82
Social expenditure	1.09***	1.04***	1.19***	0.92***
Family expenditure	5.66***	1.51***	0.18***	0.94
Wealth per capita	0.83***	1.02	1.27***	1.15***
Poverty rate	0.65***	1.03	0.70***	0.90***

Source: SHARE. Multilevel logistic regressions, unweighted, odds ratios. Parent (respondents)-adult child dyads, no coresidence. Coefficients significant at the * 0.10-, ** 0.05-, *** 0.01-level.

A8 Time

Table A8.1 Time: Countries

	Help		Care	
	Gross	*Net*	*Gross*	*Net*
Sweden	1.44***	1.79***	0.85	0.90
Denmark	1.52***	1.66***	0.79	0.81
Ireland	0.75	1.05	2.10***	2.26***
Netherlands	1.18	1.47***	1.24	1.43*
Belgium	1.27**	1.25**	0.97	1.11
France	0.75***	1.14	0.62**	0.83
West Germany				
East Germany	0.87	0.90	1.26	0.99
Poland	0.37***	0.51***	0.93	0.76
Czech Republic	0.69***	0.81	1.34	1.32
Austria	0.58***	0.64***	1.44	1.62*
Switzerland	0.97	1.14	0.69	0.70
Italy	0.42***	0.41***	1.91***	1.56**
Spain	0.33***	0.35***	1.35	1.48*
Greece	0.45***	0.49***	1.05	1.19
n	11,085	11,085	11,633	11,633

Source: SHARE. Logistic regressions, unweighted, odds ratios. Adult child (respondents)-parent dyads, no coresidence. Coefficients significant at the * 0.10-, ** 0.05-, *** 0.01-level.

Model statistics for Table A8.2

Variance (full model)		
dyads	$\pi^2/3$	$\pi^2/3$
individuals	1.44	5.52
households	3.64	2.88
countries	0.29	0.08
ICC (empty model)	0.04	0.02
n dyads	11,085	11,633
n individuals	8,971	9,425
n households	7,929	8,299
n countries	15	15

Table A8.2 Explaining time

	Help		Care	
	Gross	*Net*	*Gross*	*Net*
	Opportunity Structures			
Education: Lower (ref.)				
Medium	1.55***	1.31***	1.62**	1.91***
Higher	1.95***	1.81***	1.45*	2.23***
Income	2.19***	1.73***	0.98	0.93
Future inheritance	2.96***	2.33***	1.54**	1.51***
Health	0.58***	0.68***	1.54**	0.93
Distance	0.55***	0.55***	0.52***	0.55***
	Need Structures			
Money transfer	2.86***	2.27***	2.41**	2.21**
Age parent	1.02***	1.02***	1.18***	1.18***
Health parent	1.16*	1.43***	7.08***	6.06***
	Family Structures			
Daughter-mother (ref.)				
Daughter-father	0.91	0.87	0.48***	0.45***
Son-mother	0.64***	0.53***	0.10***	0.09***
Son-father	0.55***	0.42***	0.08***	0.07***
Married (ref.)				
Partner	0.76	0.96	1.18	1.75
Widowed	1.24	1.22	1.85	0.87
Divorced	1.05	1.01	1.27	0.93
Single	1.70***	1.21	2.57**	1.77
Partner parent	0.89	0.82**	0.29***	0.52***
Number of children	0.81***	0.91**	0.82***	0.90
Grandchild	0.64***	0.70***	1.21	0.74*
Number of siblings	0.76***	0.85***	0.85***	0.95
	Cultural-contextual Structures			
Migrant	0.19***	0.63**	0.27***	0.74
Social expenditure	1.09***	1.08**	0.93**	0.94**
Family expenditure	2.17***	2.22***	0.75	0.83
Wealth per capita	1.06	1.04	1.02	1.04
Poverty rate	0.81***	0.80***	1.09**	1.06

Source: SHARE. Multilevel logistic regressions, unweighted, odds ratios. Adult child (respondents)-parent dyads, no coresidence. Coefficients significant at the * 0.10-, ** 0.05-, *** 0.01-level.

A9 Inheritance

Table A9.1 Inheritance: Countries

	Previous inheritance		Future inheritance	
	Gross	*Net*	*Gross*	*Net*
Sweden	1.42***	1.70***	1.82***	2.20***
Denmark	1.62***	1.49***	1.75***	1.64***
Ireland	0.39***	0.39***	0.72***	1.08
Netherlands	0.78***	0.91	1.37***	1.65***
Belgium	1.58***	1.94***	1.75***	2.25***
France	0.79***	1.07	1.32***	1.49***
West Germany				
East Germany	0.40***	0.37***	0.72**	0.71**
Poland	0.21***	0.30***	0.27***	0.38***
Czech Republic	0.32***	0.39***	0.34***	0.42***
Austria	0.43***	0.42***	0.43***	0.55***
Switzerland	1.62***	2.07***	1.52***	1.75***
Italy	0.49***	0.76***	0.67***	0.98
Spain	0.50***	0.81**	0.74***	1.34***
Greece	0.69***	0.99	0.66***	0.71***
n	35,720	35,720	36,834	36,834

Source: SHARE. Logistic regressions, unweighted, odds ratios. Coefficients significant at the * 0.10-, ** 0.05-, *** 0.01-level.

Model statistics for Table A9.2

Variance (full model)		
individuals	$\pi^2/3$	$\pi^2/3$
households	0.15	3.58
countries	0.13	0.29
ICC (empty model)	0.03	0.06
n individuals	35,720	36,834
n households	25,787	26,474
n countries	15	15

Table A9.2 Explaining inheritance

	Previous inheritance		Future inheritance	
	Gross	Net	Gross	Net
	Opportunity Structures			
Education: Lower (ref.)				
Medium	1.71***	1.50***	3.70***	1.53***
Higher	2.67***	2.28***	6.65***	2.38***
Income	1.74***	1.64***	2.25***	1.59***
Previous inheritance	/	/	1.84***	1.54***
Mother alive	0.71***	0.45***	0.48***	0.60***
Father alive	0.77***	0.48***	0.66***	0.80***
Parents deceased (ref.)			0.02***	0.04***
Parents alive (ref.)	/	/		
	Need Structures			
Property	/	/	2.75***	1.40***
Age	0.98***	0.96***	0.84***	0.93***
Time transfer	/	/	3.67***	1.64***
	Family Structures			
Woman	0.88***	0.96	0.98	0.93
Married (ref.)				
Partner	0.89	0.82***	1.43***	1.09
Widowed	0.68***	1.01	0.10***	0.72***
Divorced	1.27***	1.36***	0.99	0.95
Single	1.90***	1.91***	0.84	1.17
Child	0.76***	1.02	1.13	1.06
No sibling (ref.)				
1 sibling	1.10**	0.88	1.78***	1.00
2 siblings	0.99	0.86**	1.82***	0.93
3+ siblings	0.68***	0.60***	1.25***	0.69***
	Cultural-contextual Structures			
Migrant	0.45***	0.46***	0.60***	0.63***
Social expenditure	1.08***	1.07***	1.06***	1.10***
Family expenditure	1.40***	1.38***	1.60***	1.15***
Wealth per capita	1.01*	1.10***	1.20***	1.19***
Poverty rate	0.92***	0.92***	0.87***	0.89***

Source: SHARE. Multilevel logistic regressions, unweighted, odds ratios. Coefficients significant at the * 0.10-, ** 0.05-, *** 0.01-level.

References

Aassve, Arnstein, Francesco C. Billari, Stefano Mazzuco, Fausta Ongaro 2002: Leaving Home: A Comparative Analysis of ECHP Data. In: Journal of European Social Policy, 12, 4: 259–275.

Abrahamson, Peter, Thomas P. Boje, Bent Greve 2005: Welfare and Families in Europe. Aldershot, Burlington: Ashgate.

Ahrons, Constance R., Jennifer L. Tanner 2003: Adult Children and Their Fathers: Relationship Changes 20 Years after Parental Divorce. In: Family Relations, 52, 4: 340–351.

Alber, Jens, Ulrich Köhler (eds.) 2004: Health and Care in an Enlarged Europe. Luxembourg: Office for Official Publications of the European Communities.

Albert, Isabelle, Dieter Ferring (eds.) 2013: Intergenerational Relations – European Perspectives on Family and Society. Bristol, Chicago: Policy Press.

Albertini, Marco, Martin Kohli, Claudia Vogel 2007: Intergenerational Transfers of Time and Money in European Families: Common Patterns – Different Regimes? In: Journal of European Social Policy, 17, 4: 319–334.

Albertini, Marco, Jonas Radl 2012: Intergenerational Transfers and Social Class: Inter-vivos Transfers as Means of Status Reproduction? In: Acta Sociologica, 55, 2: 107–123.

Alt, Christian 1994: Reziprozität von Eltern-Kind-Beziehungen in Mehrgenera-tionennetzwerken. In: Bien, Walter (ed.), Eigeninteresse oder Solidarität – Beziehungen in modernen Mehrgenerationenfamilien. Opladen: Leske + Budrich, 197–222.

Angelini, Viola, Anne Laferrère 2013: Parental Altruism and Nest Leaving in Europe: Evidence from a Retrospective Survey. In: Review of Economics of the Household, 11, 3: 393–420.

Angelone, Domenico, Erich Ramseier 2012: Die Kluft öffnet sich. Herkunftseffekte auf die schulischen Leistungen verstärken sich im Verlauf der Primarschule. In: Swiss Journal of Sociology, 38, 2: 223–244.

Antonucci, Toni C., James S. Jackson, Simon Biggs 2007: Intergenerational Relations: Theory, Research, and Policy. In: Journal of Social Issues, 63, 4: 679–693.

Anttonen, Anneli, Jorma Sipilä 1996: European Social Care Services: Is It Possible to Identify Models? In: Journal of European Social Policy, 6, 2: 87–100.

Aquilino, William S. 1990: The Likelihood of Parent–Adult Child Coresidence: Effects of Family Structure and Parental Characteristics. In: Journal of Marriage and the Family, 52, 2: 405–419.

Aquilino, William S. 1994a: Impact of Childhood Family Disruption on Young Adults' Relationships with Parents. In: Journal of Marriage and the Family, 56, 2: 295–313.

Aquilino, William S. 1994b: Later Life Parental Divorce and Widowhood: Impact on Young Adults' Assessment of Parent-Child Relations. In: Journal of Marriage and the Family, 56, 4: 908–922.

Arber, Sara, Claudine Attias-Donfut (eds.) 2000: The Myth of Generational Conflict – The Family and State in Ageing Societies. London, New York: Routledge.

Archer, John 1999: The Nature of Grief – The Evolution and Psychology of Reactions to Loss. London, New York: Routledge.

Ariès, Philippe 1977: L'homme devant la mort. Paris: Éditions du Seuil.

Armingeon, Klaus 2001: Institutionalising the Swiss Welfare State. In: Lane, Jan-Erik (ed.), The Swiss Labyrinth – Institutions, Outcomes and Redesign. London, Portland: Frank Cass, 145–168.

Armingeon, Klaus, Fabio Bertozzi, Guiliano Bonoli 2004: Swiss Worlds of Welfare. In: West European Politics, 27, 1: 20–44.

Arts, Wil, John Gelissen 2002: Three Worlds of Welfare Capitalism or More? A State-of-the-Art Report. In: Journal of European Social Policy, 12, 2: 137–158.

Attias-Donfut, Claudine 1995: Le double circuit des transmissions. In: Attias-Donfut, Claudine, Alain Rozenkier (eds.), Les solidarités entre générations – Vieillesse, familles, État. Paris: Nathan, 41–81.

Attias-Donfut, Claudine, François-Charles Wolff 2000: The Redistributive Effects of Generational Transfers. In: Arber/Attias-Donfut, 22–46.

Attias-Donfut, Claudine, Jim Ogg, François-Charles Wolff 2005: European Patterns of Intergenerational Financial and Time Transfers. In: European Journal of Ageing, 2, 3: 161–173.

Bäckman, Olof, Anders Nilsson 2011: Pathways to Social Exclusion – A Life-Course Study. In: European Sociological Review, 27, 1: 107–123.

Bahle, Thomas 2008: Family Policy Patterns in the Enlarged EU. In: Alber, Jens, Tony Fahey, Chiara Saraceno (eds.), Handbook of Quality of Life in the Enlarged European Union. London, New York: Routledge, 100–125.

Bambra, Clare 2007: Going Beyond the Three Worlds of Welfare Capitalism: Regime Theory and Public Health Research. In: Journal of Epidemiology and Community Health, 61, 12: 1098–1102.

Barnett, Amanda E. 2013: Pathways of Adult Children Providing Care to Older Parents. In: Journal of Marriage and Family, 75, 1: 178–190.

Bawin-Legros, Bernadette, Jean-Francois Stassen 2002: Intergenerational Solidarity: Between the Family and the State. In: Current Sociology, 50, 2: 243–262.

Becker, Rolf, Wolfgang Lauterbach (eds.) 2010: Bildung als Privileg – Erklärungen und Befunde zu den Ursachen der Bildungsungleichheit. Fourth revised edition. Wiesbaden: VS Verlag für Sozialwissenschaften.

Beckert, Jens 2008: Inherited Wealth. Princeton: Princeton University Press.

Behning, Ute 2005: Changing Long-Term Care Regimes: A Six-Country Comparison of Directions and Effects. In: Pfau-Effinger/Geissler, 73–91.

Bengtson, Vern L., Joseph A. Kuypers 1971: Generational Difference and the Developmental Stake. In: Aging and Human Development, 2, 4: 249–260.

Bengtson, Vern L., Robert E. L. Roberts 1991: Intergenerational Solidarity in Aging Families: An Example of Formal Theory Construction. In: Journal of Marriage and the Family, 53, 4: 856–870.

Bengtson, Vern L. 1993: Is the 'Contract Across Generations' Changing? Effects of Population Aging on Obligations and Expectations Across Age Groups. In: Bengtson,

Vern L., W. Andrew Achenbaum (eds.), The Changing Contract Across Generations. New York: Aldine de Gruyter, 3–24.

Bengtson, Vern L. 2001: Beyond the Nuclear Family: The Increasing Importance of Multigenerational Bonds. In: Journal of Marriage and Family, 63, 1: 1–16.

Bengtson, Vern L., Roseann Giarrusso, J. Beth Mabry, Merril Silverstein 2002: Solidarity, Conflict, and Ambivalence: Complementary or Competing Perspectives on Intergenerational Relationships? In: Journal of Marriage and Family, 64, 3: 568–576.

Bernheim, B. Douglas, Andrei Shleifer, Lawrence H. Summers 1985: The Strategic Bequest Motive. In: Journal of Political Economy, 93, 6: 1045–1076.

Bernheim, B. Douglas, Sergei Severinov 2003: Bequests as Signals: An Explanation for the Equal Division Puzzle. In: Journal of Political Economy, 111, 4: 733–764.

Berry, Brent 2008: Financial Transfers from Living Parents to Adult Children – Who Is Helped and Why? In: American Journal of Economics and Sociology, 67, 2: 207–239.

Bertogg, Ariane, Marc Szydlik 2016: The Closeness of Young Adults' Relationships with Their Parents. In: Swiss Journal of Sociology, 42, 1: 41–59.

Bertogg, Ariane 2016: Zwischen Autonomie und Verbundenheit: Junge Erwachsene und ihre Eltern. University of Zurich: Dissertation thesis.

Bertram, Hans 2000: Die verborgenen familiären Beziehungen in Deutschland: Die multilokale Mehrgenerationenfamilie. In: Kohli, Martin, Marc Szydlik (eds.), Generationen in Familie und Gesellschaft. Opladen: Leske + Budrich, 97–121.

Billari, Francesco C., Dimiter Philipov, Pau Baizán 2001: Leaving Home in Europe: The Experience of Cohorts Born Around 1960. In: International Journal of Population Geography, 7, 5: 339–356.

Billari, Francesco C., Aart C. Liefbroer 2007: Should I Stay or Should I Go? The Impact of Age Norms on Leaving Home. In: Demography, 44, 1: 181–198.

Blanc, David le, François-Charles Wolff 2006: Leaving Home in Europe: The Role of Parents' and Children's Incomes. In: Review of Economics of the Household, 4, 1: 53–73.

Blau, Peter M. 1964: Exchange and Power in Social Life. New York: Wiley.

Blome, Agnes, Wolfgang Keck, Jens Alber 2009: Family and the Welfare State in Europe – Intergenerational Relations in Ageing Societies. Cheltenham, Northampton: Edward Elgar.

Blossfeld, Hans-Peter 2009: Educational Assortative Marriage in Comparative Perspective. In: Annual Review of Sociology, 35: 513–530.

BMFSFJ 2006: Familie zwischen Flexibilität und Verlässlichkeit – Perspektiven für eine lebenslaufbezogene Familienpolitik (Siebter Familienbericht). Berlin: Deutscher Bundestag und Bundesministerium für Familie, Senioren, Frauen und Jugend (written by Jutta Allmendinger, Hans Bertram, Wassilios E. Fthenakis, Helga Krüger, Uta Meier-Gräwe, C. Katharina Spieß and Marc Szydlik).

Bonoli, Giuliano 1997: Classifying Welfare States: A Two-Dimension Approach. In: Journal of Social Policy, 26, 3: 351–372.

Bonoli, Giuliano, Silja Häusermann 2011: Swiss Welfare Reforms in a Comparative European Perspective – Between Retrenchment and Activation. In: Trampusch/Mach, 186–204.

Bordone, Valeria 2009: Contact and Proximity of Older People to Their Adult Children: A Comparison Between Italy and Sweden. In: Population, Space and Place, 15, 4: 359–380.

Börsch-Supan, Axel, Hendrik Jürges (eds.) 2005a: Health, Ageing and Retirement in Europe – Methodology. Mannheim: Mannheim Research Institute for the Economics of Ageing.

Börsch-Supan, Axel, Karsten Hank, Hendrik Jürges 2005b: A New Comprehensive and International View on Ageing: The Survey of Health, Ageing and Retirement in Europe. Mannheim: University of Mannheim.

Boudon, Raymond 1974: Education, Opportunity and Social Inequality – Changing Prospects in Western Society. New York: Wiley.

Bourdieu, Pierre, Jean-Claude Passeron 1971: Die Illusion der Chancengleichheit – Untersuchungen zur Soziologie des Bildungswesens am Beispiel Frankreichs. Stuttgart: Klett.

Bourdieu, Pierre 1979: La Distinction – Critique sociale du jugement. Paris: Les Éditions de Minuit.

Braiker, Harriet B., Harold H. Kelley 1979: Conflict in the Development of Close Relationships. In: Burgess, Robert L., Ted L. Huston (eds.), Social Exchange in Developing Relationships. New York: Academic Press, 135–168.

Brandt, Martina, Marc Szydlik 2008: Soziale Dienste und Hilfe zwischen Generationen in Europa. In: Zeitschrift für Soziologie, 37, 2: 301–320.

Brandt, Martina 2009: Hilfe zwischen Generationen – Ein europäischer Vergleich. Wiesbaden: VS Verlag für Sozialwissenschaften.

Brandt, Martina, Klaus Haberkern, Marc Szydlik 2009: Intergenerational Help and Care in Europe. In: European Sociological Review, 25, 5: 585–601.

Brandt, Martina, Christian Deindl 2013: Intergenerational Transfers to Adult Children in Europe: Do Social Policies Matter? In: Journal of Marriage and Family, 75, 1: 235–251.

Buchmann, Marlis, Irene Kriesi 2010: Schuleintritt und Schulleistungen im mittleren Primarschulalter. In: Swiss Journal of Sociology, 36, 2: 325–344.

Buchmann, Marlis, Irene Kriesi 2011: Transition to Adulthood in Europe. In: Annual Review of Sociology, 37: 481–503.

Bucx, Freek, Frits van Wel, Trudie Knijn, Louk Hagendoorn 2008: Intergenerational Contact and the Life Course Status of Young Adult Children. In: Journal of Marriage and Family, 70, 1: 144–156.

Buhl, Heike M. 2009: My Mother: My Best Friend? Adults' Relationships with Significant Others Across the Lifespan. In: Journal of Adult Development, 16, 4: 239–249.

Bühlmann, Felix, Céline Schmid Botkine, Peter Farago, François Höpflinger, Dominique Joye, René Levy, Pasqualina Perrig-Chielio, Christian Suter (eds.) 2012: Sozialbericht 2012: Fokus Generationen. Zürich: Seismo.

Canary, Daniel J., William R. Cupach, Susan J. Messman 1995: Relationship Conflict –Conflict in Parent-Child, Friendship, and Romantic Relationships. Thousand Oaks et al.: Sage.

Castles, Francis G. (ed.) 1993: Families of Nations – Patterns of Public Policy in Western Democracies. Aldershot et al.: Dartmouth.

Castles, Francis G. 1995: Welfare State Development in Southern Europe. In: West European Politics, 18, 2: 291–313.

Cerami Alfio 2006: Social Policy in Central and Eastern Europe – The Emergence of a New European Welfare Regime. Berlin: LIT.

Cheal, David 1987: 'Showing Them You Love Them': Gift Giving and the Dialect of Intimacy. In: The Sociological Review, 35, 1: 150–169.

Choi, Namkee G. 2003: Coresidence Between Unmarried Aging Parents and Their Adult Children – Who Moved in with Whom and Why? In: Research on Aging, 25, 4: 384–404.

Clarke, Edward J., Mar Preston, Jo Raksin, Vern L. Bengtson 1999: Types of Conflicts and Tensions Between Older Parents and Adult Children. In: The Gerontologist, 39, 3: 261–270.

Collins, Randall 1975: Conflict Sociology – Toward an Explanatory Science. New York: Academic Press.

Colombo, Francesca, Ana Llena-Nozal, Jérôme Mercier, Frits Tjadens 2011: Help Wanted? Providing and Paying for Long-Term Care. Paris: OECD (http://dx.doi.org/10.1787/9789264097759-en).

Connidis, Ingrid Arnet, Julie Ann McMullin 2002a: Sociological Ambivalence and Family Ties: A Critical Perspective. In: Journal of Marriage and Family, 64, 3: 558–567.

Connidis, Ingrid Arnet, Julie Ann McMullin 2002b: Ambivalence, Family Ties, and Doing Sociology. In: Journal of Marriage and Family, 64, 3: 594–601.

Connidis, Ingrid Arnet 2015: Exploring Ambivalence in Family Ties: Progress and Prospects. In: Journal of Marriage and Family, 77, 1: 77–95.

Cordón, Juan Antonio Fernández 1997: Youth Residential Independence and Autonomy. In: Journal of Family Issues, 18, 6: 576–607.

Coser, Rose Laub 1966: Role Distance, Sociological Ambivalence, and Transitional Status Systems. In: American Journal of Sociology, 72, 2: 173–187.

Cox, Donald 1987: Motives for Private Income Transfers. In: Journal of Political Economy, 95, 3: 508–546.

Cox, Donald, Oded Stark 2005: On the Demand for Grandchildren: Tied Transfers and the Demonstration Effect. In: Journal of Public Economics, 89, 9–10: 1665–1697.

Curran, Sara R. 2002: Agency, Accountability, and Embedded Relations: 'What's Love Got to Do with It?' In: Journal of Marriage and Family, 64, 3: 577–584.

Daatland, Svein O. 2001: Ageing, Families and Welfare Systems: Comparative Perspectives. In: Zeitschrift für Gerontologie und Geriatrie, 34, 1: 16–20.

Daatland, Svein Olav, Katharina Herlofson 2003a: Norms and Ideals about Elder Care. In: Lowenstein/Ogg, 125–163.

Daatland, Svein Olav, Katharina Herlofson 2003b: Families and Welfare States: Substitution or Complementarity. In: Lowenstein/Ogg, 281–305.

Daatland, Svein O., Ariela Lowenstein 2005: Intergenerational Solidarity and the Family-Welfare State Balance. In: European Journal of Ageing, 2, 3: 174–182.

Davies, James B., Susanna Sandström, Anthony Shorrocks, Edward N. Wolff 2007: Estimating the Level and Distribution of Global Household Wealth. United Nations University, World Institute for Development Economics Research (UNU-WIDER). Research Paper 2007/77.

De Graaf, Paul M., Tineke Fokkema 2007: Contacts Between Divorced and Non-Divorced Parents and Their Adult Children in the Netherlands: An Investment Perspective. In: European Sociological Review, 23, 2: 263–277.

Deindl, Christian 2010: Finanzielle Leistungen zwischen betagten Eltern und ihren Kindern im europäischen Vergleich. In: Ette et al., 283–300.

Deindl, Christian 2011: Finanzielle Transfers zwischen Generationen in Europa. Wiesbaden: VS Verlag für Sozialwissenschaften.

Deindl, Christian, Martina Brandt 2011: Financial Support and Practical Help Between Older Parents and Their Middle-Aged Children in Europe. In: Ageing & Society, 31, 4: 645–662.

DeWit, David J., B. Gail Frankel 1988: Geographic Distance and Intergenerational Contact: A Critical Assessment and Review of the Literature. In: Journal of Aging Studies, 2, 1: 25–43.

DiMaggio, Paul, Eszter Hargittai, W. Russell Neuman, John P. Robinson 2001: Social Implications of the Internet. In: Annual Review of Sociology, 27: 307–336.

Dykstra, Pearl A., Tineke Fokkema 2011: Relationships Between Parents and Their Adult Children: A West European Typology of Late-Life Families. In: Ageing & Society, 31, 4: 545–569.

Easterlin, Richard A. 1980: Birth and Fortune – The Impact of Numbers on Personal Welfare. New York: Basic Books.

Elmelech, Yuval 2005: Attitudes Toward Familial Obligation in the United States and in Japan. In: Sociological Inquiry, 75, 4: 497–526.

Emery, Thomas 2013: Intergenerational Transfers and European Families: Does the Number of Siblings Matter? In: Demographic Research, 29, 10: 247–274.

Engstler, Heribert, Oliver Huxhold 2010: Beeinflusst die Beziehung älterer Menschen zu ihren erwachsenen Kindern die räumliche Nähe zwischen den Generationen? Wechselbeziehungen zwischen Wohnentfernung, Kontakthäufigkeit und Beziehungsenge im Längsschnitt. In: Ette et al., 175–197.

Ermisch, John, Markus Jäntti, Timothy Smeeding (eds.) 2012: From Parents to Children – The Intergenerational Transmission of Advantage. New York: Russell Sage Foundation.

Esping-Andersen, Gøsta 1990: The Three Worlds of Welfare Capitalism. Cambridge: Polity Press.

Esping-Andersen, Gøsta 1999: Social Foundations of Postindustrial Economies. Oxford: Oxford University Press.

Ette, Andreas, Kerstin Ruckdeschel, Rainer Unger (eds.) 2010: Potenziale intergenerationaler Beziehungen – Chancen und Herausforderungen für die Gestaltung des demografischen Wandels. Würzburg: Ergon.

Fenger, H.J.M. 2007: Welfare Regimes in Central and Eastern Europe: Incorporating Post-Communist Countries in a Welfare Regime Typology. In: Contemporary Issues and Ideas in Social Sciences, 3, 2: 1–30.

Ferge, Zsuzsa 2008: Is There a Specific East-Central European Welfare Culture? In: Oorschot et al., 141–161.

Ferrera, Maurizio 1996: The 'Southern Model' of Welfare in Social Europe. In: Journal of European Social Policy, 6, 1: 17–37.

Ferrera, Maurizio 1998: The Four 'Social Europes': Between Universalism and Selectivism. In: Rhodes, Martin, Yves Mény (eds.), The Future of European Welfare – A New Social Contract? London: Macmillan, 81–96.

Ferring, Dieter, Tom Michels, Thomas Boll, Sigrun-Heide Filipp 2009: Emotional Relationship Quality of Adult Children with Ageing Parents: On Solidarity, Conflict and Ambivalence. In: European Journal of Ageing, 6, 4: 253–265.

Ferring, Dieter 2010: Intergenerational Relations in Aging Societies: Emerging Topics in Europe. In: Journal of Intergenerational Relationships, 8, 1: 101–104.

Finch, Janet, Jennifer Mason 1990: Filial Obligations and Kin Support for Elderly People. In: Ageing & Society, 10, 2: 151–175.

Fingerman, Karen L. 2000: 'We Had a Nice Little Chat': Age and Generational Differences in Mothers' and Daughters' Descriptions of Enjoyable Visits. In: Journal of Gerontology: Psychological Sciences, 55B, 2: 95–106.

Fingerman, Karen L., Lindsay Pitzer, Eva S. Lefkowitz, Kira S. Birditt, Daniel Mroczek 2008: Ambivalent Relationship Qualities Between Adults and Their Parents: Implications for the Well-Being of Both Parties. In: Journal of Gerontology: Psychological Sciences, 63B, 6: 362–371.

Fingerman, Karen L., Kyungmin Kim, Eden M. Davis, Frank F. Furstenberg Jr., Kira S. Birditt, Steven H. Zarit 2015: 'I'll Give You the World': Socioeconomic Differences in Parental Support of Adult Children. In: Journal of Marriage and Family, 77, 4: 844–865.

Finley, Nancy J., M. Diane Roberts, Benjamin F. Banahan, III 1988: Motivators and Inhibitors of Attitudes of Filial Obligation Toward Aging Parents. In: The Gerontologist, 28, 1: 73–78.

Flaquer, Lluís 2000: Is There a Southern European Model of Family Policy? In: Pfenning/ Bahle, 15–33.

Foa, Edna B., Uriel G. Foa 1980: Resource Theory – Interpersonal Behavior as Exchange. In: Gergen, Kenneth J., Martin S. Greenberg, Richard H. Willis (eds.), Social Exchange – Advances in Theory and Research. New York, London: Plenum Press, 77–94.

Foa, Uriel G., John Converse, Jr., Kjell Y. Törnblom, Edna B. Foa (eds.) 1993: Resource Theory – Explorations and Applications. San Diego, London: Academic Press.

Fokkema, Tineke, Susan ter Bekke, Pearl A. Dykstra 2008: Solidarity Between Parents and Their Adult Children in Europe. Netherlands Interdisciplinary Demographic Institute (NIDI), Report No. 76. Amsterdam: KNAW.

Frank, Hallie 2007: Young Adults' Relationship with Parents and Siblings: The Role of Marital Status, Conflict and Post-Divorce Predictors. In: Journal of Divorce & Remarriage, 46, 3/4: 105–124.

Frankel, B. Gail, DeWit, David J. 1986: Geographic Distance and Intergenerational Contact: An Empirical Examination of the Relationship. In: Journal of Aging Studies, 3, 2: 139–162.

Fritzell, Johan, Carin Lennartsson 2005: Financial Transfers Between Generations in Sweden. In: Ageing & Society, 25, 3: 397–414.

Gal, John 2010: Is There an Extended Family of Mediterranean Welfare States? In: Journal of European Social Policy, 20, 4: 283–300.

Gans, Daphna, Merril Silverstein 2006: Norms of Filial Responsibility for Aging Parents Across Time and Generations. In: Journal of Marriage and Family, 68, 4: 961–976.

Gapp, Patrizia 2007: Konflikte zwischen den Generationen? Familiäre Beziehungen in Migrantenfamilien. In: Weiss, Hilde (ed.), Leben in zwei Welten – Zur sozialen Integration ausländischer Jugendlicher der zweiten Generation. Wiesbaden: Verlag für Sozialwissenschaften, 131–153.

Giarrusso, Roseann, Michael Stallings, Vern L. Bengtson 1995: The 'Intergenerational Stake' Hypothesis Revisited: Parent-Child Differences in Perceptions of Relationships 20 Years Later. In: Bengtson, Vern L., K. Warner Schaie, Linda M. Burton (eds.), Adult Intergenerational Relations – Effects of Societal Change. New York: Springer, 227–263.

Giarrusso, Roseann, Merril Silverstein, Daphna Gans, Vern L. Bengtson 2005: Ageing Parents and Adult Children: New Perspectives on Intergenerational Relationships. In: Johnson, Malcolm L., Vern L. Bengtson, Peter G. Coleman, Thomas B. L. Kirkwood (eds.), The Cambridge Handbook of Age and Ageing. Cambridge: Cambridge University Press, 413–421.

Goldscheider, Frances K., Julie DaVanzo 1989: Pathways to Independent Living in Early Adulthood: Marriage, Semiautonomy, and Premarital Residential Independence. In: Demography, 26, 4: 597–614.

Greenwell, Lisa, Vern L. Bengtson 1997: Geographic Distance and Contact Between Middle-Aged Children and Their Parents: The Effects of Social Class Over 20 Years. In: Journal of Gerontology: Social Sciences, 52B, 1: 13–26.

Gruber, Siegfried, Patrick Heady 2010: Domestic Help. In: Heady/Kohli, 83–125.

Grundy, Emily, Nicola Shelton 2001: Contact Between Adult Children and Their Parents in Great Britain 1986–99. In: Environment and Planning A, 33, 4: 685–697.

Grundy, Emily, John C. Henretta 2006: Between Elderly Parents and Adult Children: A New Look at the Intergenerational Care Provided by the 'Sandwich Generation'. In: Ageing & Society, 26, 5: 707–722.

Guo, Guang, Hongxin Zhao 2000: Multilevel Modeling for Binary Data. In: Annual Review of Sociology, 26: 441–462.

Haberkern, Klaus, Marc Szydlik 2008: Pflege der Eltern – Ein europäischer Vergleich. In: Kölner Zeitschrift für Soziologie und Sozialpsychologie, 60, 1: 78–101.

Haberkern, Klaus 2009: Pflege in Europa – Familie und Wohlfahrtsstaat. Wiesbaden: VS Verlag für Sozialwissenschaften.

Haberkern, Klaus, Marc Szydlik 2010: State Care Provision, Societal Opinion and Children's Care of Older Parents in 11 European Countries. In: Ageing & Society, 30, 2: 299–323.

Haberkern, Klaus, Tina Schmid, Marc Szydlik 2015: Gender Differences in Intergenerational Care in European Welfare States. In: Ageing & Society, 35, 2: 298–320.

Halbwachs, Maurice 1925: Les cadres sociaux de la mémoire. Paris: Félix Alcan.

Hank, Karsten 2007: Proximity and Contacts Between Older Parents and Their Children: A European Comparison. In: Journal of Marriage and Family, 69, 1: 157–173.

Hareven, Tamara K. 1995: Historical Perspectives on the Family and Aging. In: Blieszner, Rosemary, Victoria Hilkevitch Bedford (eds.), Handbook of Aging and the Family. Westport, London: Greenwood Press, 13–31.

Hartnett, Caroline Sten, Frank F. Furstenberg, Kira S. Birditt, Karen L. Fingerman 2012: Parental Support During Young Adulthood: Why Does Assistance Decline with Age? In: Journal of Family Issues, 34, 7: 975–1007.

Häusermann, Silja 2010: The Politics of Welfare State Reform in Continental Europe – Modernization in Hard Times. Cambridge: Cambridge University Press.

Heady, Patrick, Martin Kohli (eds.) 2010: Family, Kinship and State in Contemporary Europe. Volume 3: Perspectives on Theory and Policy. Frankfurt/Main, New York: Campus.

Henz, Ursula 2010: Parent Care as Unpaid Family Labor: How Do Spouses Share? In: Journal of Marriage and Family, 72, 1: 148–164.

Hocker, Joyce L., William W. Wilmot 2014: Interpersonal Conflict. Ninth edition. New York: McGraw-Hill.

Hoff, Andreas 2007: Patterns of Intergenerational Support in Grandparent-Grandchild and Parent-Child Relationships in Germany. In: Ageing & Society, 27, 5: 643–665.

Hogerbrugge, Martijn J.A., Aafke E. Komter 2012: Solidarity and Ambivalence: Comparing Two Perspectives on Intergenerational Relations Using Longitudinal Panel Data. In: The Journals of Gerontology, Series B: Psychological Sciences and Social Sciences, 67, 3: 372–383.

Holdsworth, Clare 2005: 'When Are the Children Going to Leave Home!': Family Culture and Delayed Transitions in Spain. In: European Societies, 7, 4: 547–566.

Höpflinger, François 1999: Generationenfrage – Konzepte, theoretische Ansätze und Beobachtungen zu Generationenbeziehungen in späteren Lebensphasen. Lausanne: Éditions Réalités sociales.

Höpflinger, François, Valérie Hugentobler 2005: Familiale, ambulante und stationäre Pflege im Alter – Perspektiven für die Schweiz. Bern: Huber.

Howse, Kenneth 2007: Long-Term Care Policy: The Difficulties of Taking a Global View. In: Ageing Horizons, 6: 1–11.

Hox, Joop 1995: Applied Multilevel Analysis. Amsterdam: TT-Publikaties.

Huber, Manfred, Ricardo Rodrigues, Frédérique Hoffmann, Katrin Gasior, Bernd Marin 2009: Facts and Figures on Long-Term Care – Europe and North America. Vienna: European Centre for Social Welfare and Research.

Huinink, Johannes 1995: Warum noch Familie? Zur Attraktivität von Partnerschaft und Elternschaft in unserer Gesellschaft. Frankfurt/Main, New York: Campus.

Igel, Corinne, Martina Brandt, Klaus Haberkern, Marc Szydlik 2009: Specialization Between Family and State – Intergenerational Time Transfers in Western Europe. In: Journal of Comparative Family Studies, 40, 2: 203–226.

Igel, Corinne, Marc Szydlik 2011: Grandchild Care and Welfare State Arrangements in Europe. In: Journal of European Social Policy, 21, 3: 210–224.

Igel, Corinne 2012: Großeltern in Europa – Generationensolidarität im Wohlfahrtsstaat. Wiesbaden: VS Verlag für Sozialwissenschaften.

Imhof, Kurt 2006: Sonderfall Schweiz. In: Swiss Journal of Sociology, 32, 2: 197–223.

Isengard, Bettina, Marc Szydlik 2012: Living Apart (or) Together? Coresidence of Elderly Parents and Their Adult Children in Europe. In: Research on Aging, 34, 4: 449–474.

Isengard, Bettina 2013: 'The Apple Doesn't Live Far from the Tree': Living Distances Between Parents and Their Adult Children in Europe. In: Comparative Population Studies – Zeitschrift für Bevölkerungswissenschaft, 38, 2: 237–262 (German version: 263–290).

Isengard, Bettina 2015: Nähe oder Distanz? Verbundenheit von Familiengenerationen in Europa. University of Zurich: Habilitation thesis.

Kalmijn, Matthijs, Chiara Saraceno 2008: A Comparative Perspective on Intergenerational Support – Responsiveness to Parental Needs in Individualistic and Familialistic Countries. In: European Societies, 10, 3: 479–508.

Kalmijn, Matthijs 2015: How Childhood Circumstances Moderate the Long-Term Impact of Divorce on Father–Child Relationships. In: Journal of Marriage and Family, 77, 4: 921–938.

Kaufmann, Franz-Xaver 2003: Varianten des Wohlfahrtsstaats – Der deutsche Sozialstaat im internationalen Vergleich. Frankfurt/Main: Suhrkamp.

Keck, Wolfgang 2008: The Relationship Between Children and Their Frail Elderly Parents in Different Care Regimes. In: Saraceno, 147–169.

Keister, Lisa A., Stephanie Moller 2000: Wealth Inequality in the United States. In: Annual Review of Sociology, 26: 63–81.

Keister, Lisa A., Hang Young Lee 2014: The One Percent: Top Incomes and Wealth in Sociological Research. In: Social Currents, 1, 1: 13–24.

Kenrick, Douglas T., Vladas Griskevicius, Steven L. Neuberg, Mark Schaller 2010: Renovating the Pyramid of Needs: Contemporary Extensions Built Upon Ancient Foundations. In: Perspectives on Psychological Science, 5, 3: 292–314.

Kiecolt, K. Jill, Rosemary Blieszner, Jyoti Savla 2011: Long-Term Influences of Intergenerational Ambivalence on Midlife Parents' Psychological Well-Being. In: Journal of Marriage and Family, 73, 2: 369–382.

King, Lawrence P., Iván Szelényi 2005: Post-Communist Economic Systems. In: Smelser, Neil J., Richard Swedberg (ed.), The Handbook of Economic Sociology. Second edition. Princeton: Princeton University Press, 205–229.

Klaus, Daniela 2009: Why Do Adult Children Support Their Parents? In: Journal of Comparative Family Studies, 40, 2: 227–241.

Kohli, Martin 1999: Private and Public Transfers Between Generations: Linking the Family and the State. In: European Societies, 1, 1: 81–104.

Kohli, Martin, Harald Künemund, Andreas Motel, Marc Szydlik 2000a: Families Apart? Intergenerational Transfers in East and West Germany. In: Arber/Attias-Donfut, 88–99.

Kohli, Martin, Harald Künemund, Andreas Motel-Klingebiel, Marc Szydlik 2000b: Generationenbeziehungen. In: Kohli, Martin, Harald Künemund (eds.), Die zweite Lebenshälfte – Gesellschaftliche Lage und Partizipation im Spiegel des Alters-Survey. Opladen: Leske + Budrich, 176–211.

Kohli, Martin, Marc Szydlik 2000: Einleitung. In: Kohli, Martin, Marc Szydlik (eds.), Generationen in Familie und Gesellschaft. Opladen: Leske + Budrich, 7–18.

Kohli, Martin 2005: Generational Changes and Generational Equity. In: Johnson, Malcolm L., Vern L. Bengtson, Peter G. Coleman, Thomas B. L. Kirkwood (eds.), The Cambridge Handbook of Age and Ageing. Cambridge: Cambridge University Press, 518–526.

Kollmorgen, Raj 2009: Postsozialistische Wohlfahrtsregime in Europa – Teil der 'Drei Welten' oder eigener Typus? Ein empirisch gestützter Rekonzeptualisierungsversuch. In: Pfau-Effinger, Birgit, Sladana Sakač Magdalenić, Christof Wolf (eds.), International vergleichende Sozialforschung – Ansätze und Messkonzepte unter den Bedingungen der Globalisierung. Wiesbaden: VS Verlag für Sozialwissenschaften, 65–92.

König, Ronny 2015a: Educational Inequality and the Welfare State. In: Journal of Research on Contemporary Society, 1, 1: 1–20.

König, Ronny 2016: Bildung, Schicht und Generationensolidarität in Europa. Wiesbaden: Springer VS.

Korpi, Walter 2000: Faces of Inequality: Gender, Class and Patterns of Inequalities in Different Types of Welfare States. In: Social Politics, 7, 2: 127–191.

Korupp, Sylvia E., Marc Szydlik 2005: Causes and Trends of the Digital Divide. In: European Sociological Review, 21, 4: 409–422.

Kosmann, Marianne 1998: Wie Frauen erben – Geschlechterverhältnis und Erbprozeß. Opladen: Leske + Budrich.

Kotlikoff, Laurence J., Avia Spivak 1981: The Family as an Incomplete Annuities Market. In: Journal of Political Economy, 89, 2: 372–391.

Kotlikoff, Laurence J., John N. Morris 1989: How Much Care Do the Aged Receive from Their Children? A Bimodal Picture of Contact and Assistance. In: Wise, David A. (ed.), The Economics of Aging. Chicago, London: University of Chicago Press, 151–175.

Künemund, Harald, Martin Rein 1999: There is More to Receiving than Needing: Theoretical Arguments and Empirical Explorations of Crowding In and Crowding Out. In: Ageing & Society, 19, 1: 93–121.

Künemund, Harald, Andreas Motel 2000: Verbreitung, Motivation und Entwicklungsperspektiven privater intergenerationeller Hilfeleistungen und Transfers. In: Kohli, Martin, Marc Szydlik (eds.), Generationen in Familie und Gesellschaft. Opladen: Leske + Budrich, 122–137.

Künemund, Harald, Andreas Motel-Klingebiel, Martin Kohli 2005: Do Intergenerational Transfers from Elderly Parents Increase Social Inequality Among Their Middle-Aged Children? Evidence from the German Aging Survey. In: Journal of Gerontology: Social Sciences, 60B, 1: 30–36.

Künemund, Harald 2008: Intergenerational Relations Within the Family and the State. In: Saraceno, 105–122.

Künemund, Harald, Marc Szydlik (eds.) 2009: Generationen – Multidisziplinäre Perspektiven. Wiesbaden: VS Verlag für Sozialwissenschaften.

Lauterbach Wolfgang 1995: Die gemeinsame Lebenszeit von Familiengenerationen. In: Zeitschrift für Soziologie, 24, 1: 22–41.

Lauterbach, Wolfgang, Kurt Lüscher 1996: Erben und die Verbundenheit der Lebensverläufe von Familienmitgliedern. In: Kölner Zeitschrift für Soziologie und Sozialpsychologie, 48, 1: 66–95.

Lawton, Leora, Merril Silverstein, Vern L. Bengtson 1994: Solidarity Between Generations in Families. In: Bengtson, Vern L., Robert A. Harootyan (eds.), Intergenerational Linkages – Hidden Connections in American Society. New York: Springer, 19–42.

Lee, Gary R., Jeffrey W. Dwyer 1996: Aging Parent-Adult Child Coresidence – Further Evidence on the Role of Parental Characteristics. In: Journal of Family Issues, 17, 1: 46–59.

Leibfried, Stephan 1992: Towards a European Welfare State? On Integrating Poverty Regimes into the European Community. In: Ferge, Zsuzsa, Jon Eivind Kolberg (eds.), Social Policy in a Changing Europe. Frankfurt/Main, New York: Campus, 245–279.

Leisering, Lutz 2000: Wohlfahrtsstaatliche Generationen. In: Kohli, Martin, Marc Szydlik (eds.), Generationen in Familie und Gesellschaft. Opladen: Leske + Budrich, 59–76.

Leitner, Sigrid 2003: Varieties of Familialism – The Caring Function of the Family in Comparative Perspective. In: European Societies, 5, 4: 353–375.

Lendon, Jessica P., Merril Silverstein, Roseann Giarrusso 2014: Ambivalence in Older Parent–Adult Child Relationships: Mixed Feelings, Mixed Measures. In: Journal of Marriage and Family, 76, 2: 272–284.

Lennartsson, Carin, Merril Silverstein, Johan Fritzell 2010: Time-for-Money Exchanges Between Older and Younger Generations in Swedish Families. In: Journal of Family Issues, 31, 2: 189–210.

Leopold, Thomas, Thorsten Schneider 2010: Schenkungen und Erbschaften im Lebenslauf – Vergleichende Längsschnittanalysen zu intergenerationalen Transfers. In: Zeitschrift für Soziologie, 39, 4: 258–280.

Leopold, Thomas, Marcel Raab 2011: Short-Term Reciprocity in Late Parent-Child Relationships. In: Journal of Marriage and Family, 73, 1: 105–119.

Lessenich, Stephan 1994: 'Three Worlds of Welfare Capitalism' – oder vier? Strukturwandel arbeits- und sozialpolitischer Regulierungsmuster in Spanien. In: Politische Vierteljahresschrift, 35, 2: 224–244.

Lettke, Frank 2004: Subjektive Bedeutungen des Erbens und Vererbens. Ergebnisse des Konstanzer Erbschafts-Surveys. In: Zeitschrift für Soziologie der Erziehung und Sozialisation, 24, 3: 277–302.

Lewis, Jane 1992: Gender and the Development of Welfare Regimes. In: Journal of European Social Policy, 2, 3: 159–173.

Lipszyc, Barbara, Etienne Sail, Ana Xavier 2012: Long-Term Care: Need, Use and Expenditure in the EU-27. Economic Papers 469. Brussels: European Commission.

Litwak, Eugene 1985: Helping the Elderly – The Complementary Roles of Informal Networks and Formal Systems. New York, London: The Guilford Press.

Litwak, Eugene, Merril Silverstein, Vern L. Bengtson, Ynez Wilson Hirst 2003: Theories about Families, Organizations and Social Supports. In: Bengtson, Vern L., Ariela Lowenstein (eds.), Global Aging and Challenges to Families. New York: Aldine de Gruyter: 27–53

Logan John R., Glenna D. Spitze 1996: Family Ties – Enduring Relations Between Parents and Their Grown Children. Philadelphia, PA: Temple University Press.

Lowenstein, Ariela, Jim Ogg (eds.) 2003: OASIS – Old Age and Autonomy: The Role of Service Systems and Intergenerational Family Solidarity. Final Report. University of Haifa.

Lowenstein, Ariela 2007: Solidarity–Conflict and Ambivalence: Testing Two Conceptual Frameworks and Their Impact on Quality of Life for Older Family Members. In: Journal of Gerontology: Social Sciences, 62B, 2: 100–107.

Luetzelberger, Therese 2014: Independence or Interdependence – Norms of Leaving Home in Italy and Germany. In: European Societies, 16, 1: 28–47.

Lüscher, Kurt, Karl Pillemer 1998: Intergenerational Ambivalence: A New Approach to the Study of Parent-Child Relations in Later Life. In: Journal of Marriage and the Family, 60, 2: 413–425.

Lüscher, Kurt 2002: Intergenerational Ambivalence: Further Steps in Theory and Research. In: Journal of Marriage and Family, 64, 3: 585–593.

Lye, Diane N. 1996: Adult Child-Parent Relationships. In: Annual Review of Sociology, 22: 79–102.

Mackenbach, Johan P., Irina Stirbu, Albert-Jan R. Roskam, Maartje M. Schaap, Gwenn Menvielle, Mall Leinsalu, Anton E. Kunst 2008: Socioeconomic Inequalities in Health in 22 European Countries. In: The New England Journal of Medicine, 358, 23: 2468–2481.

Majamaa, Karoliina 2013: The Effect of Socio-economic Factors on Parental Financial Support from the Perspectives of the Givers and the Receivers. In: European Societies, 15, 1: 57–81.

Mannheim, Karl 1952: The Problem of Generations. In: Kecskemeti, Paul (ed.), Essays on the Sociology of Knowledge. London: Routledge & Kegan Paul, 276–322. Original publication: Mannheim, Karl 1928: Das Problem der Generationen. In: Kölner Vierteljahrshefte für Soziologie, 7, 2: 157–185; 3: 309–330.

Marí-Klose, Pau, Francisco Javier Moreno-Fuentes 2013: The Southern European Welfare Model in the Post-Industrial Order – Still a Distinctive Cluster? In: European Societies, 15, 4: 475–492.

Maslow, Abraham H. 1943: A Theory of Human Motivation. In: Psychological Review, 50, 4: 370–396.

Maslow, Abraham H. 1954: Motivation and Personality. New York, Evanston, London: Harper & Row.

Mauss, Marcel 1950: Essai sur le don. Paris: Presses Universitaires de France.

Max-Neef, Manfred A., Antonio Elizalde, Martin Hopenhayn 1991: Development and Human Needs. In: Max-Neef, Manfred A., with contributions from Antonio Elizalde, Martin Hopenhayn (eds.), Human Scale Development – Conception, Application and Further Reflections. New York, London: Apex Press, 13–54.

May, Christina 2013: Generation in Itself or for Itself? The Conflict Potential of Cohorts in the German, Dutch and British Pension Systems Compared. In: European Societies, 15, 1: 4–25.

Mayer, Karl Ulrich 2001: The Paradox of Global Social Change and National Path Dependencies – Life Course Patterns in Advanced Societies. In: Woodward, Alison, Martin Kohli (eds.), Inclusions and Exclusions in European Societies. London, New York: Routledge, 89–110.

Mayer, Karl Ulrich 2004: Whose Lives? How History, Societies, and Institutions Define and Shape Life Courses. In: Research in Human Development, 1, 3: 161–187.

McGarry, Kathleen, Robert F. Schoeni 1995: Transfer Behavior in the Health and Retirement Study – Measurement and the Redistribution of Resources Within the Family. In: The Journal of Human Resources, 30, Supplement: S184-S226.

McGarry, Kathleen 1999: Inter Vivos Transfers and Intended Bequests. In: Journal of Public Economics, 73, 3: 321–351.

Meinert, Karin 1996: Mit Dreißig noch im Kinderzimmer – Wie man Nesthocker los wird, bevor es zu spät ist. Frankfurt/Main: Eichborn.

Merton, Robert K., Elinor Barber 1963: Sociological Ambivalence. In: Tiryakian, Edward A. (ed.), Sociological Theory, Values, and Sociocultural Change – Essays in Honor of Pitirim A. Sorokin. New York, Evanston: Harper & Row, 91–120.

Merz, Eva-Maria, Ezgi Özeke-Kocabas, Frans J. Oort, Carlo Schuengel 2009: Intergenerational Family Solidarity: Value Differences Between Immigrant Groups and Generations. In: Journal of Family Psychology, 23, 3: 291–300.

Millar, Jane, Andrea Warman 1996: Family Obligations in Europe. London: Family Policy Studies Centre.

Mood, Carina 2010: Logistic Regression: Why We Cannot Do What We Think We Can Do, and What We Can Do About It. In: European Sociological Review, 26, 1: 67–82.

Motel, Andreas, Marc Szydlik 1999: Private Transfers zwischen den Generationen. In: Zeitschrift für Soziologie, 28, 1: 3–22.

Motel-Klingebiel, Andreas, Clemens Tesch-Römer, Hans-Joachim von Kondratowitz 2005: Welfare States Do Not Crowd Out the Family: Evidence for Mixed Responsibility from Comparative Analyses. In: Ageing & Society, 25, 6: 863–882.

Motel-Klingebiel, Andreas, Clemens Tesch-Römer 2006: Familie im Wohlfahrtsstaat – zwischen Verdrängung und gemischter Verantwortung. In: Zeitschrift für Familienforschung, 18, 3: 290–314.

Nauck, Bernhard 2009: Patterns of Exchange in Kinship Systems in Germany, Russia, and the People's Republic of China. In: Journal of Comparative Family Studies, 40, 2: 255–278.

Nauck, Bernhard, Anja Steinbach 2010: Intergenerational Relationships. In: German Data Forum (RatSWD) (ed.), Building on Progress – Expanding the Research Infrastructure for the Social, Economic, and Behavioral Sciences. Opladen, Farmington Hills, MI: Budrich UniPress, 1057–1080 (www.ratswd.de/publikationen/building-on-progress).

Nave-Herz, Rosemarie 1998: Die These über den 'Zerfall der Familie'. In: Friedrichs, Jürgen, M. Rainer Lepsius, Karl Ulrich Mayer (eds.), Die Diagnosefähigkeit der Soziologie. Sonderheft 35 der Kölner Zeitschrift für Soziologie und Sozialpsychologie. Opladen: Westdeutscher Verlag, 286–315.

Nave-Herz, Rosemarie (ed.) 2002: Family Change and Intergenerational Relations in Different Cultures. Würzburg: Ergon.

Neuberger, Franz, Klaus Haberkern 2014: Structured Ambivalence in Grandchild Care and the Quality of Life Among European Grandparents. In: European Journal of Aging, 11, 2: 171–181.

Neuberger, Franz 2015: Kinder des Kapitalismus – Subjektivität, Lebensqualität und intergenerationale Solidarität in Europa. Berlin: Edition Sigma.

Noack, Peter, Heike M. Buhl 2004: Child-Parent Relationships. In: Lang, Frieder R., Karen L. Fingerman (eds.), Growing Together – Personal Relationships Across the Life Span. Cambridge: Cambridge University Press, 45–75.

Nollert, Michael 2007: Sonderfall im rheinischen Kapitalismus oder Sonderweg im liberalen Wohlfahrtskapitalismus? Zur Spezifität des Sozialstaats Schweiz. In: Eberle, Thomas S., Kurt Imhof (eds.), Sonderfall Schweiz. Zürich: Seismo, 153–171.

Norris, Joan E., Joseph A. Tindale 1994: Among Generations – The Cycle of Adult Relationships. New York: Freeman.

Novak, Mojca 2001: Reconsidering the Socialist Welfare State Model. In: Woodward, Alison, Martin Kohli (eds.), Inclusions and Exclusions in European Societies. London, New York: Routledge, 111–126.

Obinger, Herbert 1998: Politische Institutionen und Sozialpolitik in der Schweiz – Der Einfluß von Nebenregierungen auf Struktur und Entwicklungsdynamik des schweizerischen Sozialstaates. Frankfurt/Main: Peter Lang.

Obinger, Herbert, Klaus Armingeon, Giuliano Bonoli, Fabio Bertozzi 2005: Switzerland – The Marriage of Direct Democracy and Federalism. In: Obinger, Herbert, Stephan Leibfried, Francis G. Castles (eds.), Federalism and the Welfare State – New World and European Experiences. Cambridge: Cambridge University Press, 263–304.

O'Connor, Julia S. 1993: Gender, Class and Citizenship in the Comparative Analysis of Welfare State Regimes: Theoretical and Methodological Issues. In: The British Journal of Sociology, 44, 3: 501–518.

OECD 1999: Classifying Educational Programmes: Manual for ISCED-97 Implementation in OECD Countries. Paris: OECD.

OECD 2008: Growing Unequal? Income Distribution and Poverty in OECD Countries (www.oecd.org/els/social/inequality/GU). Data retrieved on 08/07/2013.

OECD 2010a: PISA 2009 Results: What Students Know and Can Do – Student Performance in Reading, Mathematics and Science. Volume I (http://dx.doi.org/10.1787/9789264091450-en).

OECD 2010b: PISA 2009 Results: Overcoming Social Background – Equity in Learning Opportunities and Outcomes. Volume II (http://dx.doi.org/10.1787/9789264091504-en).

OECD 2012: OECD National Accounts Statistics (http://stats.oecd.org/BrandedView.aspx?oecd_bv_id=na-data-en&doi=na-data-en). Data retrieved on 22/03/2014.

Oesch, Daniel 2008: Stratifying Welfare States: Class Differences in Pension Coverage in Britain, Germany, Sweden and Switzerland. In: Swiss Journal of Sociology, 34, 3: 533–554.

Oorschot, Wim van, Michael Opielka, Birgit Pfau-Effinger (eds.) 2008: Culture and Welfare State – Values and Social Policy in Comparative Perspective. Cheltenham, Northampton: Edward Elgar.

Opielka, Michael 2008: Christian Foundations of the Welfare State: Strong Cultural Values in Comparative Perspective. In: Oorschot et al., 89–114.

Orloff, Ann Shola 1993: Gender and the Social Rights of Citizenship: The Comparative Analysis of Gender Relations and Welfare States. In: American Sociological Review, 58, 3: 303–328.

Österle, August (ed.) 2011: Long-Term Care in Central and South Eastern Europe. Frankfurt/Main: Peter Lang.

Parkes, Colin Murray, Holly G. Prigerson 2010: Bereavement – Studies of Grief in Adult Life. London, New York: Routledge.

Parsons, Talcott 1942: Age and Sex in the Social Structure of the United States. In: American Sociological Review, 7, 5: 604–616.

Parsons, Talcott, Robert F. Bales 1956: Family, Socialization and Interaction Process. London: Routledge & Kegan Paul.

Perrig-Chiello, Pasqualina, François Höpflinger 2005: Aging Parents and Their Middle-Aged Children: Demographic and Psychosocial Challenges. In: European Journal of Ageing, 2, 3: 183–191.

Perrig-Chiello, Pasqualina, Sara Hutchison 2010: Family Caregivers of Elderly Persons – A Differential Perspective on Stressors, Resources, and Well-Being. In: The Journal of Gerontopsychology and Geriatric Psychiatry, 23, 4: 195–206.

Pett, Marjorie A., Nancy Lang, Anita Gander 1992: Late-Life Divorce – Its Impact on Family Rituals. In: Journal of Family Issues, 13, 4: 526–552.

Pfau-Effinger, Birgit 2005: Culture and Welfare State Policies: Reflections on a Complex Interrelation. In: Journal of Social Policy, 34, 1: 3–20.

Pfau-Effinger, Birgit, Birgit Geissler (eds.) 2005: Care and Social Integration in European Societies. Bristol: Policy Press.

Pfenning, Astrid, Thomas Bahle (eds.) 2000: Families and Family Policies in Europe – Comparative Perspectives. Frankfurt/Main: Peter Lang.

Piketty, Thomas 2014: Capital in the Twenty-First Century. Translated by Arthur Goldhammer. Cambridge, MA, London: Belknap Press of Harvard University Press.

Pillemer, Karl, J. Jill Suitor 2002: Explaining Mothers' Ambivalence Toward Their Adult Children. In: Journal of Marriage and Family, 64, 3: 602–613.

Pillemer, Karl, J. Jill Suitor, Steven E. Mock, Myra Sabir, Tamara B. Pardo, Jori Sechrist 2007: Capturing the Complexity of Intergenerational Relations: Exploring Ambivalence Within Later-Life Families. In: Journal of Social Issues, 63, 4: 775–791.

Pillemer, Karl, Christin L. Munsch, Thomas Fuller-Rowell, Catherine Riffin, J. Jill Suitor 2012: Ambivalence Toward Adult Children: Differences Between Mothers and Fathers. In: Journal of Marriage and Family, 74, 5: 1101–1113.

Pinnelli, Antonella 2001: Determinants of Fertility in Europe: New Family Forms, Context and Individual Characteristics. In: Pinnelli, Antonella, Hans-Joachim Hoffmann-Nowotny, Beat Fux (eds.), Fertility and New Types of Households and Family Formation in Europe. Population Studies 35. Strasbourg: Council of Europe, 47–101.

Qureshi, Hazel, Alan Walker 1989: The Caring Relationship – Elderly People and Their Families. Basingstoke: Macmillan.

Rainer, Helmut, Thomas Siedler 2012: Family Location and Caregiving Patterns from an International Perspective. In: Population and Development Review, 38, 2: 337–351.

Reher, David Sven 1998: Family Ties in Western Europe: Persistent Contrasts. In: Population and Development Review, 24, 2: 203–234.

Reil-Held, Anette 2006: Crowding Out or Crowding In? Public and Private Transfers in Germany. In: European Journal of Population, 22, 3: 263–280.

Roberts, Robert E. L., Leslie N. Richards, Vern L. Bengtson 1991: Intergenerational Solidarity in Families: Untangling the Ties that Bind. In: Pfeifer, Susan K., Marvin B. Sussman (eds.), Families: Intergenerational and Generational Connections. New York, London: Haworth, 11–46.

Rosenbaum, Heidi 1982: Formen der Familie – Untersuchungen zum Zusammenhang von Familienverhältnissen, Sozialstruktur und sozialem Wandel in der deutschen Gesellschaft des 19. Jahrhunderts. Frankfurt/Main: Suhrkamp.

Rosenmayr, Leopold, Eva Köckeis 1961: Sozialbeziehungen im höheren Lebensalter. In: Soziale Welt, 12, 3: 214–229.

Rosenmayr, Leopold, Eva Köckeis 1963: Propositions for a Sociological Theory of Aging and the Family. In: International Social Science Journal, 15, 3: 410–426.

Rossi, Alice S., Peter H. Rossi 1990: Of Human Bonding – Parent-Child Relations Across the Life Course. New York: Aldine de Gruyter.

Rossi, Giovanna 1997: The Nestlings: Why Young Adults Stay at Home Longer: The Italian Case. In: Journal of Family Issues, 18, 6: 627–644.

Rusconi, Alessandra 2006: Leaving the Parental Home in Italy and West Germany: Opportunities and Constraints. Aachen: Shaker.

Rys, Vladimir 2001: Transition Countries of Central Europe Entering the European Union: Some Social Protection Issues. In: International Social Security Review, 54, 2–3: 177–189.

Sackmann, Reinhard, Ansgar Weymann 1995: Die Technisierung des Alltags – Generationen und technische Innovationen. Frankfurt/Main, New York: Campus.

Sackmann, Reinhard, Oliver Winkler 2013: Technology Generations Revisited: The Internet Generation. In: Gerontechnology, 11, 4: 493–503.

Sainsbury, Diane (ed.) 1994: Gendering Welfare States. London et al.: Sage.

Sandberg-Thoma, Sara E., Anastasia R. Snyder, Bohyun Joy Jang 2015: Exiting and Returning to the Parental Home for Boomerang Kids. In: Journal of Marriage and Family, 77, 3: 806–818.

Saraceno, Chiara (ed.) 2008: Families, Ageing and Social Policy – Intergenerational Solidarity in European Welfare States. Cheltenham, Northampton: Edward Elgar.

Saraceno, Chiara, Wolfgang Keck 2010: Can We Identify Intergenerational Policy Regimes in Europe? In: European Societies, 12, 5: 675–696.

Sarasa, Sebastian, Sunnee Billingsley 2008: Personal and Household Caregiving from Adult Children to Parents and Social Stratification. In: Saraceno, 123–146.

Sarkisian, Natalia, Naomi Gerstel 2008: Till Marriage Do Us Part: Adult Children's Relationships with Their Parents. In: Journal of Marriage and Family, 70, 2: 360–376.

Sarkisian, Natalia, Naomi Gerstel 2012: Nuclear Family Values, Extended Family Lives – The Power of Race, Class, and Gender. New York, London: Routledge.

Schenk, Niels, Pearl A. Dykstra, Ineke Maas 2010: The Role of European Welfare States in Intergenerational Money Transfers: A Micro-Level Perspective. In: Ageing & Society, 30, 8: 1315–1342.

Schlomann, Heinrich 1992: Vermögensverteilung und private Altersvorsorge. Frankfurt/ Main, New York: Campus.

Schmid, Tina, Martina Brandt, Klaus Haberkern 2012: Gendered Support to Older Parents: Do Welfare States Matter? In: European Journal of Ageing, 9, 1: 39–50.

Schmid, Tina 2014: Generation, Geschlecht und Wohlfahrtsstaat – Intergenerationelle Unterstützung in Europa. Wiesbaden: Springer VS.

Schubert, Klaus, Simon Hegelich, Ursula Bazant (eds.) 2009: The Handbook of European Welfare Systems. London, New York: Routledge.

Schulz, Erika, Reiner Leidl, Hans-Helmut König 2001: Starker Anstieg der Pflegebedürftigkeit zu erwarten – Vorausschätzungen bis 2020 mit Ausblick auf 2050. In: Wochenbericht des DIW Berlin, 68: 65–77.

Schupp, Jürgen, Marc Szydlik 2004a: Inheritance and Gifts in Germany – The Growing Fiscal Importance of Inheritance Tax for the Federal States. In: Economic Bulletin, 41, 3: 95–102.

Schupp, Jürgen, Marc Szydlik 2004b: Zukünftige Vermögen – wachsende Ungleichheit. In: Szydlik, Marc (ed.), Generation und Ungleichheit. Wiesbaden: Verlag für Sozialwissenschaften, 243–264.

Schwarz, Beate 2013: Intergenerational Conflict: The Case of Adult Children and Their Parents. In: Albert/Ferring, 131–145.

Segrin, Chris, Jeanne Flora 2011: Family Communication. Second edition. New York, London: Routledge.

Seltzer, Judith A., Suzanne M. Bianchi 2013: Demographic Change and Parent-Child Relationships in Adulthood. In: Annual Review of Sociology, 39: 275–290.

Seltzer, Judith A., Esther M. Friedman 2014: Widowed Mothers' Coresidence with Adult Children. In: The Journals of Gerontology, Series B: Psychological Sciences and Social Sciences, 69, 1: 63–74.

Sev'er, Aysan, Jan E. Trost 2011: Introduction: Opening Closets, Rattling Family Skeletons: What Will They Say? In: Sev'er, Aysan, Jan E. Trost (eds.), Skeletons in the Closet – A Sociological Analysis of Family Conflicts. Waterloo, Ontario: Wilfrid Laurier University Press, 1–32.

Shapiro, Adam 2003: Later-Life Divorce and Parent-Adult Child Contact and Proximity – A Longitudinal Analysis. In: Journal of Family Issues, 24, 2: 264–285.

Silverstein, Merril, Leora Lawton, Vern L. Bengtson 1994: Types of Relations Between Parents and Adult Children. In: Bengtson, Vern L., Robert A. Harootyan (eds.), Intergenerational Linkages – Hidden Connections in American Society. New York: Springer, 43–76 (Appendix: 252–264).

Silverstein, Merril, Vern L. Bengtson 1997: Intergenerational Solidarity and the Structure of Adult Child–Parent Relationships in American Families. In: American Journal of Sociology, 103, 2: 429–460.

Silverstein, Merril, Daphna Gans, Ariela Lowenstein, Roseann Giarrusso, Vern L. Bengtson 2010: Older Parent–Child Relationships in Six Developed Nations: Comparisons at the Intersection of Affection and Conflict. In: Journal of Marriage and Family, 72, 4: 1006–1021.

Silverstein, Merril, Roseann Giarrusso 2012: Aging Individuals, Families, and Societies: Micro-Meso-Macro Linkages in the Life Course. In: Settersten, Richard A., Jr., Jacqueline L. Angel (eds.), Handbook of Sociology of Aging. New York: Springer, 35–49.

Simmel, Georg 2009: Sociology – Inquiries into the Construction of Social Forms. Translated and edited by Anthony J. Blasi, Anton K. Jacobs, Mathew Kanjirathinkal. Leiden: Brill. Original publication: Simmel, Georg 1908: Soziologie – Untersuchungen über die Formen der Vergesellschaftung. Berlin: Duncker & Humblot.

Smits, Annika, Ruben I. van Gaalen, Clara H. Mulder 2010: Parent–Child Coresidence: Who Moves in with Whom and for Whose Needs? In: Journal of Marriage and Family, 72, 4: 1022–1033.

Snijders, Tom A. B., Roel J. Bosker 2012: Multilevel Analysis – An Introduction to Basic and Advanced Multilevel Modeling. Second edition. London et al.: Sage.

Soldo, Beth J., Martha S. Hill 1993: Intergenerational Transfers: Economic, Demographic, and Social Perspectives. In: Annual Review of Gerontology and Geriatrics, 13: 187–216.

Soldo, Beth J., Martha S. Hill 1995: Family Structure and Transfer Measures in the Health and Retirement Study. In: The Journal of Human Ressources, 30, Supplement: S108-S137.

Stamm, Isabell, Peter Breitschmid, Martin Kohli (eds.) 2011: Doing Succession in Europe – Generational Transfers in Family Businesses in Comparative Perspective. Zürich, Basel, Genf: Schulthess, also Opladen & Farmington Hills: Budrich UniPress.

Stark, Oded 1995: Altruism and Beyond – An Economic Analysis of Transfers and Exchanges Within Families and Groups. Cambridge: Cambridge University Press.

Steinbach, Anja 2008: Intergenerational Solidarity and Ambivalence: Types of Relationships in German Families. In: Journal of Comparative Family Studies, 39, 1: 115–127.

Steinbach, Anja, Johannes Kopp 2010: Determinanten der Beziehungszufriedenheit: Die Sicht erwachsener Kinder auf die Beziehungen zu ihren Eltern. In: Ette et al., 95–116.

Steinbach, Anja 2012: Intergenerational Relations Across the Life Course. In: Advances in Life Course Research, 17, 3: 93–99.

Steinbach, Anja 2013: Family Structure and Parent–Child Contact: A Comparison of Native and Migrant Families. In: Journal of Marriage and Family, 75, 5: 1114–1129.

Stierlin, Helm 1974: Separating Parents and Adolescents – A Perspective on Running Away, Schizophrenia, and Waywardness. New York: Quadrangle/New York Times Book.

Suitor, J. Jill, Karl Pillerner 1991: Family Conflict when Adult Children and Elderly Parents Share a Home. In: Pillemer, Karl, Kathleen McCartney (eds.), Parent-Child Relations Throughout Life. Hillsdale, NJ: Erlbaum, 179–199.

Suitor, J. Jill, Megan Gilligan, Karl Pillemer 2011: Conceptualizing and Measuring Intergenerational Ambivalence in Later Life. In: The Journals of Gerontology, Series B: Psychological Sciences and Social Sciences, 66, 6: 769–781.

Suitor, J. Jill, Jori Sechrist, Megan Gilligan, Karl Pillemcr 2012: Intergenerational Relations in Later-Life Families. In: Settersten, Richard A., Jr., Jacqueline L. Angel (eds.), Handbook of Sociology of Aging. New York: Springer, 161–178.

Swartz, Teresa Toguchi 2009: Intergenerational Family Relations in Adulthood: Patterns, Variations, and Implications in the Contemporary United States. In: Annual Review of Sociology, 35: 191–212.

Szinovacz, Maximiliane E., Adam Davey (eds.) 2008: Caregiving Contexts: Cultural, Familial, and Societal Implications. New York: Springer.

Szydlik, Marc 1994: Incomes in a Planned and a Market Economy: The Case of the German Democratic Republic and the 'Former' Federal Republic of Germany. In: European Sociological Review, 10, 3: 199–217.

Szydlik, Marc 1995: Die Enge der Beziehung zwischen erwachsenen Kindern und ihren Eltern – und umgekehrt. In: Zeitschrift für Soziologie, 24, 2: 75–94.

Szydlik, Marc 1996: Parent-Child Relations in East and West Germany Shortly After the Fall of the Wall. In: International Journal of Sociology and Social Policy, 16, 12: 63–88.

Szydlik, Marc 2000: Lebenslange Solidarität? Generationenbeziehungen zwischen erwachsenen Kindern und Eltern. Opladen: Leske + Budrich.

Szydlik, Marc 2002: Vocational Education and Labour Markets in Deregulated, Flexibly Coordinated, and Planned Societies. In: European Societies, 4, 1: 79–105.

Szydlik, Marc 2004: Inheritance and Inequality: Theoretical Reasoning and Empirical Evidence. In: European Sociological Review, 20, 1: 31–45.

Szydlik, Marc, Jürgen Schupp 2004: Wer erbt mehr? Erbschaften, Sozialstruktur und Alterssicherung. In: Kölner Zeitschrift für Soziologie und Sozialpsychologie, 56, 4: 609–629.

Szydlik, Marc 2008a: Intergenerational Solidarity and Conflict. In: Journal of Comparative Family Studies, 39, 1: 97–114.

Szydlik, Marc 2008b: Flexibilisierung und die Folgen. In: Szydlik, Marc (ed.), Flexibilisierung – Folgen für Arbeit und Familie. Wiesbaden: VS Verlag für Sozialwissenschaften, 7–22.

Szydlik, Marc 2011a: Bequests: Motives, Model, Money. In: Stamm et al., 153–170.

Szydlik, Marc 2011b: Erben in Europa. In: Kölner Zeitschrift für Soziologie und Sozialpsychologie, 63, 4: 543–565.

Szydlik, Marc 2012a: Von der Wiege bis zur Bahre: Generationentransfers und Ungleichheit. In: Bühlmann et al., 58–71.

Szydlik, Marc 2012b: Generations: Connections Across the Life Course. In: Advances in Life Course Research, 17, 3: 100–111.

Tartler, Rudolf 1961: Das Alter in der modernen Gesellschaft. Stuttgart: Enke.

Therborn, Göran 1993: Beyond the Lonely Nation-State. In: Castles, 329–340.

Thomson, David 1989: The Welfare State and Generation Conflict: Winners and Losers. In: Johnson, Paul, Christoph Conrad, David Thomson (eds.), Workers Versus Pensioners: Intergenerational Justice in an Ageing World. Manchester, New York: Manchester University Press, 33–56.

Timonen, Virpi, Catherine Conlon, Thomas Scharf, Gemma Carney 2013: Family, State, Class and Solidarity: Re-Conceptualising Intergenerational Solidarity through the Grounded Theory Approach. In: European Journal of Ageing, 10, 3: 171–179.

Todd, Emmanuel 1983: La Troisième Planète – Structures Familiales et Systèmes Idéologiques. Paris: Éditions du Seuil.

Todd, Emmanuel 1990: L'Invention de L'Europe. Paris: Éditions du Seuil.

Tomassini, Cecilia, Stamatis Kalogirou, Emily Grundy, Tineke Fokkema, Pekka Martikainen, Marjolein Broese van Groenou, Antti Karisto 2004: Contacts Between Elderly Parents and Their Children in Four European Countries: Current Patterns and Future Prospects. In: European Journal of Ageing, 1, 1: 54–63.

Trampusch, Christine, André Mach (eds.) 2011: Switzerland in Europe – Continuity and Change in the Swiss Political Economy. London, New York: Routledge.

Treas, Judith, Zoya Gubernskaya 2012: Farewell to Moms? Maternal Contact for Seven Countries in 1986 and 2001. In: Journal of Marriage and Family, 74, 2: 297–311.

Trifiletti, Rossana 1999: Southern European Welfare Regimes and the Worsening Position of Women. In: Journal of European Social Policy, 9, 1: 49–64.

Tyrell, Hartmann 1976: Konflikt als Interaktion. In: Kölner Zeitschrift für Soziologie und Sozialpsychologie, 28, 2: 255–271.

Usita, Paula M. 2001: Interdependency in Immigrant Mother-Daughter Relationships. In: Journal of Aging Studies, 15, 2: 183–199.

Usita, Paula M., Barbara C. Du Bois 2005: Conflict Sources and Responses in Mother-Daughter Relationships: Perspectives of Adult Daughters of Aging Immigrant Women. In: Journal of Women & Aging, 17, 1/2: 151–165.

Valentine, Christine 2008: Bereavement Narratives – Continuing Bonds in the Twenty-First Century. London, New York: Routledge.

Van Gaalen, Ruben I., Pearl A. Dykstra 2006: Solidarity and Conflict Between Adult Children and Parents: A Latent Class Analysis. In: Journal of Marriage and Family, 68, 4: 947–960.

Viazzo, Pier Paolo 2010: Macro-regional Differences in European Kinship Culture. In: Heady/Kohli, 271–294.

Walker, Alan 1996: Intergenerational Relations and the Provision of Welfare. In: Walker, Alan (ed.), The New Generational Contract – Intergenerational Relations, Old Age and Welfare. London: UCL, 10–36.

Walker, Robert 2005: Social Security and Welfare – Concepts and Comparisons. Maidenhead, Birkshire: Open University Press.

Ward, Russell, John Logan, Glenna Spitze 1992: The Influence of Parent and Child Needs on Coresidence in Middle and Later Life. In: Journal of Marriage and the Family, 54, 1: 209–221.

Ward, Russel A., Glenna Spitze, Glenn Deane 2009: The More the Merrier? Multiple Parent-Adult Child Relations. In: Journal of Marriage and Family, 71, 1: 161–173.

Ward, Russell, Glenn Deane, Glenna Spitze 2014: Life-Course Changes and Parent–Adult Child Contact. In: Research on Aging, 36, 5: 568–602.

White, Lynn 1994: Coresidence and Leaving Home: Young Adults and Their Parents. In: Annual Review of Sociology, 20: 81–102.

White, Lynn, Debra Peterson 1995: The Retreat from Marriage: Its Effect on Unmarried Children's Exchange with Parents. In: Journal of Marriage and the Family, 57, 2: 428–434.

Wicki, Martin 2001: Soziale Sicherung in der Schweiz: Ein europäischer Sonderfall? In: Kraus, Katrin, Thomas Geisen (eds.), Sozialstaat in Europa – Geschichte, Entwicklung, Perspektiven. Wiesbaden: Westdeutscher Verlag, 249–272.

Wilkinson, Richard, Kate Pickett 2010: The Spirit Level – Why Equality Is Better for Everyone. London: Penguin Books.

Willson, Andrea E., Kim M. Shuey, Glen H. Elder, Jr., K.A.S. Wickrama 2006: Ambivalence in Mother-Adult Child Relations: A Dyadic Analysis. In: Social Psychology Quarterly, 69, 3: 235–252.

Zissimopoulos, Julie M., James P. Smith 2011: Unequal Giving: Monetary Gifts to Children Across Countries and over Time. In: Smeeding, Timothy M., Robert Erikson, Markus Jäntti (eds.), Persistence, Privilege, and Parenting – The Comparative Study of Intergenerational Mobility. New York: Russell Sage Foundation, 289–328.

Zukowski, Maciej 2009: Social Policy Regimes in the European Countries. In: Golinowska, Stanislawa, Peter Hengstenberg, Maciej Zukowski (eds.), Diversity and Commonality in European Social Policies: The Forging of a European Social Model. Warsaw: Wydawnictwo Naukowe Scholar and Friedrich-Ebert-Stiftung, 23–32.

Index